Go North, Young Man, Go North!

ROBERT WAYNE MUMFORD

◆ FriesenPress

Suite 300 - 990 Fort St
Victoria, BC, V8V 3K2
Canada

www.friesenpress.com

ISBN
978-1-5255-5985-3 (Hardcover)
978-1-5255-5986-0 (Paperback)
978-1-5255-5987-7 (eBook)

1. BIOGRAPHY & AUTOBIOGRAPHY, PERSONAL MEMOIRS

Distributed to the trade by The Ingram Book Company

Table of Contents

I dedicate this book to my grandchildren:
Tarec, Tyne, MacKenzie, Jared, Rory, & Blake

Life is a long journey ... Choose the right path!

Cooling Down A Bit, Eh?

When I stepped off the Greyhound bus in Prince George that mid January morning in 1961, my first inclination was to step right back on and head south as fast as the legal speed limit would allow. Cold! That's what registered in my quickly numbing brain, cold. It was a brilliant, blue sky morning. The air was full of what I would later learn were ice crystals. I would also learn that twenty degrees below zero F. was prime logging weather and not really considered that cold at all! Not until that thermometer edged down toward the 40 below zero (F) mark, would the hardy Canadians start buttoning up, pulling down ear flaps, and greet one another with "How's it going, eh? Cooling down a bit, eh?" as they shuffled by, eyebrows and beards covered with frost.

But for a transplanted 19 year old American, who had climbed aboard a bus 2 days earlier in the Willamette Valley city of Springfield, Oregon, where a relatively warm rain was falling, and the temperature was a balmy 45 degrees above zero, it felt mighty cold.

Well the first instinct is survival, so I raced across the street to that bastion of Canadian history, the Hudson Bay Company store, and bought a coat. The plan had been to wait until I was actually in the land of eternal ice and snow so I would buy the right kind. The truth of the matter was that for a wet behind the ears kid just fresh from the good old U.S.A. with no particular goal in mind, there were a lot of things more important to consider than what kind of coat to buy!

As the bus rattled along the frozen gravel road through the mostly unoccupied 60 miles of bush toward the small farming and lumbering town of Vanderhoof, there was plenty of time to think. As I gazed out the window at the changing landscape and broken terrain coming out of Prince George, the country began to open up into long rolling hills of endless jackpine, spruce, and poplar. The great interior plateau, an immense land that at that time was virtually untouched.

It was a little unsettling. This looked a little too much like Daniel Boone country to me! I was into rock and roll and Elvis Presley, not beaver trapping and pioneering! As I bumped along across the flattening poplar covered countryside, the thought occurred to me that two years previous, this would have been the last place in the world I would have expected to be!

As the bus descended the hill into Vanderhoof, the little town nestled along the banks of the Nechako River, little did I know that for the next 45 years the Nechako Valley would be home. The people of this valley would extend friendship and kindness to a young guy with no particular focus in life. They would take me into their homes, supply me with a job, and by word (sometimes pretty straightly spoken) and example, show what a contributing member of society was supposed to act like! But this was all in the future.

Right then, my goal was to get off that bus, meet my cousins, the Jones family, who had just moved up a couple of months earlier from Oregon, and find a place with a roaring fire so I could get warm! So how did this whole performance of coming to Vanderhoof, British Columbia, the exact geographical center of nowhere in the western-most province of Canada, come to be?

It all started with my cousins next door neighbour, Tom Curl. Tom was an interesting guy. Part Cherokee Indian, he was born of parents who came from the state of Oklahoma. Tom had read a Canadian National Railroad advertisement promoting land in central B.C., Canada. He was a logger, and looking to the future, he felt there was a good chance his job would be at risk because of the newly mechanized loading methods. He piled his wife, Inez, and 3 kids in the car, and took a vacation to check out the North Country. He ended up buying a ½ section of good land with a lot of timber and a somewhat livable house for $3,000 a few miles south of Vanderhoof in what was called the Lakes District. He returned to Oregon with glowing reports of this new land. The stories Tom brought back sparked an irresistible urge in Red Jones, to see this new frontier. As soon as possible, he headed north and was sold on what he found. He traveled up, bought 160 acres on the west end of Sinkut Lake, right beside Tom Curl's ½ section, and got ready to move to Canada.

The ¼ section Red bought was a nice piece of property. The building site, three hundred feet above the lake, had a full south slope that looked straight south across Sinkut Lake to where a high, flat bench rose up from the lake on the far side, then swept up to the top of Sinkut Mountain, a 4,000 foot, perfectly shaped peak. When you looked out the window at the constantly changing colours and shadows on the lake and mountain, it was like watching a movie picture.

Fall was an especially nice time of the year. The brilliant yellow and red leaves of the poplar and birch stood out in bright contrast to the distant deep blue of Sinkut Mountain. To make the scene complete, it was not uncommon to look across the lake in the evening and see three or four moose feeding together in the willows.

There were five kids in the Jones family. Ed, the oldest, had come up the summer before and built a rough sawed lumber house for the family to move into that fall. It was a good house. Ed was a sharp guy and tended to be a little on the moody side like his Dad. He was a year or two older than I was. Dick was next. He was a quick witted joker, and took after his Mom's side, the Mumfords. Carma was the only girl in the bunch and pretty well ruled the roost. She was a petite little thing, but knew how to hold her own in a rowdy bunch of brothers. Dwayne was a few years younger than I was and had faced some major health problems as a kid. I always had a lot of respect for him, and though he was a quiet type guy, could come up with some good one liners and thoughts. Donnie, the youngest, was a real natural for the business world because of his personality.

We all originally came from a mixed farming area in the south, central part of the state of Iowa, in the Midwestern United States, where I was born in the small town of Lacona, on July 24, 1941. To understand how I ever happened to be on that Greyhound bus in B.C., I will have to recall some family history.

Cowboys and Indians

"Iowa, the Corn and Hog state", is what it said on the vehicle license plates. Hot, humid summers, where the sweat ran off you in streams, even when you were sitting in the shade in the evening. Thunderstorm country, that charged the air with nitrogen and really made the corn grow! Farmers, that's what they all were, grandpas, grandmas, uncles, aunts, cousins, neighbours, you name it. Straw hat, bib overall farmers. At the time we left Iowa, my Dad, Charles Wayne Mumford, was still farming with horses. He was renting a farm, but he was restless. The war was just over, and you could feel change in the air. He was born and raised on the farm, and had to take over when his Dad died, which was a big responsibility for a sixteen year old. Now in his early thirties, with his wife, Lois Marie Batman Mumford, and three kids, Ronald Lee 10, Sharon Marie (Judy) 8, Robert Wayne (Bobby) 6, he was ready for a change.

His relationship with his mother-in-law, Nora Batman, was probably the deciding factor. She had a very strong personality, with considerably higher aspirations for a son-in-law than this coon hunting, fiddle playing backwoods boy. By this time, Dad knew the only way to save the marriage was to hit the road.

As luck would have it, Dad's first cousin Maxine, had married Red Jones, who had been raised in the area. Red had left a few years previously and spent quite a bit of time in Alaska and the northwest. He was a logger, a timber faller, and had built a house out in the backwoods, north of Sweet Home, Oregon.

When Red & Maxine came back to Iowa for a visit, a few exciting tales of working in the woods, falling and bucking in the big virgin growth Douglas Fir, was all it took. We were moving to Oregon, where a man could make as much in a six- hour day as a farmer could make in a month, and only work half as hard! To Dad, it looked like the perfect chance to make the break. He painted up his machinery, had a farm sale, and we headed west, where we would all live happily ever after! Actually, the first stages went pretty well as planned. How Dad ever pulled it off is a mystery to me to this day. But there were conditions! Every summer, Mom & us kids were to come back to Iowa for a visit. I still clearly remember the morning we left. We had spent the night at Dad's brother Theo's house. Theo was a bear of a man with black craggy eyebrows and I had always seemed to be a favourite. On a hot Saturday afternoon when every body was in town, he would take me to a little pop stand and buy me a bottle of ice cold Orange Crush for a nickel.

Wayne & Lois Mumford on the farm near Lacona, Iowa 1942

Brothers: Donald, Theo, Wayne Mumford

It was a miserable day when the time came to leave, snowing and blowing. We had spent the night at Uncle Theo & Aunt Carol's house and they were doing their best to convince Dad that he was crazy to take a wife and three young kids out on a day like that. It was at this point in the conversation that I made a contribution that didn't really help my Dads' cause! In heartbroken words I said, "I don't got no home no more". Well, my poor uncle, though he was a rough old farmer on the outside, he could not handle that! We ended up staying one more night. My brother Ron, and sister Judy, were not so soft hearted, and let me know right quick they were not impressed with my lack of courage! My cousin Duane, Theo's son, told me years later that as they watched us leave the next morning his Dad said "he'll be back"! But it never happened. Though we visited, we never moved back to Iowa.

––––––––

The trip out west was a roaring success! By the time we had dropped down and hit the famous old Route 66 and headed west, it was sunshine all the way to California. Dad had an almost new Chrysler 4 door Sedan, with big overstuffed seats, so we travelled in style. No comparison to those who had fled the Oklahoma dust bowl in the depression years of the 1930's. It was truly an adventure that seemed like it would never end.

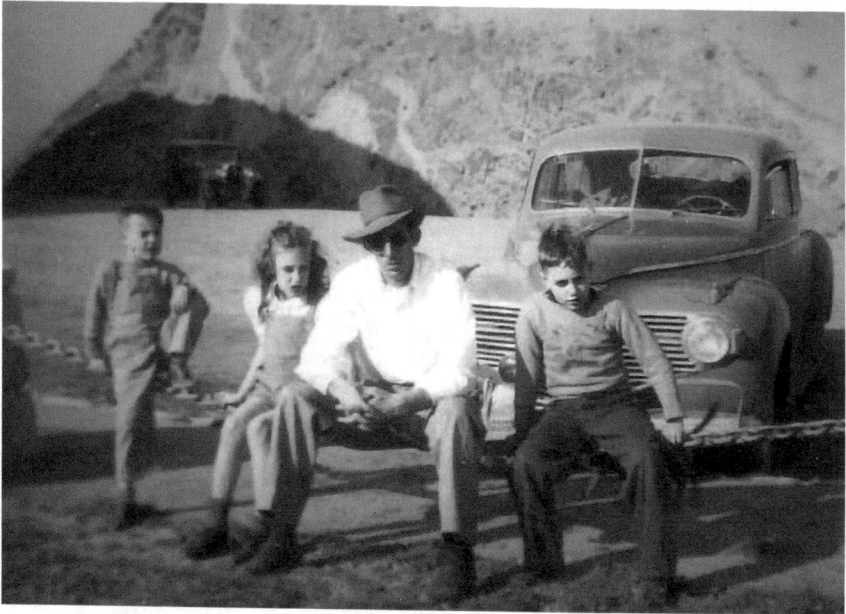

On the road to Oregon in 1947, Bobby, Judy, Wayne & Ronald Lee

We stopped for breakfast at a little restaurant out of Amarillo and had just sat down at a back corner table, when the door swung open and in walked 3 north Texas cowboys. We were awe struck. This wasn't Roy Rogers, Gene Autry, and Hopalong Cassidy. This was the real thing! One had fingers missing, one had a black patch over the spot where his eye had been, and the 3rd looked like a horse hoof had rearranged his face. They all radiated the smell of cows, horses, sweat, and whisky. We were wearing cowboy outfits, complete with hats, vests, and chaps, that Mom had bought before heading west. When the cowboys came in they couldn't believe their eyes when they saw us kids! With their heavy, dusty, chaps swinging and big roweled spurs clinking they came over and asked Dad where we were headed for. When they found out we were moving from Iowa to Oregon they invited us out to the ranch. This was beyond our wildest dreams! Those cowboys loved us kids and couldn't do enough for us. It was a real genuine working ranch a few miles out of town. This was the real raw west in all its glory, a Charles Russel or Frederic Remington painting. The smell of horses, cows, sagebrush and dust in the cold clean air. The sound of cattle bawling, men shouting, a cowboy riding in holding a calf in his arms. The last thing they did before we left was show us the bunkhouse. There was a long table down the middle, and bunks scattered along the walls. Right in the middle of the long table was a bottle of Four Roses Whiskey. The cowboys insisted that Dad have a drink before he left so he took a big swig to show his appreciation for their hospitality! They came out to the car to see us off and shake our hands before we left. We would never forget their kindness!

In New Mexico a big Mexican policeman pulled us over and told Dad he had failed to stop at a stop sign. Dad got in a big argument with him and we had to follow him back to the police station. I think Dad was lucky to get away with only a fine.

As we travelled through Arizona we stopped at the Grand Canyon which was quite a contrast to the corn fields of Iowa. We also saw a native woman wrapped in a colourful Navajo blanket standing on the shoulder of the road. We were all pretty excited as this was the first genuine Indian we had ever seen except in the movies. We stopped and as Dad backed up she turned her back to us. When Dad offered her $5.00 she was quite willing to turn around and have her picture taken.

When we arrived in Los Angeles, California. Dad took a wrong turn and we ended up going in the wrong direction on the freeway. Not hard to do when you are an Iowa farmer!

———

When we finally got to Red & Maxine's place in Oregon, it was a new ball game. All of a sudden reality set in. Red was in the process of building a new house. There were seven people in the Jones family, Red, Maxine, and 5 kids, Ed, Dick, Carma, Dwayne, and Donnie. The arrangement (not to my Mother's liking), was that we would live with them until Red and Dad got our house built at the foot of the hill going up to their place. So instead of seven being in their house, there would be twelve. Well, needless to say, it was quite a party! We were a long way back in the hills and between Red's fondness for making home brew, and Dad's dedication to shooting deer out of season, it was a pretty busy place.

Eddie, Judy, Ron, Carma, Bobby, Dick

One incident that didn't improve family relations happened when a good pair of Red's pants, hanging on the clothesline, were cut off at the knees, by one of the kids. They gave us all a good grilling but no one would confess. They lined all 8 of us up in the front room from the oldest to the youngest. They should have taken a picture! We were told that no one would be punished if they confessed. Well, how do you beat a deal like that. After mulling it over for about two seconds I confessed. I must have seemed too eager because they didn't believe me. It turned out that Dick was the culprit, and peace was once again restored.

10

Well we somehow managed to live together until Red and Dad got our house built. It wasn't anything too elaborate. In fact, it was half a house with the foundation being two big fir logs. Half a house with a lean-to for a bedroom built off the back. But we were happy. When I look at the pictures of us in our ragged bib overalls, we would probably be classed as deprived in today's world. But I don't think we were too hard done by. We spent endless hours in Strawberry Creek, a little stream a few feet wide a couple of hundred feet north of our house, which was full of crawdads and cutthroat trout.

There were several families that had came out to Oregon from Iowa, and almost every weekend they had a blow-out party at the Jones house. My Dad was a fiddle player and when they all got together, they would really raise the roof.

Red Jones & Wayne Mumford

11

Some You Win --- Some You Lose

We lived in what was known as the McDowell Creek area, on a little road that ran off to the south from the McDowell Creek Road, a couple of miles east of the schoolhouse. It was a fairly short road, maybe a ½ mile long, that wound around a bit before it went by our place, and ended at the Jones' home. It was really back in the boondocks. We were a few miles north of the logging town of Sweet Home.

There were probably ½ dozen families scattered along the road. Joe Heinz, a big German logger had the first place, a neat, well-kept farm back off the road. His son, Skipper, was about my age, though quite a bit taller, and always had plenty to say. The next place was right on the road, and was owned by old man Wagner. I don't remember his first name, but he was quite the story teller. His son, Gale, suffered from shell shock and had a steel plate from a serious head wound received during World War II.

Just up around the corner from the Wagners were our next-door neighbours, the Mack McTimmonds. I couldn't know it at time, but his kind, patient, long suffering wife, Effie, would have a profound effect on our family, the Jones family, and many other people she would befriend down through the years.

It was an interesting community. Out to the west of where we lived, the country opened up a little more, and there at a crossroads, was the McDowell Creek School. McDowell creek itself was a beautiful clear, rocky stream 30 or 40 feet wide, that flowed out of the Cascade Mountains to the east. We crossed it every day on our way to school. Church and school were a big part of our lives. I clearly recall our teacher for the first year at McDowell Creek School. Her name was Mrs. Patch. She was a big heavy woman who always dressed in black, wore her hair in a bun, and ruled with an iron hand. Our school was typical for that time, a one teacher, Grade 1 – 8 country school. It must have been a real challenge for her, as we were a pretty unsophisticated bunch. Dick and I were in Grade1 and Mrs. Patch was a hardliner. One of her cardinal rules was that you had to get permission when you were in class to go to the outhouse. You raised your hand and first finger if you had to go for a pee break, and two fingers for anything more serious. One day, Dick was feeling the urgent need for a two finger trip, and she didn't pay any attention to him. Maybe it was because he was sitting on an outside row next to the wall that she didn't notice him waving his hand, or maybe she was just ignoring him. Dick had a ruddy complexion under any circumstances, but now that he was getting to the panic stage, it had turned brick red. Frantically waving his arm with the two finger sign, he was reaching the extreme emergency zone. Finally, Mrs. Patch looked his way and asked him what he wanted. So, he told her exactly what he had to do. Well! This rattled even Mrs. Patch, and she hustled him out the door in high gear! After that little explosion, she kept a pretty close eye on him, and even if he reached up to scratch his ear, she was right there to see what he wanted!

Our next teacher, Mrs. Miller, was a slender, soft-spoken lady who held us all in the palm of her hand. Every day after lunch and noon recess, she would read gripping stories of the west that held us spellbound. What I remember the best about her was how she instilled in me a lifelong enjoyment of books and reading. She and her husband owned a horse ranch, and over a period of time, she took every kid that was old enough home with her to spend a weekend.

One incident that was on the comical side, was my battle with Skipper Heinz. Skipper lived on a little higher financial plane than us hillbillies at the end of the road. He actually had his own bike to ride to school, while in our family, we had managed to piece together one piece of junk for all three of us. Even at that, it was a great improvement over the old baby buggy we had finally ridden into total oblivion coming down the Jones' hill above our place. It happened on a mid winters afternoon, with 6 inches of sloppy, wet snow on the road. My brother, sister, and I, along with the Jones' kids, were trudging along about half way home from school. Most of the time, we were pretty good friends with Skipper, but on this day, he was riding along beside us on his good quality bike giving us a hard time because he could ride, and we had to walk.

Finally, in a moment of thoughtless bravado, I made a nice solid wet snowball and without ever considering it would hit him, let it fly! He had just opened his mouth and said, "don't you dare throw that!" when it hit him square in the mouth! I can still see the look of surprise and disbelief that crossed his face. He was off that bike in a split second, dug the snowball out of his mouth, and down into the mud and snow we went. I didn't stand a chance. He was taller and heavier than I was. But by some strange fluke, as we battled in the snow and slop, I managed to get on top of him. My brother and sister and the Jones' kids gathered around and cheered me on, and finally Skipper yelled, "calf rope!" Now back in that time and place "calf rope" meant you gave up. Well, for all the rest of the way home I was the hero of the day. Unfortunately, when I opened the door of the school house the next morning, he was waiting, and his bony fist hit me square in the nose and brought my reigning championship to an end!

We lived in Oregon and went to the McDowell Creek School for four years with the Jones' kids. Overall it was a good time, except for one incident I remember. I'm still not sure why the Cunders' kids had it in for us. There were three kids, George, the oldest, and most easy going of the bunch. Ronnie was in the middle, and pure mean from one end to the other. Their sister Jackie was a little younger than Ronnie, with the same personality. Both Ronnie and Jackie seemed to have inherited their Mom's personality, as she was pretty hard to deal with. They lived in the house on Clarence Bates' farm about half way home from school, just across the first bridge we had to cross.

The situation came to the point where the teacher sent them home from school ahead of us, reasoning, I guess that their Mom would keep them under control. That never happened. It came to a climax on a day when, after giving us the gears as we crossed the bridge, they followed us up the road. My older brother, Ron, was the main object of harassment by Ronnie Cunders. My brother had made a small leather quirt for protection in case all three jumped him; and when Ronnie went after him, he let him have it across the leg with the quirt. Then they fell down into the grader ditch and went at it no holds barred.

My brother had thrown his quirt down on the road when the battle began, and George had picked it up and was cutting it to pieces with his pocket knife. By this time, my brother Ron was on top of the other Ronnie and giving him a pretty good overhaul. It was at this point that Ronnie Cunders began to yell at his brother, "Stab 'im, Georgie, stab 'im!" This scared me right out of my wits because Georgie began to move toward them in the ditch with his pocket knife in his hand. I was four years younger than my brother and that day at school, a bunch of us younger kids had been playing dinosaur. This was a big rage in the movies at that time. I had an oblong shaped lunch box with dual handles that met in the middle. Scared right out of my tree, I knew one thing for sure, nobody was going to stab my brother! With a cry like a Tyrannosaurus Rex dinosaur, I sprang onto Georgie's back and began to beat him over the head with my lunch bucket. To this day I don't know what would have happened if Dad had not come along. Both he and Mrs. Cunders arrived at the scene at the same time.

"Get those boys out of that ditch," she screamed, "and my boy will whip your boy!" Dad was always a fair- minded type, so they got the boys untangled and up out of the ditch, and both Ronnie and Georgie headed for home as fast as they could run. Unfortunately, that was not the end of the story. Dad left to continue his way to town, never suspecting the whole thing wasn't over. I don't know how he knew what was coming, but my brother told me to give him my lunch box and get home as fast as I could.

When he came limping home later, he was bruised and blood from head to toe. The only thing that saved him from very serious injury was that lunch box, and it was squashed as flat as a pancake. The Cunder boys had come back on their bikes and really beat him up. Ron had used the lunch box to deflect the biggest rocks they had thrown at him. This brought things to a head, and from then on, we went home first. Not long after they left the area, and hopefully at some point in time, got things together a little better in neighbourly relations.

Grab Bags and Pocket Knives

I'm not sure when the McDowell Creek area was settled, it may have been a spill over from the settlers that came west on the Oregon Trail. Located east of the flat, fertile Willamette Valley, it was beautiful country, with rolling hills and farmland. There was a lot of German people in the area with their neat, prosperous farms, and well organized ways.

We all went to the McDowell Creek School together, and my sister, Judy, became very good friends with Susan Swink. Susan's Dad, Albert Swink, had a large turkey farm that bordered the McDowell Creek Road. We passed it every day on our way to and from school. Every time we went by, I couldn't help but think of Christmas and Thanksgiving dinner. He had a nice home, lawn, and landscaping. It was a totally different world than our back- woods way of life.

Ready for Church: Ron, Bobby, Judy, Mom

The Swinks were a hard working, church attending family, and possibly because of the girls' friendship, they took a very dedicated interest in taking us to Sunday School. In case there was any lingering doubt about the German presence in the area, the name of the church they attended was called Berlin! We loved going to the Berlin Church. The sermons could get a little long and boring, but they made it pretty plain what was right and what was wrong.

The highlight for us kids was an event that took place in the church sanctuary that you could take part in if you faithfully attended Sunday School so many weeks in a row. It was called "The Grab Bag", a box with a hole in the top just big enough for your hand, and was full of different kinds of candy, small toys, and trinkets. But best of all, somewhere down in there were some single bladed pocket knives! The rules of this reward time were pretty strict. You walked to the front of the church, and with the eyes of the whole congregation boring into your back, quickly reached in, grabbed a handful of whatever you got, and headed back to your seat.

Like most small boys at that time, I had a real fascination with knives. If you had a pocket knife, you had arrived. As luck would have it, there were two kinds of pocket knives in that Grab Bag. They were identical, simple, single bladed pocket knives, one with a black plastic simulated bone handle, the other a beautiful white simulated pearl handle. I wanted the one with the pearl handle in the worst way. The Sunday finally came. My name was called, and I headed up the aisle. The sombre eyes of all those stern faced German elders fastened on me from the front, the eyes of the whole church congregation from the back. I plunged my hand into the Grab Bag. All I could feel were pieces of candy and trinkets. The pressure was intense, but I began my search, feeling, sorting, until finally the elders began to clear their throats and shuffle in their chairs. That's when I felt it, the unmistakable shape of a pocket knife! I think it was about then that our Sunday School teacher pointed out that this was a "Grab Bag", not a "Search Bag". By this time, I was a nervous wreck, so clutching my knife, I headed back to my seat, but I had missed the prize! The knife I held in my hand was not the treasured pearl handled one but the one with the black simulated bone handle.

The Way It Was

In later years, especially after coming to Canada, I have often reflected on the influence some people have had on my life. In the early years, its something that was always there, although it may take a lot of water under the bridge before you appreciate its value. Those straight laced German farmers were that kind of people. But they also had a sense of humour, at least that's the only reason I can think of for what Albert Swink did one morning on the way to church. To really understand this whole episode, it is necessary to understand the difference between the way established law- abiding farmers and the out-of-season outlaws viewed hunting deer.

I'm sure the early pioneers in Oregon simply shot deer when they needed them. Then, as they prospered and developed herds of cattle, flocks of turkeys, and other livestock, their dependence on wild game fell off and hunting seasons were put in place; that was the norm. I think Dad, Red Jones, and the rest of the new immigrants from Iowa saw themselves as pioneers. Shooting deer out of season was a fairly common practice at that time. Spot lighting was the method a lot of people used. They would use a spotlight at night to catch the reflection of the deer's eyes, and then shoot them with a .22 caliber rifle to keep the noise level down. But that wasn't the way my Dad hunted.

My Dad, Wayne Mumford, was a born outdoorsman and hunter. As a kid, growing up in Iowa, he would sit in school during the winter months and imagine himself as a trapper in the great fur laden country of the Canadian North. With his first cousin, Edwin, a big, tall, strapping kid about the same age, he was always on the trail of some mink, skunk, or raccoon in the broken hills and fields around the little town of Oakley where they grew up. They usually had a Hound or Rat Terrier with them. When we were kids, at one time we had 32 hounds on the farm. That included a litter or two of pups, I think, but it was still quite a pile of dogs. But they were there for a purpose; you could sell the pups.

One of my favourite pictures is one of Dad and Shorty Ryan, a neighbour he hunted with a lot, taken beside the end of a shed covered with pelts from animals they had caught.

Dad & Shorty with raccoon & mink pelts

In the Midwest, during the 1930's, things on the farm weren't real prosperous. You ate well, but cash money was hard to come by, and mink and coon hides equalled cash money. When we arrived in Oregon, we weren't broke, but we weren't rich either. With all those growing kids to feed, and with the hills crawling with blacktail deer, what was a man to do? To the best of my knowledge, Dad got somewhere between 22 and 25 deer before he ever shot a legal one. When he got his first legal buck, it was a beauty. I still remember like yesterday, going in to help pack it out. Not that us kids were any help, but we all got to go along just for the excitement. In later years, my brother Ron, who is the hunting and gun pro in the family, took the head from this trophy buck up to Columbia Falls, Montana, where he lives, and had it remounted for Dad. It scored in the top ratings in the Boone and Crockett Record Book, but was disallowed because they thought it might be a blacktail, mule deer cross.

But that didn't affect the flavour. We lived on deer meat. We also lived in fear of being caught! Even though we lived back in the sticks, people were fairly regularly caught for shooting deer out of season. Somewhere, Dad had bought a 30/40 Krag. I'm sure that all of our reasonably close neighbours knew what was going on with the deer population. A 30/40 Krag is not a BB gun, and as far as I know that's the only gun Dad ever used.

The Jones' kids and us were constantly warned to never say anything to anyone about shooting deer out of season. You would have thought that living in this constant atmosphere of being aware of what you say would have made it second nature for us to never give the slightest hint that anything illegal was going on. But no, as in all great crimes, someone has to make the fatal slip, and this is where Albert Swink pulled his little prank!

It happened on the way to Sunday School. We were riding along in the back of Albert's car. I was probably giving some serious thought about my next chance at a pearl handled pocket knife from the Grab Bag, when out of the blue came the question, "has your Dad been shooting any deer lately?" Lulled into complacency by the soft car seat and far off dreams of Grab Bags and pocket knives, I replied just as casually "yeah, he just got one yesterday." Dead silence. I had said it. My brother and sister looked at me in total shock and disbelief. I had betrayed the family! We drove on in silence. From that day on, we lived in gnawing apprehension, no one more than me. When we got home that day, I really got the gears. All the rest of the time we lived in McDowell Creek, we continued to go to the Berlin Church with the Swinks, and never another word was said about shooting deer. I've often wondered if maybe that was Albert's subtle way of letting us know he was aware of what was going on.

———

Another valuable lesson impressed on me during the time we lived on McDowell Creek, was respect for your elders. As mentioned earlier, one of our neighbours was old man Wagner. I think that's all anyone ever called him. He was quite a character, and famous in the community for his tall tales. He would sit outside on a warm afternoon when the Jones kids, Virgil McTimmonds, and my brother and sister and I would be coming home from school, and invite us to come over and talk for a little while. During these visits, he would tell some tall tale that couldn't possibly be true, but back in those days, story telling was a fine art, and didn't have to be true as long as it was entertaining!

As we stood there listening to old man Wagoner that day, it was probably my desire to impress the crowd that led to my mistake, or maybe it was the fact that everyone in the neighbourhood was saying it, just not out in the open. Whatever the case, at some point, as we all stood around listening to old man Wagoner's tall tale, I summoned the courage to tell him he was a "lying old coyote"! Oh, the price of bravery, honesty, and stupidity! That night, when Dad came home, I learned in a right quick way by the old leather belt, that even if some old man was a "lying old coyote", it wasn't the job of a 7 year old kid to tell him so!

Hillbilly Hazards

The small, out of the way world that we lived in, was filled with hazards. It's not my intention to belittle or downplay the safety conscious parents and society that we live in today, but a lot of this protective gear is of fairly recent invention and, without a doubt, has prevented no end of injuries, and saved countless lives. But at that time they were simply not there, so you learned through experience to figure out what you could get by with and still survive, with not too many parts missing. We played Tarzan of the Apes across the road from our house in the vine maples. We could swing from tree to tree for long distances, yelling out the Tarzan call. "Tarzan" was my brother's role, as he was the one with the official leather "G" string, which he had made out of an old leather jacket of Dads. My sister of course, was "Jane" the wife, and depending on the day or the need, I was given the lowly role of "Boy", the son, or, worse yet, "Cheetah", the monkey. I got to the point of being able to do a pretty good job of either one, especially "Cheetah".

My sister Judy was a real tomboy. One Christmas, someone from Iowa had sent her a beautiful big doll. She was totally heart broken, and would have nothing to do with that doll for weeks. What she had wanted for a Christmas present was not some sissy doll, but a Red Ryder BB gun!

One implement that was always laying around was an axe. At some point in time every kid that lived in the backwoods had to learn how to use an axe. Somehow, it seemed that at a certain time in your life, you just picked it up, and saw what you could do with it. If parents, brothers or sisters had warned you to leave it alone, that only added more incentive to the temptation to give it a try. I'm sure it was Ron's job to split the kindling and keep the wood box full, because by this time, he was13 years old, and went to a boys club at church called The Kings Teens.

Unfortunately for her, my sister decided one evening to split the kindling with our long handled double bit axe. The worst possible kind for a kid to be cutting wood with, but like car seats and seat belts and a hundred other things, it was something you didn't worry about. Being the tomboy type she was probably also going to show my brother she could split kindling just as good as he could. Whatever the reason, she brought the edge of the axe straight down on that block of fir wood, holding the big axe in one hand, and the block of wood with the other, and clipped a neat ½ inch off the end of her thumb. She dropped the axe, and with a blood curdling howl, ran for the house.

Judy, Ron, & Bobby

The first thing to do, of course, was to stop the bleeding. When that was accomplished, someone suddenly realized that if we got the end of her thumb, we could rush her into the hospital and get it sewn back on. That's where the fun began. We had a dozen or so free range chickens that were constantly patrolling around looking for some tidbit to eat, and as luck would have it, one of them had spotted that piece of thumb. Then the race was on! We would almost catch the chicken that had the thumb, and it would drop it and before we could grab it, another chicken would snatch it up, and the race was on again! Sadly, the chickens were all the same colour, and in the wild melee, we finally lost track of which one had the thumb, and which one didn't! Needless to say, we were a little queasy about eating eggs for few days, but life has to go on. It was really too bad we weren't able to retrieve the end of her thumb, because it took weeks of going to the doctor to have the proud flesh removed, and weeks of suffering before the end of her thumb finally healed.

————

In the slam bang of daily adventure, somebody was always getting cut, or bruised, or loosing some hide. My cousins, Ed, Dick, and I were like brothers. We were basically the same age and pretty much fought and played together on a daily basis, since they lived on the hill just above us. Their house was a king's palace compared to our humble two-room home. It wasn't that I envied them, they just had a lot more room to play inside. Their basement was pretty much off limits due to the home brew crocks and the hanging illegal deer, but being a 3 story house, the whole top story was pretty much theirs. On the third floor, they had, with the help of their Dad, set up an incredible electric train track. You name it, from bridge to whistles, it was all there.

As a kid I was always a homebody. When the sun went behind the hill and dark came, I wanted to be home. It was probably the lure of that train track that prompted me to agree to come up and spend the night with them. After all, it was only a good rock throw from their place to our yard at the foot of the hill. So, with great bravado, the adventure began. But along about bedtime, I began to get this intense yearning to be in my own bed at home. They begged, they pleaded, but there was only one answer. I was going home! So, against all their wishes and cautions, I went out, crawled on the family bike, and headed for home. The road down to our house was steep. When the road was built, all the big fir stumps were rolled out and pushed on the down hill side of the road. When I left their house that night, it was pitch black. I completely missed the junction where their driveway hit the main road, and sailed over the edge out into the darkness and fir stumps far below. That's the last thing I remember.

When I came to, I was sitting on a chair in our kitchen at home, and the bike was parked out in the front yard with the kick stand down. I was a very fortunate kid! To this day I don't have the slightest idea how I got home. The only thing I can assume is that I was half cold conked, but still awake enough to drag that bike out and somehow get home! On top of that, the bike wasn't damaged, and by some miracle, neither was I!

The Family Bike

Our parents had to warn us kids about black bears, and it wasn't unheard of to hear a cougar scream at night. We lived in a little open area, in a vast forest of untouched wilderness. Across the road from our house, an old logging trail wandered back into the standing timber. It was over grown with thistles and tall grass, and slowly returning to the surrounding forest. About a hundred feet down this old trail was a big, half rotten, moss covered fir log. It was rolled off to one side, and left because of some defect. A story began to circulate that farther down that road was a giant fir tree that was hollow inside. I don't recall all the particulars now, but it raised the spirit of exploration and discovery in my cousin, Dick Jones, and I. Why we ever took Carma along, I will never know. Probably because she threatened to tell on us if we didn't. As we slowly moved into the deeper timber, every bear and cougar story we had ever heard began to crowd into our over active minds. We finally decided this whole story about a big hollow tree was just a figment of someone's imagination, and we slowly began the return journey, taking a quick look back over our shoulders every now and then as a precaution.

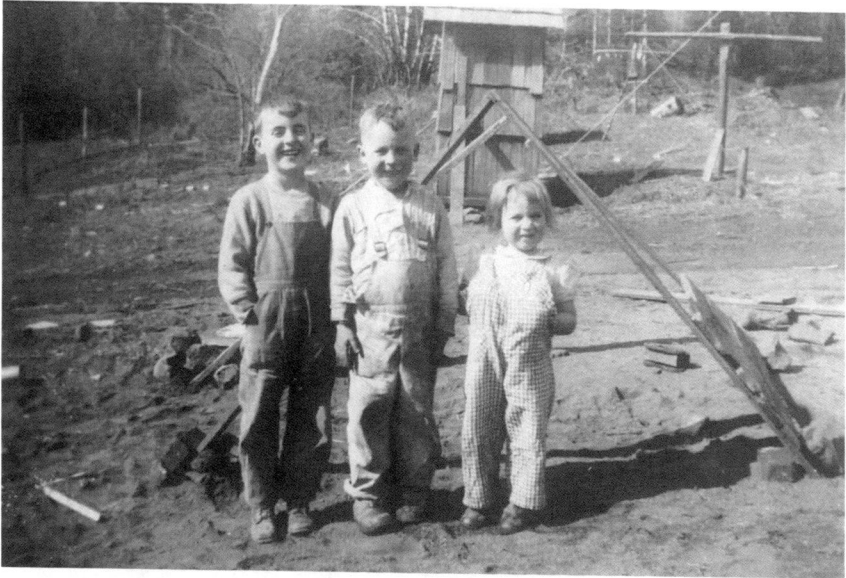

Bobby, Dick, & Carma

We had just gotten to the middle of the old rotten fir log, that we had passed earlier, when from behind that log came the most heart stopping, adrenalin generating growl you could imagine! For one zero part of a second,

Dick and I stood frozen in our tracks, then we were gone. I don't think our feet even hit the ground until we were a hundred feet up the trail, and we had totally abandoned poor little Carma! Tangled up in the weeds and grass, she was screaming and crying, and scared to death. She eventually made it out on her own. But I don't think she ever trusted us again! We found out later that my Dad had seen us head off on our great expedition, and decided this was a perfect time to put the fear in us. He hid behind the old log and made the growl, so that we would stay where we belonged. I think he believed that Dick and I should have had the decency to take Carma with us when we made our hasty retreat!

The Good Times

We had our accidents and catastrophes on McDowell Creek, but there were good times along with the bad. Picnics, music jams, berry picking, 4th of July celebrations and crawdad feeds were some of the good times. The 4th of July was a real literal blow out for us. Maybe because it was not that long after the end of the war. It's a wonder we didn't set the whole state on fire with the Roman Candles and every other kind of exploding, flame throwing gadget you could buy! I was a complete nut case when it came to fire crackers! By all early indications, I should have become a demolitions expert! "Fire cracker crazy" was my nickname. It was a pure miracle we got through that stage of growth with all 10 fingers and undamaged eye sight, but practice leads to perfection, and it was amazing how handy we became.

It was Mack McTimmonds idea to have the Crawdad feed. For someone not familiar with crawdads, they are simply a small freshwater version of a lobster. As kids, we spent endless hours laying across some wet log on Strawberry Creek, luring crawdads or crayfish out of their hiding places with a piece of bacon rind, tied on the end of a string. Strawberry Creek was loaded with them, and when the great Crawdad Day Festival arrived, we had a couple of big buckets filled with these miniature lobsters; a seething mass crawling over the backs of each other, trying to escape. Down by the creek we had a bucket of water over a roaring fire. Mack was the master chef and would reach in the bucket and grab a crawdad, and drop it into the boiling water. He was pretty handy at that because you had to grab them just behind their arms, or they could give you a nasty pinch.

We were having quite a feast, the Jones clan, our family, and Mack as the chef. Everybody was pulling off tails and pinchers, the edible parts, and throwing the main body in a separate bucket. Someone noticed that Donnie Jones, who was much younger than the rest of us, was throwing the good parts away, and was buried right up to his nose in the bright orange of whatever it was, that was contained in the body cavity! This caused great howls of laughter from the rest of us kids, who by this time considered ourselves great connoisseurs of crawdad etiquette. His peculiar culinary tastes didn't seem to have any ill effects on him, but it became a family joke that was never forgotten!

———

My Grandparents, Uncle Robert, and some of Dads first cousins had never been out west. In the first few years they came out to Oregon to visit a couple of times. I think they were impressed with Oregon, but it wasn't their kind of country, too raw, too untamed, too wild. Those were good times, especially for us kids. They were really good to us, and always brought us some new toys and clothes. As a young woman, my maternal grandmother, Nora Francis Batman, lost a baby boy at birth, and a few years later lost twin boys at 1 year of age. The loss of the baby boys had a lasting effect on my grandmother, and she had an almost obsessive love for my brother Ron and I. Truthfully, it was me even more than my brother. I think that partly came from the fact that my Mom had some serious complications, and was in the hospital for quite a while after I was born, so Grandma Batman took care of me. I've often thought pity may have played a big part as well, because I was not a very cute baby at 10+ pounds, and it looked like 9 pounds of that was nose! It wasn't that she ignored my older brother and sister, but I seemed to be her favourite. That, of course, is never a healthy situation.

Grandma & Grandpa Batman were mixed farmers in Iowa. Like most farms back then they grew corn, raised hogs and beef, chickens, ducks, geese... you name it. They milked a few cows by hand and separated the cream. They were hard working people, and when you sat down to eat, every meal was a king's banquet, and a cardiovascular, cholesterol nightmare! Everything you could possibly want was on that table. I guess they must have burned it off because both grandparents lived to a fairly good old age. They were real mid-westerners; my Grandmother was into politics and very outspoken. Grandpa Arthur Emery Batman was as quiet as my Grandmother was loud and I always thought he resembled Abraham Lincoln. On a soft summer evening he would sit out on the porch and play the old songs on his harmonica, and it felt like the whole world was at peace.

Grandparents Arthur & Nora Batman with Lois (my Mom) and Uncle Robert 1944.

We were never able to spend a lot of time with our Grandma Ethel Mumford as she lived in a small house in Chariton. She was very close to Donald, her youngest son, and his family. When Donald moved his family to Lebanon, Oregon for a couple of years, Grandma Mumford came out to visit us all, and was there for my 7th birthday in July 1948, and the birth of our baby sister, Janice Kae, in August 1948.

Kay & Francis Williams, in-law relatives, who had also moved out from Iowa to Lebanon, Oregon, were good friends with our family. I don't recall the reason now, but I went to stay with Kay and Francis for a few days.

During that time, Kay and I went on a shopping trip to Lebanon, a main business and shopping center for the area. It was where my younger sister, Janice-Kay, was born; my older sister Judy, had her thumb repaired; and where my cousins, Ed & Dick Jones, and I, had our tonsils removed, and I got my first pair of blue jeans. It seemed the practice at that time was to get your tonsils removed at a certain age. The incentive for this operation in my case was that I would get my first pair of genuine Penny's "Foremost" blue jeans! They couldn't get me to the hospital fast enough! Even as the ether mask was being lowered over my face, I was already in La La Land dreaming of pulling on the first pair of "real" blue jeans.

Grandma Mumford, Mom, Ron, Bobby, Judy

On our trip to Lebanon, Kay Williams and I happened to walk by a western clothing store. In the front display window, where I could almost touch it, was a genuine pearl grey Stetson hat with a 4" brim, and I mean genuine Stetson! It looked exactly like the one Roy Rogers wore. I pointed this out to Kay, who didn't really seem to see how important that was, so I think I mentioned it again several times over the next couple of days.

Our heroes back then were pretty much limited to Roy Rogers and Trigger, Gene Autry and Champion, Tarzan and Jane. The movies were almost always shoot'em up westerns featuring Roy or Gene. Roy and his horse Trigger were far and away my favourites. Somehow Roy had just the right kind of squint-eyed look a real cowboy should have, and Trigger was the perfect horse.

A couple of days later, we went to Lebanon again, and just happened to go by that western store. You guessed it! Lo and behold, that hat was still in the window! I quickly pointed this out to Kay, and this time he stopped, looked it over, and we went in. That day, I was wearing one of those little, red, felt slouch hats with about a 2" brim. All kinds of people wore them. They were simply called an Oregon Red Hat. They were a favourite hat with loggers, and was the main hat they wore before the tin hat came along. Well, the long and the short of it was that Kay Williams bought that Roy Rogers Stetson hat for me that day! It cost him plenty; $40.00 was a pile of money in those days! When we left that fancy clothing store and headed down the main street, I had on that pearl grey Stetson hat that fit clear down over my ears, and Kay had my little, Oregon Red Hat perched on top of his red head. We both had a grin that went from one ear to the other, and everyone we met on the sidewalk did too! I treasured that hat for years.

Dogs, Lesson Learned, Tragedy

Dogs and dog fights were a never ending source of entertainment and concern for us. We had two small dogs. The oldest, Brownie, was a little female rat terrier we had brought with us from Iowa in 1947. The youngest, was her fully grown pup, Butch. He was hard to describe, about as homely as they come; solid built with short legs and a long body, and big ears that stood straight up. Butch had long black hair that hung to the ground because of his short legs, and a white patch on his belly, and on the end of each foot. He had a brown patch over each eye and a long straight tail. He might have been homely but he was all heart.

Ron holding Butch, Judy standing by

Butch never knew what it meant to back down from a fight. When Virgil McTimmonds walked by our place with his big lab, Butch would come out to bark at them, and defend his turf. The big lab would grab him and shake him like a rat, then mop the ground with him. We would all come running to break up the fight. Butch may have been small and homely but he wasn't stupid. The opening under our house was higher at one end and lower at the other. One day when Virgil came by and the big lab took after Butch he ran for the high end of the house with the lab in hot pursuit. Butch had a plan in mind. He ran under the house with the lab right on his tail. There was plenty of room for the big dog to follow him at the beginning but the further Butch lured him under the house the tighter the spot became. Finally, the big dog was right down on his belly and had wedged himself solid under the house. Thats when Butch got his revenge. The big lab was stuck so tight he couldn't budge and Butch chewed him from one end to the other. The howls for mercy coming out from under the house was music to our ears. After that when Virgil came by, the big lab made sure he stayed on the other side of the road.

––––––––

Our neighbour, Mack McTimmonds, was a complex man. He tended to be a little on the grumpy side, but over all he seemed to like us kids. He played the guitar and taught my brother Ron how to play a few chords. Mack had the perfect voice for singing the old cowboy songs and we loved to sit and listen to him.

One day I was down in his wood shed for some reason, probably watching him split kindling or work on something. I suddenly noticed an unbelievable prize laying on a shelf against the wall. I could never have guessed it at the time, but that object would haunt me for a long time. It was a U.S. Navy combat knife. It was a beauty, full leather handle, with probably a 10" blade. Something I could never own in my wildest dreams! If I had that knife, I would be the envy of every kid in the neighbourhood.

It's not easy in this day and age, when most kids have more toys and gimmicks than they can ever possibly play with, to understand how bad I wanted that knife! It also may be hard to understand, in a world where the line between right and wrong has become more and more blurred and hazy, to understand how wrong it was to even think of stealing that knife. Those old German preachers and kind Sunday School teachers had made an indelible impression on our backwoods brains when it came to "Thou shalt not steal!" This was re-enforced by the teaching of our own parents, especially Mom. It was essentially the same with Dad when it came to a man's tools, guns or anything personal that might affect his work or whatever. But when it came to something like making home brew, shooting deer out of season, or possibly helping yourself to one of Albert Swink's turkeys, he figured there was room for adjusting the interpretation of the law a little. The first two items weren't really a big deal. It might be against the law, but it didn't hurt anyone. But when it came to taking one of Albert Swink's turkeys, you had to see it as doing him a favour. There was always a strong possibility that a turkey that was stupid enough to have wandered away from the rest of the flock, and strayed up to the edge of the road, would be picked off by some predator and not do anyone any good. So, in effect, you were doing Albert a favour by removing this genetically faulty bird from the flock so it didn't pass this wandering habit on to future generations of turkeys.

But that wasn't the case with the hunting knife. The struggle was terrible. Mack was a hard drinker, but he was also my friend. In the end, I stole the knife. It weighed a pound in my hand, and a hundred pounds on my mind. I didn't know what to do with it, I had never stolen anything before. For a while, I hid it. I would sneak it out, look at it, hold it in my hand, feel the solid strength of the leather handle, but there was no joy there. I couldn't stand to be around Mack anymore. I lived under a cloud of guilt and anxiety, afraid I'd be caught. Then I came up with what I thought was a brilliant idea! I would overhaul it. I would change the look of it so much that no one would recognize it, and say I had found it along the road.

There must be some kind of parable of life in what I tried to do with that knife. The first thing was to get rid of that leather handle. Somehow, with the aid of a hack saw, pliers, and whatever else, I managed to get all those little leather rings cut off. When I got finished, it was a mess. The leather rings were what held the hand guard tight, and now it simply rattled around on the handle. I then got the idea to wrap the handle with soldering wire. So where to get that? It doesn't take much imagination for that one. Once you start down the trail, one crime leads to another.

It never really worked. Even at the best, it was a botched job and never even came close to really working. Finally, I brought the knife out of hiding. The questions, of course, came thick and fast, and the answers didn't convince anyone. The trips to the Berlin Sunday School and the Grab Bag became trips of condemnation, not joy, because now I was not only a thief, but a liar as well. But now, it reached the point where I had enough. When I told Mack what I had done, he just looked at me. Even now, after all these years, I can remember that look.

Mack had a heavy face, with baggy, blood shot eyes. It wasn't hard to see he was a heavy drinker, and wrestled with his own demons. I don't remember that he said a word, but in his eyes was a look of sadness and disappointment. I had failed him. I had been his friend, and now I had let him down. Maybe after all these years, I'm remembering these things as a little more dramatic than they were, but I don't think so. There was a time in Mack's life when he, too, had been a young, innocent kid, and at some point had made a bad choice, and then another one. The man that looked at me then knew how things could get away on you.

———

When we came to McDowell Creek there were three sons, Billy, Virgil, Norman, and an older daughter, Ethel, in the McTimmonds family. Virgil was the same age as my brother Ron. Billy was our hero. He was a big, tall, good looking guy, and just out of the U.S. Navy. He had married a beautiful local girl, Lois Pickens, tall and graceful, with long dark hair. They were a very striking couple, and to us grimy, ragamuffin kids, they were like a Prince and Princess out of a fairy tale.

Not long after being discharged from the Navy, Billy started working on the landing for a local logging contractor. He had been working two or three days, when we got the news that Billy McTimmonds had been killed working in the woods! Stunned! That's the only word I can think of that describes how we all felt. Impossible…not Billy McTimmonds! Maybe some old, careless, broken down logger that couldn't move fast anymore, or one that had a hangover, and wasn't paying attention. But not our hero, not Billy McTimmonds, who had his whole life ahead of him, and a beautiful wife who was 4 months pregnant with a little girl that would be named Debbie. It was about this time I began to realize that life isn't always fair.

That evening, Mom, Maxine Jones, and all of us kids gathered at the McTimmonds house. I'm not sure where the men were. It was a small house, simple but neat and clean. We all mourned together, kids and Mothers, as many as could crowd in. We sang "The Old Rugged Cross", and "I Come to the Garden Alone", and at some point we even sang "Old Shep". We were not very sophisticated people, but we were certainly sincere in our desire to show them what Billy meant to us all.

The death of Billy was only another great weight added to the burden that Effie McTimmonds bore. Their youngest son, Norman, had been born with Down's Syndrome, which meant years of caregiving. Mack, her husband, was not only a hard drinking man, he could also be mean. When he really went on a full blown rampage, he was bad news! But there are some people who, because of their great faith and determination, shape their world instead of letting their world shape them. Effie McTimmonds was that kind of woman. In later years, Mack did quit drinking and became a Christian.

I have told this story to a lot of people down through the years, and I think that Effie was one of the best examples I have ever known of what the Bible says true love really is. "Love suffers long and is kind". "Bears all things, hopes all things, endures all things". "Love never fails". 1 Corinthians 13:4,7,8. Effie McTimmonds was a Seventh-day Adventist Christian. We had never heard of such a thing. Probably the strangest thing about her was that she went to church on Saturday instead of Sunday.

Other than sending us kids to Sunday School, religion wasn't a big thing in our family. Mom and Dad had gone to the Baptist Church in Iowa as young people; but that was just a social thing. Effie would come down and visit with Mom every once in a while. When Mom asked her about this Saturday church thing, Effie pointed out that at creation, and in the Ten Commandments, it was pretty plain the seventh day was Saturday. Mom had never given it much thought until Dad was laid off work, and looking at the calendar to fill in the unemployment forms, realized that Saturday was the seventh day of the week. If you were going to go by the Bible, then Saturday was the day of worship, set aside as a memorial of Creation. Mom eventually became a Seventh-day Adventist Christian. It cost her dearly. Her

38

family back home gave her a lot of opposition. But, like Effie McTimmonds, she stuck to her guns, and eventually Dad and most of us kids also became Adventist Christians. When we moved to California, she spent a good part of her life working to put us kids through the Adventist school system.

A Big Change

Dick Burl, the guy Dad worked for, moved his whole logging crew down to California with him. I have been told that the coast of northern California is the foggiest place in the world outside of London, England. After the beautiful summers at McDowell Creek, it was like having your head stuck in a 10 gallon bucket of pea soup! Oh, there was the odd day you got a faint glimmer of sun, but mostly in the years I lived there, it was grey, with fog in the summer, and rain and more fog, in the winter. The fog only extended inland for a few miles, and when you broke out of it, there was a different world. It was really noticeable in the fall during the deer hunting season. When you left the fog belt where the giant Redwoods grew, and headed up into the Coast Mountains where the Douglas Fir held sway, you could look down for endless miles on a great fluffy grey blanket.

Moving to California

When we first moved south, we lived for a short while in a motel. We were like caged animals. Traffic, people, noise, and on top of it all, that dismal grey fog. Eventually, Dad rented a place out in the country on a hill just above a little store and tavern called Clam Beach Tourist Camp, north of the town of Arcata. The house was just a small one bedroom place, but it had a cabin that had three rooms that we made into bedrooms. Our landlord's name was George Beck. George was a good guy, but was quite a drinker. You could tell by his red nose, but you never saw him drunk.

George had a bulb farm. There were a lot of them in that part of California at that time, big white Easter Lilies. He had a big, white sprawling mansion of a house, a huge shop, and a lot of top quality outbuildings. Of course, my brother and I had to explore these outbuildings on the sly, and in one of them, my brother found a Martin guitar. I think Ron made a deal with George to work off the price of the guitar in the bulb fields, and by a lot of diligent effort became a real Chet Atkins style guitar player.

Ron and his Martin guitar

41

The whole area was a big flat plateau above the ocean, where you could stand on the edge and look for miles out to sea when it was clear. The sand dunes and beach were only 1/4 of a mile away down a very steep embankment. Just south of us on this plateau, was the Arcata, California Commercial Airport. The whole area around the airport had been cleared during the Second World War to test fog dispersal equipment. Miles of pipe had been installed that blew hot air, or gas, to disperse the fog when a plane was coming in to land. This huge cleared area had now grown back to scattered brush mixed with open spaces and was loaded with California quail and rabbits.

———

Somewhere along the way, we had ended up with an old Stevens bolt action .22 rifle with no front sight. Ron figured out that we could tap a bevel headed screw into the notch where the front sight had been, file it off, bevel both sides, and just like that, we'd have a front sight. It worked like a charm, and by some strange fluke, when we tried it out, it shot right on the button! About a quarter of a mile west of us, and a quarter of a mile north, right on the sharp edge of the hill that broke over and went down to the sand dunes and beach, was the local garbage dump. It was swarming with rats. Big rats. When you crawled up to the edge of the bank and they realized you were there, it looked like the whole dump was moving as they headed for their holes. That's when we would open up on them. Strangely enough, the whole time we lived at George's place, I don't ever remember seeing a rat around his buildings, or ours. We spent all our time hunting, and a lot of that was spent at the dump.

We were miles ahead of our time when it came to recycling. There was endless numbers of pop and beer bottles to be picked out of the dump and hauled down to the little store below our house. We then used the money to buy .22 and shot gun shells to shoot rats, quail, band tail pigeons, or whatever else that was fair game.

———

Moving to California in 1952 was a big change for me. The first year I went to Dawes Prairie Elementary School. The subjects I seemed to have an aptitude for were writing, spelling, history and geography. Math and science were a hard go. When it came to sports it was football, and baseball, but I loved the simplicity of running for track and field. But mostly I loved the freewheeling simplicity of just plain running! A friend, Ron Remington, could outrun me; he wasn't a big guy but he was quite an athlete, and later became a football star when we went to Arcata High School. The next year, when I was in Grade 6, we went to the new public McKinleyville Elementary School. I've often wondered about the things that influence you in making bad decisions, or what we use as an excuse to make bad decisions in our lives. For me, it was school. School and teachers.

Buck Fever and Silver Salmon

I came down with Rheumatic Fever not too long after we moved to California. Up to that point in time, we were all a fairly healthy bunch, and I think by spending a good share of our lives scrounging through the dump shooting rats and collecting bottles to recycle, we had developed immunity to most diseases, including the Bubonic Plague! Mom took me to an Italian doctor in Arcata named Dr. Portalupe, who probably saved my skinny hide. He assured her that this was not caused by our dump foraging, but it was a situation that had to be taken very seriously, even to the point where I couldn't walk to the bathroom on my own, but had to be carried by my Dad. This was pretty humiliating for a twelve year old kid! I became a virtual skeleton, and one evening when Dad packed me off to the bathroom, I looked so pathetic that Mom began to cry. I wasn't feeling the greatest right about then, and was starting to wonder if this might be the end of the trail. Then one day just out of the blue, I knew I was on the mend, and on the road to recovery.

———

Deer hunting in the Northwest, at least in Oregon and California was a pretty big deal. Deer season was seen as the first test of manhood, and you had not achieved that status until you got your first buck. I think it was the fall following the Rheumatic Fever episode that my turn came. I was a deadly shot at that time with the old .22 with the screw for a front sight, and had burnt up a mountain of ammo with the help of our "bottle recycling for shells" business. But I had never shot anything bigger than a Jackrabbit.

That fall, we went hunting in an area called the Bald Hills, back in the Coast Range, east of where we lived. It was a beautiful area with open spaces, and scattered oak and fir timber. The Black Tail deer would fatten up on the acorns until they were real butterballs. We usually hunted in the morning until the day started to heat up, then again in the evening after it cooled down. I was desperate to get my buck, as the Rheumatic fever had left me with a physique that resembled the 97 pound weakling in the Charles Atlas ads, and I wanted to be considered a man! So, even when everybody else quit, I kept right on hunting. It was completely senseless, because in the dry oak leaves, any deer that wasn't completely deaf could hear you coming a mile away.

I was crashing along down a sharp ridge where oak trees fell away on each side, sounding like a D-8 Cat coming through the brush, when all of a sudden, a little forked horn buck jumped up from almost under my feet. I had been stumbling along, not even thinking, and he caught me completely by surprise. He must have been having a little snooze, but quickly made a few jumps, and then stopped in an opening not more than 50 yards away. I didn't have a deer rifle of my own, so I was using a little Winchester .22 Hornet that belonged to Speed Hart, the guy that Dad worked with in the woods.

A .22 Hornet was as small a legal gun as you could use to hunt deer, but at that distance I could have killed him with a rock. I had never shot the gun before, but knowing Speed, it would have been shooting right on. I didn't try anything fancy, just zeroed in behind his shoulder, and pulled the trigger. I had a little buck fever all right, but it was not completely out of control. Nothing happened! I shot twice more, and nothing happened. By this time, even this long suffering, slow to catch on buck was getting a little edgy, and I was a complete wreck. I don't remember how many times I shot, but the rest of our hunting party thought I was sending out a distress signal, because no self-respecting deer would have hung around long enough to have that much lead slung at him.

Then it happened! He just keeled over. I couldn't believe it. I let out a yell that would have made Tarzan green with envy, and headed down the hill. I can remember like yesterday how proud I was to get my first buck. But as I looked down at him, I couldn't help but see how perfect he was, every hair, every detail, eyebrows, ears, horn's, absolutely perfect, and now he was dead. As I looked down at my first deer, I felt a twinge of sorrow for what I had done.

My 1ˢᵗ Buck

Another sport we really got into was salmon fishing. In the 1950's, there was a great abundance of wild salmon on the Pacific coast, that we knew as Silvers and Chinooks. Dad had bought a 14 foot fibre glass boat and painted it up a nice green. Many Sundays we would go salmon fishing off Trinidad Head, a big rock knob just north of us that jutted out into the ocean. It had a nice protected bay and wharf on the south side. It was a pretty exciting place to go with all the sights and sounds, the smell of the ocean, people launching boats, the yelling, tide pools and starfish, and places to explore.

My brother and sister were true sailors, but I was a puker. I tried my best, put on my best front. On the way out to where we fished a couple of miles off shore, I was a hundred percent. As long as the motor was going full bore and we were ploughing through the waves, I was a real Viking. As soon as everybody got baited up and Dad cut the motor to trolling speed, we began that deadly rocking up and down, then I was in trouble. I tried everything, looking at the horizon, etc., but within an hour I was barfing, puking, and feeding the fish. I would finally be so wasted they would have to take me in.

A few years later, my Uncle Theo came out from Iowa to pay us a visit, and we went out on a regular party boat. By this time, I was older and had enough sense to take some kind of motion sickness pill, but not my dear old Uncle Theo. He was a tough old Iowa farmer, with his straw hat and bib overalls and wasn't about to take any seasick pills. We had been out quite a while, and he seemed to be doing pretty good, but then as he stood there holding his salmon rod, I could see he was getting into trouble. He turned from white to grey to green, and then out she came. I really felt for him. Uncle Theo had false teeth, and when he barfed, he barfed his teeth out! The amazing thing was that even in the condition he was in, he reached out in the spray and grabbed them! It had to be a knee jerk reaction, but he had them! I don't recall if we caught any fish on that trip, but Uncle Theo had managed to catch something a whole lot more valuable than any salmon. He still had his false teeth!

There was a time when all the rivers coming out of the Coast Mountains were loaded with salmon. It seemed completely impossible that these numberless runs of fish could ever become less than they were at that time. But as surely as the buffalo were slaughtered until none were left, the salmon also have been affected by a whole host of things. We were fortunate to live in northern California just before the decline began.

One river north of us on Highway 101 was the Klamath. This river was world famous. When the salmon were really running, it was an absolute zoo! Just a couple of hundred yards from where the mouth of the river ran into the ocean was Suicide Row; it was very aptly named. It consisted of a line of boats that were anchored side by side completely across the river, from the south bank to the north bank. You could actually walk across the river by stepping from the side of one boat onto another. It was called Suicide

47

Row because if you decided to pull up your anchor and leave the line-up, and your motor failed, or something went wrong, you would then be swept down the river and right into the maelstrom where the river mouth hit the incoming waves of the ocean. You simply wouldn't have a chance of surviving. To make things even more interesting, there usually was not one, but two of these rows, one above the other extending from bank to bank. It really got interesting if somebody hooked into a 40 or 50 pound Chinook salmon that had just come out of the surf and was spoiling for a fight. The rule when this happened was to yell "fish on", and all the other gentlemen anglers would quickly reel in their rigging so the lucky one could play his fish, and net or gaff it. What would actually happen is that a few people would reel in their rigging, but a lot wouldn't, so in no time there could be several fishermen hooked to the same fish, and it kind of went down hill from there. Fist fights and brawls were not uncommon!

I was 13 when we went up to give the Klamath a try. Fishing on a river didn't bring out the same barfing tendencies in me that fishing in the ocean did, so I was really fired up to give it a try. The Klamath was a fast flowing river just before it hit the ocean. When you fished the Klamath, one thing you never, ever, did was to hook someone's anchor rope in Suicide Row. If that should happen, the fisherman had to start his motor, try to maintain his position in the line up, pull up his anchor and disconnect your line. Then get re-established in the row again. Better to just cut your line and start over!

There were a few local Klamath Indians working as guides for fishermen. It was fascinating to watch them. They never used an outboard motor, only a set of oars, and they paddled hand over hand.. One slip, one mistake, and there would have been big trouble, but the Klamath Indians were real pro's with those oars, and never missed a stroke.

I had never hooked a salmon before, so as we started fishing that day, I kept asking Dad, "How do you know when you've got one on?" He would say, "You'll know boy, you'll know!" The rod I was using that day was a big long cane or bamboo pole, nothing very fancy, and I had on what they called a "Cherry Bobber", a fluorescent lure. Usually a salmon would strike the lure more from just being aggressive than being hungry, so they would really nail it. We had just made a sweep down the river above Suicide Row, had finished the curve, and were headed back up river, when all of a sudden my pole began to bend! My line was still in the curve above Suicide Row, and my heart went cold! We had come down the river too far, and I had hooked an anchor rope! By then, my pole was really bending and I yelled at Dad, "I'm hung up!" I no sooner yelled and he cut the motor, when a salmon exploded out of the water and I could see I was hooked onto him. The battle was on! It was quite a job, as I was pulling against the current of the river, but eventually I got him in. He was a 22 pound Silver, and I was one proud boy!

―――――

One of the most enjoyable things about going to our church in Arcata was the hikes our teachers, and parents, took us on. They were usually to the beach which was close by. One memorable hike took place when three of my friends and I went down to check out the mouth of the Mad River, just a few miles north of Arcata. At that time it was still a good salmon river. It was much smaller than the Klamath, although it too could become a rampaging torrent when the winter rains came. On this particular Saturday afternoon, both banks of Mad River were lined shoulder to shoulder with fishermen. It was the same basic principle as Suicide Row on the Klamath River, except here they were on the riverbank. There was a point, as you got toward the mouth of the river, where it was not legal to fish. As my friends and I passed this point, it made for a great day at the beach! It was probably 300 yards or so from where the "No Fishing" sign was on the river to where the river actually hit the ocean surf.

The mouth of the river that year was very shallow, with a lot of little channels spread out over a wide area. We had just got to the mouth, and started wading in some of these little channels, when out of the ocean surf burst a big salmon. He was going for broke! The spray from his tail was flying high in the air as he tried to reach deep water. Without even thinking, (I guess all the hunter/gatherer instincts kicked in) and grabbing a driftwood club, I headed for him as fast as I could go. He was just coming loose from the sand bar when I got there, so I walloped him over the head with the club and scooped him up in my arms and headed for shore!

Now, what would later turn out to be a 30 pound Chinook salmon is a pretty good handful for a young kid, and when I scooped him up, I had his head between my knees, my arms around his middle, and his tail in my face, and he was as slippery as an eel!

My buddies had arrived to try to give me a hand, as by this time, the salmon had come back to life, and it was a battle royal. He gave my face a good slapping with his tail, and I could only waddle along with his head between my knees, squeezing him as tight as I could around the middle. Eventually we got him to shore and dispatched him, and as we were packing him by the legal fisherman on our way out, they said, "Hey kid, where did ya get that fish" or, "Hey kid, I'll give ya 20 bucks for that salmon".

Those Saturday afternoon hikes and trips to the beach made me realize there was more to religion than sitting in a church pew. There was a whole world out there made for us to enjoy, although catching illegal salmon on a Sabbath afternoon nature hike was probably pushing the limits! Unfortunately, I was about to develop a major shift in attitude.

Crossroads

When I came back to McKinleyville Elementary School, after my bout with Rheumatic Fever, I had to take it easy. I think that was when I developed a real inferiority complex. This was a difficult time, as I had always had a lot of friends, and had been right in the middle of things. Our teacher that year was a big, blond, wavy haired guy who looked like Charles Atlas! He was strong on sports, so Ron Remington and the other athletes were his good buddies.

To make my presence less noticeable, at recess or lunchtime, I would hang out in the back corners, and bathroom, so no one would notice me, or give me any guff. I was in the bathroom one day, when "Charles Atlas" came in and demanded to know what I was doing. I guess he thought I was trying to vandalize the place. Then he grabbed me by the arm and told me he should shove my head in the toilet and flush it. Well, needless to say, "Charles Atlas" had a thing or two to learn about dealing with kids, and that little incident didn't improve my feelings about teachers and school!

The next school year, Mom enrolled Ron, Judy, and me in the Arcata Seventh-day Adventist Church school. To pay the school bill she started working in the bulb fields. It was hard, dirty work. She eventually became a nurse's aid and worked the night shift at Arcata Hospital for many years to give us kids the opportunity for a Christian education. Mom was always very busy but made a good home for us.

Changing schools made a world of difference to me. All my friends from Church were there, and I quickly became friends with Stanley Baldwin, Kenny Werner, and David Hiebert. I was especially interested in being friends with Stanley because he had a cute, little, blonde sister who had a perfect dimple on each cheek when she smiled. Ever since I was in grade 1, I felt that girls were a very attractive part of the human race, and this girl was special!

The only problem, again, was the teacher. I will say one thing. He ruled the roost with an iron hand. It was his personality, and it was his culture. He was a short, bald headed, hook nosed, eagle eyed man of strict German discipline, with a trim little moustache. He always wore a suit, and stood ramrod straight. He seemed to think that to crack a smile was a sign that you were losing control. We suffered through it for a couple of years, but it was not a happy time in the classroom.

In Grade 8, I thought I was a pretty important guy. Stanley Baldwin and his cute little sis had moved away, but another girl had arrived on the scene. By this time I had convinced my buddies to call me "Bob", which had a much more manly ring to it. Since girls were now becoming such an interesting part of life I didn't want to be known as "Bobby". There were four of us in the class, David Muth, a tall, serious, red haired kid, Kay Johnson, who I thought made a perfect match for David, and a new girl named Louella Kenemer, who I thought made a perfect match for me. We had a new teacher by that time, who was our next door neighbour on Baird Road, a new area we had moved to a couple of miles inland from the coast. Our new teacher tried his best, but by then I was starting into some rebellious years. When we graduated from Grade 8 into Grade 9, suddenly we were in a new classroom and at the bottom of the ladder again.

But something would happen in Grade 9 that, like Effie McTimmonds at McDowell Creek, would have a long lasting effect on my life. A new grade 9 and 10 teacher, Gray Banta, came to the school. I couldn't believe my eyes! A church school teacher who wore a cowboy shirt and cowboy boots! He was a big, dark, square jawed, easy going guy, a natural teacher, who would just sit on the edge of his desk and talk to us. He had dark, kind eyes that made every kid in the classroom feel special. One of the most obvious examples of his patience and teaching ability was that in grade 9, I passed Algebra! He had that same quiet, steady, western way and authority about him that Mrs. Miller, our teacher at McDowell Creek had.

Overall, grade 9 was a good year. Good teacher, good friends, and at least three girls close to my age that I thought were pretty cute! There were two blondes in Grade 8 (loved those blondes!) and one native girl, Vivian McCovey, who, along with her short, square built cousin, came to our school. She was a very pretty girl, with a nice personality and she and I would team up to play badminton in the gym. The one blonde was Janie Scheppler, the daughter of a doctor in our church, the other blonde was Jeanie Berg, the adopted daughter of our Grade 8 school teacher, George Berg.

We played a lot of baseball and flag football at our school, and since I seemed to be fairly adept at catching a football, I mainly played end. One day in a pile up of players, I managed to break my collar bone. At that time, I had a varsity style jacket that was dark blue with a white leather band that circled each shoulder. It was the same kind the College players wore, and when I got my collarbone taped up, I couldn't put my hand through the left sleeve as I had to keep my arm in a sling. I wore that jacket like I was a player in the National Football League! By this time, I was starting to think I was a pretty cool guy in our small school, and really used that collarbone injury to full advantage in letting the girls know what a great athlete I was!

———

Grade 9 was a relatively good year, but there was a problem. Looking back, it's plain to see that society was going into a time of social and musical revolution, and it was not to be for the better. As kids growing up, our heroes were Roy Rogers, Gene Autry, the Lone Ranger, and all the other good guys who exemplified the "Code of the West" cowboy ethics and moral values of our time. Not that we were perfect, but these heroes along with the right and wrong we were taught at home and church were about to be replaced by a new hero. He was a hip swinging singer named Elvis Presley and the music was called Rock and Roll. It took a whole generation by storm. Music was always a big part of our lives. Almost every night after supper, we had a music session; Dad on the fiddle, Ron on the guitar, and myself on the mandolin. We were raised on country and gospel music.

Elvis could sing all that and finish it off with "Blue Suede Shoes" and "You Ain't Nuthin' but a Houn' Dog"! It was especially confusing for me because I discovered I could do a pretty good job of singing like Elvis, yet at the same time I wanted to stay in the past where things were simpler, and a hero to me was a cowboy or logger. Mr. Banta with his quiet western ways was the connection to that past.

This time in my life proved to be a crossroads. Unlike my church and church school friends, who were born and raised in the Seventh-day

Adventist Church with both parents Christians, we had grown up in two different worlds. One side was the kind, conservative Christians who took us to Sunday school and Sabbath school, and tried to instill a Christian experience in our lives. On the other side was the influence of the home brew drinking, country music hoedowns, we grew up with in the Oregon backwoods. Now this whole new music scene, everywhere you looked, was Rock and Roll, Elvis, Bill Haley and the Comets, Dick Clark and American Bandstand!

Rebellion was in the air, but it was a strange mix of the old and new, that over time would evolve from Elvis and Rock and Roll, to the drug and biker culture with James Dean and Marlon Brando, and films like "Easy Rider" and "Rebel without a Cause". Then the Flower Children of Haight and Ashbury in San Francisco, with their LSD and hippy protest songs arrived, and the drug scene began to infiltrate society. So even though I deeply admired and respected Mr. Banta, I would have some hard lessons to learn.

———

I don't recall the occasion, but I think it was a Saturday night program at the church school, and someone (probably me) had managed to get their hands on a bottle of wine. Looking back, the whole thing was ridiculous. There wasn't enough wine in that small bottle to give any of the five or six boys that drank it more than a couple of good big swigs, but we managed to convince ourselves that we were on a real rampage, so we charged around and damaged some eaves trough and handrails, and generally made complete fools of ourselves. On Monday morning, we faced the judge.

The Seventh-day Adventist School was, and still is, a respected school in the community. Despite being unfortunate enough to have one hard line teacher, it was a good school and I can assure you the problems weren't always the teacher's fault. When Mr. Banta called us on the carpet, he had the same look in his eyes that old Mack McTimmonds had when I told him I had stolen the Navy combat knife. It was that same look of sadness and disappointment. He never ranted or raved, he just told us how disappointed he was and what our punishment would be.

In spite of the years of separation from God that were soon to come, it was the example of people like him, solid, down to earth people who believed in me, that would later draw me back to a life that had meaning. The members of the Arcata Seventh-day Adventist Church, were very supportive of our family from the time we first began attending.

The house and grounds we rented on Baird Road were by far the nicest place we had ever lived. There were all kinds of flower beds and a big garden area. Mom loved it as she was a born farmer and really enjoyed flowers, especially Dahlias and Roses. She also decided we needed a big garden to keep us kids occupied. Dad borrowed a horse and walking plow from Uncle Jobe, our neighbour, and broke up a big garden area and planted potatoes. I will never forget the feeling I had when I started working in that soil! It must have been the genes from my farmer ancestors that suddenly kicked in! I actually, of all things, enjoyed gardening!

Ted and Lorna Werner were also neighbours on Baird Road with three boys and two girls in their family. Their youngest son, Ken, was one of my best friends. Sadly, he died later in a motorcycle accident. Ted had a landscaping and lawn mowing business, and Kenny and I worked for him after school and during the summer. Ted was a big, roughhewn, strong faced man with a solid German work ethic. When you worked for him, he treated you more than fair if you did your job.

Lorna went back to school in midlife and became an elementary school teacher, and taught my younger sister Janice Kae for several years. Lorna was an attractive lady with high cheekbones and a beautiful smile. She had a very kind, helpful way about her and always encouraged Mom along.

One of the most prominent families in our church were the Schepplers. Their son, Dr. George Scheppler (Doc), had a medical clinic in Blue Lake, a little logging town several miles inland from Arcata. My sister Judy worked at the Blue Lake Clinic for 20 years as a Clinical nurse, and became close friends with Doc and his family. Doc Scheppler had a great sense of humour and was the life at all of our social gatherings. His wife, Bernice, was a nice person in a kind of plump, attractive, take charge sort of way. I always liked her because she would have parties at their house where we actually got to hold hands with the girls in some of the games we played! Doc Scheppler was well liked in the community and was the doctor for the Humboldt State College football team in Arcata.

Boarding School

In the fall of 1955, a new Seventh-day Adventist Boarding Academy opened in Milo, Oregon. My older sister, Sharon, attended the opening year. The next year, 1956, we both went. I was 15 and in Grade 10. Milo, Oregon was made up of a gas station and grocery store on a little winding back road highway. It ran east from Canyonville, a small logging town between Grant's Pass and Roseburg, Oregon. I think it was chosen for a couple of reasons. Its isolated location created an atmosphere where students were not distracted by worldly happenings, yet it was within reasonable driving distance of a number of fairly large southern Oregon and northern California towns and cities. Anyway, for me at 15 years old and always having been kind of a homebody, it was quite an adventure!

Before coming to Milo I thought I had reached the status of Mr. Big in our Church school in McKinleyville. But I was in for a rude awakening. In one day, I went from Mr. Big to Mr. Nobody! In a way, attending a Boarding Academy was like joining the army. You had to learn to look after yourself, and you had to learn it fast. When you arrived at the school, it was a sink or swim situation. Your Mom was no longer there to hold your hand and look after you. You were thrown into a dorm with 90 to 100 guys you had never seen before, and into a dorm room with a guy you had never met and would now live with 24 hours a day. (Like him or not!) In the bathroom you would perform all your toilet and bathing functions in full view of whoever happened to be around. It finally got to the point where you lost any semblance of bashfulness or sense of privacy, and just did whatever had to be done when it had to be done! You were awakened at 5:00 a.m. by gentle music, then met for morning worship, with breakfast at 6:00 a.m. Classes started at 7:00 a.m. and ran until 12:00 noon; then lunch until 1:00 p.m., work from 1:00 p.m. to 5:00 p.m., then supper until 6:00 p.m. There was worship again at 6:00pm to 6:30pm, and study hall from 7:00pm to 9:00pm. It was a full day! The kids whose parents lived fairly close could get a pass to go home every 3 weeks. For our group from northern California, it was 6 weeks between breaks.

I really got started off with a bang. There was a pick up ball game going on after I got settled in my room, so I thought I would go out and get acquainted. I had no sooner arrived at the ball field, when a high fly ball came my way, which I made a pretty nice catch on. I guess this tall, red haired guy thought I had robbed him, so he gave me a good cussing out! Wow! Good start to the year! We never did become buddies. Kids of course will be kids, and it wasn't long before we fell into some semblance of a routine. The first few weeks were the worst. We were kept so busy that by the time our heads hit the pillow at night and the lights went out, we were more than ready for sleep.

I was fortunate to have a good roommate at Milo Academy. His name was Gordon Klein. He was from Alaska, and to this day I wish I had taken the time to get more background information on him. But maybe in the long run, that's not what's really important. What was important to me was that he took me in as an equal. He always called me "Roommate". I don't remember what grade he was in. I'm sure it was grade 12 because he looked and acted like a grown man. Anyway, he was a great friend and mentor while we roomed together. In later years, he worked in church evangelism and married a lady named Dona Spainhower, a very accomplished recording artist. I recently heard he has passed away, but I will always remember Gordon Klein as a very patient, tolerant roommate and friend.

Milo Academy, in 1956, operated on a conservative dress and social standard. I knew before I came to Milo that they had a rule you couldn't wear blue jeans to class. I don't know where I had been, or what I had been doing when Mom bought my clothes, but I guess we didn't have the money, or she wasn't up on the latest shirt and slack fashions. When I pulled them out and put them on, I was stuck with what I thought were some very uncool combinations of clothes! Kids then and kids now can be very cruel if they think your clothes don't match the "In" fashions. I had a pair of pants and a shirt that were kind of a blue green that looked like a prison uniform, and every time I wore them, I really got the gears, so I finally threw them away. But I was just as bad to any other kid whose clothes didn't fit in.

When classes were finished for the day, I couldn't wait for noon to come. I could hardly wait, for three reasons. The first was that at all three meals we got to sit with the girls, so we could learn our social manners. Three boys and three girls sat at each table. The second was the food. I think the cooks' name was Mrs. McArty. She was a short, chubby, motherly lady that loved to cook, and I can tell you I loved to eat as much as she loved to cook! I think I grew close to 5 inches that year at Milo. They had a dairy at the school, so we had a constant supply of ice cold milk that I drank by the endless gallons. I had some real hang ups about the dress code at the school, but I sure didn't have any complaints about the food supply! The third and probably greatest reason I was glad to see noon come was that I got to put my beloved old 501 Levi blue jeans on! As mentioned earlier, we attended classes in the morning and worked in the afternoons. It was a common practice at that time in Seventh-day Adventist schools, to enable students to pay for their schooling as well as learn practical skills.

All of the buildings at the school were not yet built, so I worked on the foundation for the Music building. That part of Oregon in the winter can be one cold, wet, miserable, muddy piece of real estate. As we slogged around in the mud and slop, there was only one bright spot. The Music building was next to the girls' dorm and with a little luck you might have one of those delicate, dainty creatures walk by and have the kindness to give you a little smile!

The dorm life thing was the hardest part for me to adjust to. Some people are naturally gregarious mixers and socialites. I don't mind being around people for a while, but I'm the type of person who needs some space and quiet time alone. In a dorm full of guys, you had to adapt. I think by the time the year was half over, I was probably somewhere in the middle as far as social standing went. I was not a star athlete, and had not excelled in any dorm fist fights; in fact I had been punched out by one guy after I had bragged about how tough I was! I was not the most popular among the girls, but not the most unpopular either. But there was one thing I could do, play the guitar and sing like Elvis!

Our dorm rooms were constantly monitored for radios and tape decks; nothing of that kind was allowed. But you could have a guitar, and given a will there was a way. We would station look outs in the halls and monitor the location of the Dean and all the stool pigeons, and when everything was in the clear, we would have a rockin' good time!

Bob

But the Dean outwitted us on one little project. He lined us up to be part of a formal banquet supper program that the school put on. It was a big deal. Everyone dressed in their finest with corsages for the girls and the whole works. The Dean came and asked me if I could do a skit up on the stage of some guys sitting around in a dorm room singing Elvis songs, and he would let us sing for a bit and then come crashing in and break up the party. Well, we were more than happy to go along with that, so we decided on a fairly tame song called "When My Blue Moon Turns to Gold Again". My date for the evening was Jody Harms, a cute girl from my class. When they threw open the curtain and I started singing, most of the kids started to clap and yell. I hadn't got past "When my blue moon turns to gold again" when the Dean burst in and brought the whole thing to an end. But it was still a real kick and brought us instant fame with the girls!

———

That night was the high point of my year at Milo. Unfortunately, it was to be followed by the lowest. The next story I have to tell still makes me feel bad after all these years. It doesn't make me look too good, but I have to tell it because it shows one of the best examples of "turning the other cheek" Christianity I have ever experienced. It all started at the gym. They had installed a new hardwood floor and on certain nights, the boys got to go in and roller skate. I loved it. I was pretty good on roller skates, kind of a skate boarder of the Fifty's! Our assistant Dean's son, Carl Hanson, was a good Christian kid. He just did everything right. It wasn't that he acted like he was better than you, or put on the dog. He was just an all right guy, the kind that stayed on the right side of the track. One of Carl's big things was weight lifting. I don't know how much he could lift, but he was built like a Sherman tank. He was so muscle bound that when he put his roller skates on and started around the gym, he looked like he was going in slow motion. Under normal circumstances I just flew past him with a nod and went on my merry way because I had nothing against him. But this night, a couple of the Grade 12 guys were sitting on the side lines and motioned me over. Always eager to see what an upper class man might want, I skidded in to see what was up.

Their plan was that I should harass Carl by skating around and bumping into him. I'm sure they hoped this would aggravate him enough that he would get fed up and beat me to a pulp while they sat by innocently on the sidelines and watched the show! It's unbelievable what a kid will do when they want to belong, to feel accepted! In all fairness, later in life both of these guys became dedicated Christians. As a young married man, one was killed while flying in mission service in Alaska. This was their idea that night, not mine, but I didn't have the guts to tell them to get lost with their bright idea, so I began the attack. It was pathetic. Carl was so naive that at first he didn't even figure out what was going on. Then when he did figure it out, he did everything he could to avoid me, but it was hopeless. It was like a fighter plane against a slow, ponderous bomber. My buddies on the sidelines were enjoying the whole thing immensely, sitting back and egging me on. Finally, I came in from the side and tripped him and down he went like a ton of bricks. I skidded to a stop, and as he tried to get up, I did something to him that went against everything that I had ever been taught about fair fighting. I cussed him out and punched him in the nose while he still had his glasses on. I didn't hit him that hard, because on roller skates, it's pretty difficult to throw a hard punch, but it knocked his glasses off and made his nose bleed. The best thing he could have done right then would have been to knock me cold. Instead he got up, gave me a look of pity and forgiveness, and slowly skated away.

I was too small to apologize and the rest of the year I couldn't even look at him. When I left the gym and went back to the dorm room that night, I felt like dirt. Even today after telling this story I get those same bad feelings, and when I hear of the cruelty of bullying, I know it's the same, with kids trying to fit in, trying to belong, trying to do something that will make them accepted and look big to others.

———

I had two favourite teachers at Milo. The first was Harley Cordiss. He was a middle aged man who ran the power house for the school. It was located down behind the laundry. He was the mechanics and shop teacher and we called him "Old Dirty Face", but that was behind his back. It was a term of affection, not disrespect. He always looked the same whether he was in the middle of working on a boiler, teaching a class, or standing in a church pew. He was a big man with a crew cut and sloping shoulders, who always wore bib overalls except on Sabbath. He was totally dedicated to the school.

The second was Elder W.V. Schoepflin. He was, of all things, a Bible teacher. For some strange reason, I seemed to have been born with a theological bent, or interest. But this was not to surface until a few tumultuous years later. I think it all went back to those German Sunday School teachers, and the things I was taught in church and church school, and not just in the classroom.

I still remember walking home from school at McDowell Creek with my brother and sister and cousins, crawling through the fence of a neighbour's field, and walking into a stand of old growth Cascade Mountain Douglas Fir. They were monstrous trees, and the longer you stood there, the smaller you felt. It seemed like a sacred place. It made you feel small, like when you looked up at the Milky Way at night and you realized you were less than nothing on a world that was nothing, in a great universe. You realized even as a kid, that all this order, all these things could not just come from nothing.

Elder Schoepflin was an incredible teacher. He was a very distinguished looking man, with a full head of iron grey hair, slightly receding at the temples. He wore tortoise shell rimmed glasses, had clear grey eyes, and when he looked at you and taught you, it was with a straight forward, mild mannered authority. Always impeccably dressed, he was a humble man, and to cross him was unthinkable. He had an almost magical way of transmitting biblical truth. It may not have affected everyone the same, but to me he made things very easy to understand. His voice was a deep baritone with almost a Scottish burr that was very easy to listen to. On top of all that, he could come up with a pretty good joke now and then to keep things in perspective. In a lot of ways, he was like Mr. Banta, our Grade 9 teacher back in California. Probably the biggest difference was that he didn't wear a cowboy shirt and cowboy boots! So, in spite of my overall aversion to school and teachers, there were some I couldn't help but like and respect.

The school year finally came to an end and I couldn't wait to get away. But at the same time, in spite of my rebellious attitude and immaturity, Milo was a good school, with many of the kids, and members of the staff who really lived their Christian faith.

Iowa Summer

When I came home from Milo, Oregon in June 1957, I decided to go back to Iowa for the summer. After being cooped up back in the boondocks for so long, I felt like I needed to get out and cover some ground.

My Grandpa Batman picked me up at the bus station in Des Moines. I know looking back, it was an inconvenience to him. He was getting up in years, and I could see, even as clueless as I was, that age was taking its toll on him. It was a typical hot, humid, corn growing Iowa day, when we left Des Moines and headed south to the farm. The smells of Iowa are incredible. The rich soil, hay, corn, farm ponds, cattle, hot humid air, and oh yes, the hog farms. As we rode along, I could sense there was a distance between us that had never been there before. I'm sure the fact that I had an Elvis Presley haircut, and a leather jacket on in the 100 degree weather, didn't help bridge the generation gap! After a few words of greeting, we mostly travelled in silence, but I was quite intrigued by his driving technique. It must have come from back in the horse and buggy days when men would spit on their hands to keep a better grip on the reins. Every once in awhile, as he kept his eyes focused straight ahead on the road, he would take one hand off the wheel, and give a little spit into the palm of his hand, slap it back on the steering wheel, and after a while do the same with the other hand. This would happen every 5 or 10 minutes just like some old teamster driving a team of horses.

After we arrived home and got reacquainted, we managed to get back on the same wave length again, and it turned out to be a pretty good summer. My Grandparents, Uncle Robert, my Mom's older brother, his wife Maymie, their two kids, Arthur Harry and Mary Francis all lived and worked together on the farm. It was especially good to see Mary Francis again. She had become quite a young lady.

A few years before, two accidents had happened on their farm that could have cost them their lives. One night during a bad thunder storm, their house was struck by lightning. Fortunately, they were all in bed and no one was touching anything that was grounded, but it literally blew the house to pieces. They had to rent another farm house for a couple of months while the Insurance Company rebuilt their house. But at least no one was injured.

Mary Francis & brother Arthur Harry

The other tragedy happened to Mary Francis when she was 2 years old. She was always a tiny, delicate little thing; had the most beautiful soft brown eyes, and cutest mischievous smile. It was a raw, cold spring day when Uncle Robert took her with him on the old, open deck, steel seated Allis Chalmers tractor. She was dressed in a snow suit against the cold and was sitting on his lap, with his arm around her as they bounced along. He was discing, you can lose concentration when you're discing. Time goes by, your mind wanders, you get cold, the slamming and bouncing of the tractor. He hit a bad bump and suddenly in one heart stopping second, she was gone! But it was too late! The first gang of disks had already run over her. A farm disk is an absolutely brutal piece of machinery, its purpose is to do one thing – chop things to pieces. The only thing that saved Mary Francis was the soft ground and her snow suit that prevented the disc blades from cutting through the material. One disc went across her forehead, completely through her nose and chin, and through the roof of her mouth, and then hit the snowsuit material and crushed and bruised from there on. The disc completely missed both eyes and the nerves to both eyes. The discs that went over the rest of her body, broke her pelvis, both collar bones, and bruised internal organs. The Doctors at the hospital were sure she would die. But, by what I believe was a miracle of God, she recovered and still has those same beautiful, soft brown eyes with the mischievous twinkle, and the cute smile.

———

Once I got settled in that summer, I decided I was a big boy now, so I better find a job and not just live off the relatives. At that time, they were building an addition to the Hy-Vee Food Store warehouse in Chariton, which was the main shopping center for Lucas County. A neighbour named Carol Schneider was working there, so I checked it out and managed to get a job. Carol was a great guy. He was a big, easy going, heavy set man with a slow, easy smile. He wasn't a drinking man, but I managed to talk him into buying us each a bottle of Schlitz beer every night on the way home from work. I had a little construction experience by this time from working at Milo and even though I was just a kid, I was a good worker and could hold my own when it came to shovel and wheel barrow work. We earned our dollars that summer. It was pouring concrete floors, right out in that good old scorching hot Iowa sun. Our foreman's name was Vern Condun. He was a driver, always pushing to go a little faster. His father-in-law, W.H. Grabau, was the owner of the construction company, and I guess Vern was trying to impress him. Mr. Grabau was older, and from what little I saw of him, seemed to be a nice guy. In the later part of the summer, another young guy named Vern Halferty came to work on the job. He had an Irish name, and looked every inch an Irishman, with a square jaw and mop of red-brown hair. He wasn't the easiest guy to get along with at first, because he was a real competitor. Vern was a rugged looking guy, bigger than me. But I hung in there and we got to be good friends. He was born in July 1940, and was just a year older than I was. He had no way of knowing that in a few short years, his determination and will would be tested to the limit. At 28 years of age, in 1968, he would lose one leg at the hip to cancer. Given an 8% chance of survival, he battled back, went to college, and became a medical technologist and later, a Biology teacher. He now lives happily in Waveland, Mississippi; an amazing guy.

———

We worked like dogs that summer. We were brown as Indians. Nobody worried about skin cancer, or wearing sunscreen. You just fried. We finally got rained out one day, so Vern and I decided we would take a little run down to Lineville, Missouri. I don't know why we decided to go to Lineville of all places, maybe just so we could say we had been in another state, but first we had to fuel up and that meant buying a bottle of Jack Daniels whiskey. That must have been his idea, because I usually just stuck to beer, but if I was going to drink whiskey, it had to be Jack Daniels. There was an old friend of Dad's in Chariton, by the name of Ernie Teeters. We called him "Teetering Teeters". He was a retired farmer who now spent all of his time in the bar. Every once in a while, I would get him to buy me some beer. He didn't like to do it but as a favour to his old friend, my Dad, he would. So, we looked him up this day and he did us the favour. On the way to Lineville, we stopped by my Grandparent's house to let them know where we were going. Even now, I can't imagine what I was thinking. They were church going Baptist people. I'm sure they didn't have any alcohol in their house. We must have already had a pretty good buzz on, because we brought our jug right into the house and set it in the middle of the kitchen table and offered my Granddad a drink. He was very gracious, and out of a sense of old southern hospitality he had a small drink with us. But I know without a doubt from later experience in life, they were saddened, and knew this was not a good thing.

But we were on a roll. Look out Lineville! Here come the Irishmen! We got there in the mid afternoon. We went into a little juke box café that was crammed full of kids. By this time, I was definitely feeling no pain. The juke box in the corner was playing the song "Unchained Melody". I was mesmerized by that song. I can still remember the whole thing like yesterday even in the condition I was in! I am deeply moved by music. I make no apology for that. When we were small kids in the backwoods on McDowell Creek and crowded around the radio to listen to the "Lone Ranger" on the radio, the introduction to the program was "The William Tell Overture". I still get goose bumps when I hear that song, and can still see the Lone Ranger and Tonto coming over the hill! Believe it or not, the song "Unchained Melody" is one of the most recorded songs of the 20th century! Elvis Presley included it in his last public appearance. I loved that song. That day in Lineville, I played it over and over, and looking back, as laughable and ridiculous as it seems, I came to a momentous decision. I decided I was going to go to New York City. I would hitch hike to New York and I would become a famous singer. I would get up on stage before great crowds of people and sing songs like "You Ain't Nothin' but a Houn' Dawg", and "Unchained Melody", and I would be famous just like Elvis. At this point Vern reluctantly left me to my own devices and went back to Chariton. Given the state I was in at that moment, all this seemed very possible, so I staggered over to the phone and called my Uncle Robert and told him of my plan. He told me in very plain, easy to understand farmer language to get my rear end home, and get it home fast!! Well this sobered me up considerably!

Now evening was coming on, a major thunderstorm was brewing, and I didn't even have a coat. I was a long, long ways from home. I went to a clothing store and bought a good warm dark green jacket. Then I was flat broke, so I started hitch hiking. Destination: Chariton, Iowa (not New York City.) By then it was dark. I hitch hiked for about an hour before the storm hit and when it hit, it was a beauty. A thunderstorm doesn't usually last too long. This one went on for hours. It sounded like a war zone. They had curbs along the sides of the highways and the water was running half way to my knees, it was raining that hard. I'm sure people couldn't even see me with that green jacket on. I should have just tried to find a place to hole up until it was over but you couldn't see anything. It was a wonder I didn't get ironed out. What a mess. The storm finally quit and it started to lighten up in the east. I can tell you, as I slogged along that desolate road, those earlier visions of cheering crowds and worldly fame seemed very far away.

I was pretty well done for by this time, so when I spotted a shed alongside the highway with a high board fence around it, I thought I would jump over the fence and maybe find a place I could zonk out for a while. I managed to climb up on top of the fence and drop down into the pen on the other side. But when I hit bottom, I just about had a heart attack. What I didn't know, because it was too dark to see inside the pen, was that I had dropped right into a big pen full of hogs! When I landed, they all jumped up and started squealing, and grunting, and woofing and chomping their jaws and ripping around the pen. These were big, full grown hogs. I don't think my feet even touched the ground before I was up and over the top of that 12 foot fence and never touched a board! But I did manage to get into the loft of the shed from another angle and stretch out in about 3 inches of dust and chicken manure and sleep for a couple of hours.

When I got up and started hitch hiking again, my uncle came along and picked me up, as he had been looking for me. He complimented me on my neat appearance and efficient method of travelling around the country. When we got to the farm I was received with open arms by the whole family. In some simple way that probably only had meaning to me, it reminded me of the old Bible story of the return of the prodigal son.

Street Rod & Fat Lip

When I got back to California, it took some time to re-adjust. I had been living and working in a man's world, doing a man's job, even though I was still a kid, having just turned 16 in July 1957. Now here I was back in high school again and still into that Rock and Roll music. I had a long time friend, Les Goodier, who had a real good voice and we would sing together by the hour, trying to imitate Elvis and all the other pop singers of the day. He was a tall thin guy like myself, with a head of black curly hair so thick he had to brush it rather than comb it! His friendship and Christian influence over a long period of years have meant a lot to me.

It was also about that time that I bought my first car. A 1932 Ford Coupe with the original fenders. But this was in the days when you wanted it to look like a street rod, and I didn't have either the money or expertise to go through all the fancy expensive steps. I just wanted to get the fenders chopped off that thing, get a coat of bright coloured paint of some kind on it and get it on the road to impress the neighbourhood girls! I didn't actually have a drivers' license yet, so I just drove it on our street. It didn't take long to get Uncle Jobe Lukins, our neighbour, to cut the fenders off and for me to take a paint brush and slop a couple of coats of bright purple paint on. Then Bingo! Just like that, I had a street rod! Granted, it didn't have the chrome accessories and exhaust pipes like they had in those fancy street rod magazines, but it was good enough for me! The old Ford still ran fairly good, but there was one small problem. The rear seal on the motor leaked like a sieve! In my desire, to keep that buggy on the road as many hours of the day as possible, I just couldn't spare the time to get it changed. So I came up with a real ingenious solution. Rather than wasting my money on repairs or buying new oil to pour in the crankcase, I would get used oil from Uncle Jobe, or wherever else I could scrounge it, and store it in quart jars in the back window! Brilliant idea! There was another advantage to this scheme. The whole blacktop road from in front of our house for probably a mile down the road to where I turned off to Les Goodiers' place was always kept freshly oiled!

Les Goodier

Over a period of time Ron had a lot of influence on my life. Not that I blame him, we all make our choices. As a younger brother, I always looked up to my older brother. If he was Tarzan, I was Boy. If he was Batman, I was Robin. When he started chewing Copenhagen or "snoose" I saw it as the "manly" thing to do. In todays, enlightened world, chewing, like smoking is recognized for what it is – a dirty, dangerous, expensive habit. When I first tried chewing, I just took a few grains. No problem I thought! So, the next time I really loaded up! Bad move! I thought being seasick was bad, but I gritted my teeth, persevered, and finally made the grade. I could chew right up there with the cowboys and the loggers!

I had been mouthing off about how tough I was and Ron decided it was time to tone me down a little. It was just to be a friendly wrestling match so we cleared the kitchen table out of the way, and squared off. He came in low and fast, grabbed me around the middle and pinned both arms to my sides, then rolled backwards. We had a cement floor in our house and when he rolled back the force of the roll drove my smiling face right into the concrete floor! Well, it didn't knock me completely out, but there were a lot of tweety birds singing in my head and I wasn't sure which planet I was on for a while! The biggest concern when the birds quit singing was that when my face hit the floor, it drove 3 or 4 teeth on the left side completely through my lower lip. It had bent them back some, but luckily not broken them off so away we went to get a few stitches in the lower lip. Ah, the next morning...what a sight! Lip completely turned inside out, teeth aching. But as you can imagine, I didn't pick any scraps with my brother for a while!

My brother, Ron, was a fit, husky built guy and had been working in the woods since his high school graduation. By this time he was an accomplished guitar player and played in local bars and beer joints with the Henshaw brothers. They eventually became known as the Northwest Troubadours, with Ron on vocals and playing rythm guitar.

In November 1956 Ron married a local girl, Cleah Overly. Cleah was a lovely girl and the whole family liked her. Several years later Ron joined the U.S. Army, and served in Germany. Ron and Cleah had 2 boys, Wayne and Rafe, born in 1959 and 1960.

Ron & Cleah with sons, Wayne & Rafe

I started Grade 11 in Arcata Public High School in 1957. It started off pretty good because I really didn't know anyone to get in trouble with. We were still living on Baird Road at that time and Les Goodier was also going to Arcata High. We chummed around some together after school, but I was not going to church anymore.

Later in the school year, I ended up running around with a motley crew of friends. One night we raided one of the taverns on the town square in Arcata. Lucky for us, there were some sons of the town fathers in the group and a few basketball stars, or we would have all ended up in the clink for sure.

It all started out innocently enough, just two or three cars cruising around for a few hours, looking for something to do. One of the boys mentioned he had a job as a janitor at one of the taverns on the square and had a key. We couldn't believe our good fortune. As soon as the tavern closed, we slipped down the back alley with our 3 cars, unlocked the door, and we were in business! A couple of guys got behind the bar to set 'em up for the boys, and the shuffle board games and pinball machines got into full swing and while this was going on, another whole crew was packing cases of beer from the cooler and filling the trunks of the cars. Two of the cars had left when guess who arrived on their nightly patrol? The town cops! They were not impressed. They made us clean everything up, pack all the beer back in, gave us a good tongue lashing, told us if it ever happened again, it would be life imprisonment. They let us go, because as mentioned, we had some basketball stars and town father's kids in the group! (pays to know the right guys!) Then they told us to get out of town!

We met up with the other 2 cars that had the beer and hid it out on the side of a hill not too far north of Arcata near Azalea Avenue. We had enough excitement by then for one night, so agreed to meet there the next day and haul our booty off to a Boy Scout camp at the end of an out of the way road and polish it off.

The next day we went back to the hillside, loaded the beer up, just got settled in for a nice little party, when a car drove up and parked behind us. I was sitting in the front seat between a couple of basketball stars and I looked in the rear view mirror and guess who was walking up to the car on the drivers' side. It was Paul Fleming, my old Pathfinder leader from church school days! Just who I wanted to see! We had hidden the beer right across the draw from his house and he had sat and watched the whole recovery operation! Now he was here to plead with me to mend my ways! He was smart enough not to single me out specifically, but I knew who he was talking to. The guy on the driver's side slowly rolled his window down and Paul began his spiel. I didn't even let on that I knew him. I can tell you, I wished right then that I was a million miles away. Another thing I can tell you is that the short, dumpy little man with his round face, rimless glasses, and funny looking haircut was one of the bravest, most selfless people I have ever known. He didn't care what he looked like. He didn't care what we thought of him. All he cared about was us. I would carry that selfless image in my mind for a lot of years before I had the opportunity to thank him for his concern for us that day.

Hound Dog Man

When our family moved to the new place we rented on Azalea Avenue, just north of Arcata, I ended up with a whole new group of friends. Dave Sutter, Mel Mattila, and Bill McInnis; you could have called us the Four Musketeers. Dave lived just north of us about a ¼ of a mile, Mel just across the road, and Bill a mile south of us.

Dave and I were the closest friends, closer than brothers. He was a tall, solid built kid, a year younger than I was, with the ruddy good looks of someone who spends a lot of time outdoors. We really hit it off, probably because his folks had a dairy farm and I had spent a lot of summers growing up on my grandparents farm in Iowa. Next would have been Mel. He was a great guy, short, stocky and easy going, always ready with a laugh. His mother was an especially nice person, and his father was a hard working logging truck driver. The last of the group was Bill McInnis. He was a tall, lanky guy with a brush cut on top and long hair on the sides, with a more reserved personality.

Dave's parents, Pete and Mary Sutter, were Dutch Catholics. They were wonderful people. Pete was a typical big, strapping, hardworking Dutchman with ruddy cheeks, and a belly that hung over his belt. He always had a ready smile and never seemed to stop working. We avoided him as much as possible because the minute he laid eyes on you he had a job for you to do! Mary, Dave's mother, was the kindest lady imaginable. We would be lounging around the kitchen table and Pete would be trying to conscript us into some job. Mary would be saying, "Now Pete, now Pete, these boys need something to eat." Her specialty was thick slices of strong cheddar cheese slathered with salad dressing on homemade bread! Well, after you had eaten a couple of those, you couldn't even get out of the chair, much less work, so that brought that threat to an end!

One good thing that came from my friendship with Dave was that he broke me forever of any propensity to gamble. Having been brought up a Christian, gambling had simply never been a problem in our family. One day Dave asked if I would like to play a hand of poker. I said, "Sure, how do you do it?" He explained the procedure and after losing about ten dollars at ten cents a game, I could plainly see that Lady Luck was not on my side and that Las Vegas and Reno were not for me. In spite of all the other stupid things I got involved in, that was one addiction I never had to overcome!

———

One thing Dave and I hit it off on was hunting with hounds. As I mentioned earlier, I came from a long line of coon hunting hound dog men that went a long way back in our family history. It would have been on Dad's side; as when the early settlers started their homesteads, hounds were part of the picture. They kept them as watch dogs to track down the "varmints" that got into their crops, as well as bear and mountain lion that could be a threat to their lives. We viewed hunting with hounds as a sport. We failed to catch anything a lot more times than we succeeded. But there's no sweeter music to a hound man's ears than the voices of his dogs. It was a legal sport, so I guess the game department felt it had some game control value to it.

Most of our hunts were fairly uneventful, and took place early Sunday morning after a Saturday night of living it up, so by Sunday night after a long day of chasing hounds, we were pretty well bagged. Sometimes we hunted with John and Jack Matlock, whose Dad, "Dude" Matlock came from Oklahoma. They were a couple of solid built "Okie" boys with close set eyes and a direct look that let you know they took hound hunting and most everything else pretty serious. They were a couple of years older than Dave and I, and really good guys when you got to know them. About a year down the road, they were to come in real handy as backup men in a scrape I found myself at a local Dance Hall!

Sometimes during the week, Dave and I would hunt coons on his Dad's farm. But on the weekends, we would go inland from the coast to hunt bobcat and bear as well as raccoons. One of our favourite places to hunt was Red Wood Creek. Inland about 20 miles, the Seventh-day Adventist Church had a Church Camp in that area, where I was baptized when I was 12, along with a group of my Christian friends. We hunted on property that belonged to Redwood Creek Ranch. On this particular day, it was late afternoon when we went by the ranch house, down along Redwood Creek, and headed up through the open pasture land and scattered timber, to the solid stands of timber on top of the ridges.

I don't know why we didn't just go home. It was late, we were hungry, it was starting to rain, and we were bone tired. But Dave was a real hound man and could be pretty set in his ways when it came to giving up on a days' hunting, so we decided to stay until dark. He had three Red Bone hounds; Rusty, a big, deep chested male, Judy, a more delicate built female, and Old Dixie, a toothless, half blind, heavy bodied old female who bawled her head off every step and was excellent for training young dogs.

When we got into standing timber at the higher elevation we got into serious trouble. The logging road we were on ran through the standing timber 200 hundred yards in from a big block that had been recently logged. What had started out as a few showers had turned into a full blown coastal storm, and when we hit a big mud puddle that soaked the motor of Dave's old 1937 Chevy hunting car, the motor died. Then we were in a real fix. He had taken the back seat out of the car and filled it with straw for a place for the dogs to stay so we left them there.

We were about to starve by this time. We had some matches, so decided to shoot a deer, start a fire, and roast some of it. When we got out into the logged off area, there were deer everywhere, so getting one was no problem. We didn't have any rain gear, and by then, I don't think it would have even mattered. We were beyond being soaked through. It was just one solid wall of driving water coming down. We couldn't even begin to get a fire going. When we took the matches out, the heads just fell off when you tried to light them. We finally gave up and headed back to the car. By then it was almost dark, and the wind and rain were unreal. We crawled into the back and huddled up in the straw with the dogs. It was just one big tangle of dogs and humans all huddled up together trying to stay warm. It was one long, sleepless night!

Our main concern was that one of those big fir trees would blow down across the car; we could hear them coming down all around us. When morning finally came, we realized how fortunate we had been. There were trees down everywhere! We made the long walk down to Redwood Creek Ranch where they stuffed us full of grub, and let us phone home just as our Dads were heading out to look for us.

A Close Call

In the late part of the winter, December 1958, Dad bought me a 1949 Ford 4 door sedan. I wasn't 18 yet, I wouldn't be until the 24th of July, but this was Dad's way of ushering me into a man's world of responsibility. The 1949 Ford was a light green colour and immaculate. The motor needed some work, so Dad arranged for that to be done. I was one excited kid and really thought I had arrived! It wasn't the coolest car at school, but after I got the front end lowered to give, what at that time was called a "rakish" look, (with the front low and the back high), it looked pretty sharp. A big improvement over the 1932 Ford hot rod! I was flying high at that point, and everything seemed to be going along really well.

I was setting in Mr. Smith's History class when I got a call to come to the administration office. I was puzzled, as I couldn't think of anything I had done wrong recently. When I got there, they told me "Your Dad has been hurt in the woods and has been flown to the hospital in Eureka by Air Ambulance." That's all they knew, so I tore out of there and headed for Eureka, which was about 20 minutes south. When I got up to the hospital room, Mom was sitting in a chair beside the bed. She worked as a nurses aid at the Arcata Hospital, so was used to being around injured people. They had Dad so doped up, he didn't know what was going on. He had been hit by a snag, or dead tree, that was 60 feet long and 10 inches across on the small end. It had hit him a glancing blow across the small of his back on the right hand side. The whole right side of his lower back, rear end, and back of his leg down to his ankle was totally black. If the tree had hit him solid, it would have without a doubt killed him on the spot. It was a freak accident. Dad and his long time working partner Speed Hart, were working out of Orleans, a little logging town 70 miles or so east of the coast. They would camp out during the week and come home early on Friday. On the day of the accident, Dad was bucking down in a draw and Speed was clear up on the side of the hill, a long ways from where Dad was. They were both careful loggers, not "High Ballers" like some falling/bucking partners were called. Speed had fell a green tree that hit a standing snag that fell and hit another standing snag. The top snapped out of it, and that was the piece that came down into the draw that Dad was in. It was a one in a million accident. Dad said later that if he had just stayed where he was, it would have missed him, but he tried to out run it and that's when it got him. Fortunately, there weren't any broken bones, but it took about 6 months of rehab before he could work again.

Of course, as soon as he could, Speed came in to see Dad. Words couldn't come close to telling how bad he felt. Speed was a big old Swede, big in a lot more ways than just size. His birth name was Willis, but he was called "Speed" because he moved so slow. Speed and Dad had hunted and worked together for years, and after this accident they would go on to hunt and work together for many more years without any loss of confidence in each other.

When I drove back from Eureka that day I realized I was one lucky kid. Dad had come within a hairs breadth of being killed or crippled for life. I was lucky in a lot of ways. He was a good Dad. Both our parents were straight forward, honest, hardworking people. They set a good moral example in all areas of life. Dad wasn't a drinking man. Sure, back in the McDowell Creek days when he was younger, at the weekend hoedown he could get carried away, but that was years ago. From my Mother's perspective, my Dad's greatest vice was hunting. She saw that as an absolute total waste of time, energy, and most of all money. One Fall before duck hunting season he decided that buying shot gun shells a box at a time was pure foolishness the way we went through them, so he went out and bought a whole case. I don't know how Mom found out, but when she did she hit the roof! My Mother had a pretty fiery temper, so to even things up she went out and bought a brand new refrigerator! As far as I can remember that was the last case of shot gun shells that Dad ever bought; he found it was quite a bit cheaper to just buy them a box or two at a time so no one noticed!

When we were growing up, men didn't tell their boys in so many words that they loved them, at least not in the society we lived in. They had other ways of letting you know like kicking you in the butt, punching you in the shoulder, messing up your hair, tickling you, putting you in a headlock, wrestling with you, but never actually telling you they loved you. That was sissy stuff. You wouldn't have known what to do and neither would they. In a lot of our old family pictures, Grandma and Grandpa, and especially uncles would be holding us boys. So, we knew that they cared. Another way our Dad showed us he cared was, as mentioned, taking us hunting and fishing, and teaching us how to use and look after a gun and fishing tackle.

Those were the good times I remembered as I drove back home that day from the hospital in Eureka. I didn't know it then but within a short while I would need all the good memories I could recollect, because I was about to hit a rough stretch in life that, due to my own stupidity, would last almost 5 years. For a while, I rejected all the values that I was brought up with. I'm sure I'm not the only kid who went over "Fool's Hill", but that doesn't make it any easier to remember the disappointment I was to Mom and Dad, as well as others who had done a lot for me through the years.

Fool's Hill

There's no doubt it started with the car wreck. Not long after Dad got hurt, a bunch of us guys were out riding around Arcata one Saturday night in this guy's customized '56 Chev. He had a steady job in a Safeway grocery store, and had no end of dollars, so his car was a real show stopper. I had parked my '49 Ford in the parking lot of the Safeway store, so I suggested after a while that we take my car around for a spin. We all piled in, I think there were six of us, and headed uptown. There were two ways you could go downtown from the parking lot. One to the left along the foot of the hill below the high school, the other turned to the right and crossed a railroad track. We very seldom took the road to the right that crossed the tracks, but for some reason that night, I did. As mentioned earlier, I had the front end of my car lowered as that was the style, so it naturally shortened the distance the headlights would shine. We weren't speeding, but suddenly a rail car was right in front of us. It was a logging train. Fortunately for us, we hit a wheel on the rail car, so we didn't go under the train, or that would have been the end of the trail. The way it was, it tore the front end right off the car. Thankfully, other than being shook up pretty bad, no one was hurt. We hadn't been drinking too much that night, but that was the end of the nice little '49 Ford.

Losing my car was quite a blow and things went downhill pretty fast after that. I hadn't been doing too well in school, and it wasn't long before I got kicked out....2 weeks before grade 12 graduation in June 1959. The drinking was really getting out of hand. It was to the point where I was starting to go off and drink by myself, which is a bad sign. It finally came to a head one Saturday night when some friends brought me home and literally dumped me off. I finally managed to drag myself into the house and fall in a chair.

By this time, Dad had been home from the hospital for a while and was going for walks on our road so he could get back in shape to go to work again. Dad was a long suffering, patient man. But when he got mad, you better look for something to crawl under. Even as a kid, I would rather have Mom give me a whipping any day than have Dad give me a talking to. I can tell you I have never seen him so mad as he was that night, and he had every right in the world to be. He let me have it with both barrels. He chewed me up one side and down the other and then did it all over again. No one else was home that night so he didn't hold back. That's the night he gave up on me, maybe gave up isn't the right word, just didn't know what else to do might be a better way to put it. He had done everything he could, and had reached the end of his rope. I had failed him at the worst time. Right when I should have been there while he was recuperating from the logging accident, I was nothing but a constant worry.

––––––––

Somewhere around this time, I decided I could salvage the motor out of my wrecked 49 Ford and stick it in a junker of some kind and have some wheels again. I found a blue 49 Ford Coupe, and managed to get the motor in, and got it going. I took it to the dance at the Clam Beach Inn Dance Hall, which was just north of where we lived on Highway 101 at the George Beck place. The Clam Beach Inn Dance was quite a big deal; how I ever expected to go there in a car without a hood, and not get caught by the cops is beyond me. I hadn't been able to find a hood so just drove it without. I had done pretty good, but on the way home on Highway 101, a California Highway Patrol passed me going toward Clam Beach. I'm sure he couldn't believe his eyes! He probably thought he was in the middle of a stock car race! I quickly shut off my lights and whipped off into our old drive way, but I made the mistake of hitting the brakes instead of coasting to a stop. By then, he had turned around, came back, saw my brake lights, and I was done for.

This was the third time I had been picked up for underage drinking. The first two they had let me go with a warning. Now they were fed up. I was just under 18, so still in the Juvenile System; they took me to the Detention Center in Eureka. I was locked in a 6 x 12 cell with a heavy mesh screened window on the north side that I could climb up and look out into a high concrete walled exercise yard. They handed you your food through a hole in the door. You would have thought I had robbed Fort Knox, but I guess they were trying to make a point.

They let Mom come in to see me in the latter part of the week, and I asked her if she would buy me a pack of Lucky Strike cigarettes. She did, but against her better judgment. It was a week of pure hell for me. I was a boy of the open spaces and fresh air. They told me that they would hear my case in a week, to decide if they were going to send me to Reform School for a period of time to smarten me up. It was obvious the week of solitary confinement was a "think it over" period so I would know they were tired of playing around and meant business. I had plenty of time that week to ponder the direction I was going. I had no excuse for going down the road I was taking. Growing up, I had all the love and support from all those uncles, aunts, grandparents, and especially from my parents, that anyone could need. It was a week of some pretty deep soul searching. I won't say I came out a changed man, but I had done some thinking that had an impact later on.

When the Hearing day came and they let me out of that cell, I still remember the incredible feeling of freedom. The courtroom was big. There were 3 people in it, the Judge, me, and my Mom. She was sitting there in that big courtroom, all alone, with her head down, crying. My Mother was a very stubborn person. You might have your differences with her, but you could never doubt that she loved you. That was plain to see that day. Everyone else had had enough, but a Mother's love never fails. They let me go, gave me another chance. I couldn't believe it. I like to think that day the Good Lord answered a desperate Mother's prayer. I had dodged the bullet, now what was I going to do?

Somewhere along the line in my badly fractured senior year of high school, between car wrecks, getting kicked out of school, and spending a week in a Detention Center, I had decided to join the U.S. Air Force. With a lot of encouragement from Dad (who I know saw this as the last possible chance for me), and with 3 friends set out for the Recruiting Office in Eureka. By this time, I had just turned 18. My best friend in high school other than Dave Sutter, was Neil Baker. Neil was a big, tall, lanky, easy going guy with wavy blonde hair who always had a friendly smile on his face. You couldn't find a nicer guy to be around. Strangely enough, he wasn't a heavy drinker; he would have a few beers, but he didn't have to drink to enjoy life. We ended up in just about every class together and along with a couple of other friends, decided to join the Air Force.

The Recruiting Officers name was Sergeant White. He was an older, white haired officer and a real fatherly type of gentleman. I explained my run ins with the law. He assured me as long as I was under 18 at the time, and there was no criminal record, which there wasn't, there would be no problem. Things proceeded well and we headed for Oakland, California, to take our Physicals. I was pretty cranked up over the whole thing. I had always thought a lot of my Uncle Donald, my Dad's youngest brother who had been in the Air Force, and now I thought maybe this would be a chance to find some direction in life.

Oakland, California was a real dump. I couldn't believe how dirty the place was, at least the part we went through. The Physical went well and things were looking pretty good. I was then told to go into an office and talk to an officer who began to ask me questions. He mumbled when he talked, and it was really hard to understand what he was saying, so I kept asking him, "What did you say?" It was a very frustrating interview as I really had a hard time understanding what he was saying. I wasn't trying to be a smart guy, I wanted to get into the service pretty bad. By this time, I had put quite a bit of time and effort into it, as well as wanting to go in with my buddies. Afterwards, those of us who had the interviews rejoined the group, and they came through the room and said, "you stay", or "you go home." When the guy came to my buddies, he told them, "you stay." When he came to me, he said, "you go home." I asked him what was the reason? He said, "We feel because of your attitude towards the officer who was interviewing you, that in a military setting, you would resist authority!" That simple bit of logic sent me on a long gloomy bus ride back through the grungy streets of Oakland.

A Seed Of Doubt

When I went back to Arcata, the best way to describe the way I was living at that time was like a loose cannon. I just didn't have any direction at all. One weekend, Dave Sutter and I went to a Johnny Cash concert in Eureka. I was quite a Johnny Cash fan, but by the time we got there, I was so far gone that all I remember was when he imitated Elvis Presley. I faintly remember driving Dave's old '57 Ford home, and parking it in his folk's garage, because he was totally conked out. But when we woke up in the car the next morning, it gave us both a pretty bad scare.

Another guy I was running around with was Melvin Holden. We had been friends with Mel ever since we came to California. Mel was a tall, thin guy with thick, wavy yellow blond hair. To look at him, you would think he was skinny, but he was made of rawhide and spring steel. He would have fit right in with the old mountain men. He had a talent for mimicking people and would do this in a high falsetto voice. Mel had a very different upbringing, and it left him with a very unique personality. He was probably born 150 to 200 years too late. Mel was raised in the backwoods communities, where his Dad worked. He didn't have much to do and grew up reading Zane Grey books. His favourites were about the pioneers of the Ohio Valley, where the heroes were Jonathan Zane and Lou Wetzel. In his early years, Mel found himself a coonskin cap, and a buckskin coat, and relived the days of the pioneers as he stalked through the hills around the little lumber towns where they lived. By the time we got to know him, he had modernized quite a bit, but he was still a rather unique guy.

One adventure Mel, my brother Ron, and I, went on one early spring that didn't pan out too well, was when we were going to live off the land. Just the idea of this adventure should have been warning enough to stay home. Dad dropped us off in a wet Redwood forested area, in from the coast a few miles and was going to pick us up in 5 days. We had 1 loaf of bread, 1 slab of bacon, and 1 sack of dried beans. Not long after Dad left, it started to rain, and by the end of the second day, the only thing we hadn't eaten was the bacon rind, so we made a stew of bacon rind and fiddle head ferns. After I ate that, I got violently sick. On the morning of the third day, Mel shot a little tweety bird of some kind, with his 40 caliber Remington rolling block Heritage buffalo rifle, and you couldn't even find a feather. Then he shot a rabbit. But a pair of rabbit ears doesn't go far when you have to split it three ways. By the afternoon of the third day, the starvation march for home was in full swing. But as luck would have it, Dad had the timing figured out pretty close and came along and picked up the survivors.

———

Mel had a half-brother by the name of Stan Robson that we ran around with for a short while. It was a good thing it was only for a short while. Stan was a drifter, a real tramp logger. He had a wife and a couple of kids. I never got the whole story on him, but I know they lived a real Gypsy existence. During this time there was one beer joint where I would drink with Mel and Stan and whoever else came along. It was located on the east side of Highway 101 just north of McKinnleyville. They had dumped a big pile of rocks and gravel into a cat tail swamp along the edge of the highway, levelled it off, and built a flat roofed beer joint on it. It wasn't much for quality, but it had one thing in its favour. They didn't ask how old you were when they brought the beer! I didn't know it at the time, but I was to learn a very valuable lesson of life in that cheap tavern that even someone as young and stupid as I was couldn't help but understand.

Stan Robson was a spell binder. My brother, Ron, worked on a logging show with him for a while out of Bothel, Washington, and said that in spite of all the hot air, Stan really knew what he was doing on the job. A lot of people aren't aware that the logging business has its own culture, stories, poems, songs, language, the whole works. Especially west coast High Lead logging, which is hard, fast, dirty, brutal, dangerous work.

Stan Robson was the perfect image of a west coast logger. With curly, dark brown hair and rugged square jawed good looks, he could have came right off the silver screen. I think he knew every west coast logger and Robert Service poem that was ever written, plus all the stories and songs. As we sat there in a pleasant half-drunk stupor in that tavern out in the swamp,

I was blown away. You couldn't help but be impressed with Stan. At that time, I had a plaid white and brown Pendleton jacket. It was an expensive coat that I really liked. Somehow Stan was impressed with that coat too, so one cold, rainy night when all of us old logger buddies were drinking it up, he asked if he could borrow it. Well, of course he could borrow it! What are old logger drinking buddies for if they won't lend you their coat? That was the last time I ever saw it.

———

Over a period of time, I caught a glimpse into the tramp logger world, a world of broken promises, broken dreams, broken hearts, and broken noses. I'm no authority on the world of tramp loggers and the skid row thing, but what little time I spent around "the edge," so to speak, wasn't a pretty sight. It doesn't matter if it's on the west coast from California to Alaska or central British Columbia, it's all the same sad story. My brother Ron, took that trail for a few years, and it didn't do him, or his family any favours. There is a kind of vague code of conduct and intention to do it right, but after a few drinks, things just seem to get a little distorted and out of focus. I think that is what happened with my good Pendleton coat. Stan didn't mean to steal, he just never found a convenient time to bring it back. Maybe there was another side to this whole booze thing than what the Good Time Beer ads showed you. Somehow this incident planted a little seed of doubt that this wasn't an ideal way to live, especially if you liked Pendleton jackets!

Dance Hall Brawl

It wasn't long after, that I had the fight at the Clam Beach Inn Dance Hall. I had learned a good lesson about loaning my coat too quick, but there were a few other things to learn. Clam Beach Inn was a bar along Highway 101, north of where we lived on George Becks' place. There was a big dance hall a few hundred feet toward the beach from the bar. It was a pretty wild place on a Saturday night, and sometimes some of the boys from Humboldt State College in Arcata would come out and kick up their heels. I had developed a real negative attitude by this time and was not a very congenial person to be around. But at least back at that time in northern California, once someone was knocked out or gave up in a fight, you didn't have to worry about someone sticking a knife in you, or stomping your head in. But it could still be a little hazardous if you were on the losing end. It was to my good fortune that my old coon hunting buddies, the Matlock brothers, John and Jack, with their burly builds and serious ways, were at the dance hall that night, too.

By nature, I wasn't a fighter. I had worked myself into that frame of mind by admiring the tough guys in the movies, my older brother, and some of the guys that I ran around with. It was also cool at that time to be a tough guy. When we were kids living in the place back up Highway 101 from Clam Beach, we had a neighbour, Winnie Winkler, who had been a professional boxer. He was a logger, and along with his stepson, Wes Hale, did a lot of deer and duck hunting with us. Whatever Winnie did, he was good at, and not the least bit bashful about letting you know it. He tended to focus on his own exploits most of the time. He was short, about 5 foot 4 inches tall, and built right on the ground. His forearms were bigger than my upper leg. Somewhere along the line, he decided us boys needed to learn how to box. He took us down to his place, and put the gloves on us. When he fought, he crouched down where the only place you could hit him was right on the top of his head. But he did teach me a few basics, like a straight punch is harder to stop than a round house haymaker, and to hit 'em in the nose right off the bat, and make their nose bleed, and sometimes that would end the fight.

He was always bragging to me about a young relative of his about my age, who was the next in line to Rocky Marciano. He bragged about him all the time, and said when he came up to visit him, he would put the gloves on us and this kid would teach me a thing or two. He said he was just a chip off the old block, and I really didn't stand much of a chance. Well the day finally came, and when I met this kid, I couldn't believe my eyes! I expected him to look like King Kong. He was smaller than I was, and a real mild mannered nice guy. We hit it right off as good buddies, and took off rabbit hunting on the airport and had a great time together. But the gloves were inevitable.

He wasn't any more interested in punching me out than I was him, but this was the old boxers' chance to show off the new generation of champions in his line, so at it we went. I figured I was in a fight for my life, so I remembered all the things Winnie had taught me and after a couple of minutes, I threw a straight punch right from the shoulder, and hit him right square on the chin. I couldn't believe it. It was the first time I ever came close to knocking someone out! His eyes sort of glazed over and his hands just dropped to his sides like someone had shot him. I was scared to death. I don't remember if I ran over and grabbed him or if Winnie did, but it was quite the scene. They jerked the gloves off us, and there was everything I had done wrong and he had done right, and if this hadn't happened and that hadn't happened, it would have been different. I just wanted to get out of there. Well things turned out pretty good in the long run when they just let us be friends, and we got to hunt together for a few more days before he had to leave. It wasn't a big deal to either one of us what had happened, but it cooled Winnie's bragging down, and I noticed he lost interest in giving me anymore boxing lessons.

I came to the Dance Hall that night looking for trouble. I wasn't drunk, just enough to be brave; brave and ignorant. I started walking through the crowd inside the Dance Hall, bumping into people. But I wasn't completely stupid, I kind of sized up the ones that I bumped into and chose ones I figured I could beat. They all just ignored me, I think mostly because they had more important things to do, or just didn't want to be bothered!

Then as I got toward the band stand, there was this big guy with a Humboldt State College Varsity jacket on. I made a point of leaving plenty of room between us as I started to go by, and wouldn't you know it, just as I went by, somebody shoved me right into him. Well things went downhill pretty fast from there. He must have come out there for the same purpose I did, because before you knew it, we were headed for the door. When I looked back over my shoulder, I knew I was in big trouble. It looked like Hulk Hogan trailing along behind.

But it was too late to back out because too many people had seen the altercation. Somewhere along the way, the Matlock boys showed up, and John, the older, biggest one asked me if I wanted them to come along. Well! Did I want them to come along? I couldn't very well hug him right there with all the people around, but I told him, "Sure, be glad to have you!" My sparring partner had brought along three or four of his own buddies to watch the massacre, so I was more than happy to have the Matlock boys there to pick up the pieces.

When we got outside and toward the stomping grounds at the back of the Dance Hall it was fairly dark, and when I looked over my shoulder again, I thought I had made a very big mistake. I was six foot four inches tall at that time, and probably weighed 180 pounds, and was in fairly good shape. I never did find out for sure, but this guy must have been a football or basketball player. He was six foot six or taller and weighed well over 200 pounds. He was one big boy, and I was one scared tough guy! When we stopped, I peeled off my leather coat with my back to him and when I turned around, I hit him as hard as I could right in the face. It didn't even faze him. He was on me in a second and over we went with him on top. Well, needless to say, I was not in the best position. There was only one thing that saved my neck that night. As I went over backwards and hit the ground, by some miracle I got my knees or shins under his arm pits, and by raising my rear end off the ground, I could lever him up high enough that he couldn't hit me. But it was close, man, was it ever close! Every time he took a swing, it just whistled by the end of my nose. If he had ever hit me, it would have been lights out for sure. This was not a stand-up Winnie Winkler by the rules, kind of fight, this was a rough and tumble, behind the Dance Hall brawl. I knew I couldn't stay in that position forever, and I guess I must have had him a little off balance, because I just gave one big sideways heave and rolled him over. Then, for just a minute, I was on top. He was a lot bigger than I was, but he was slower and when I got on top, I knew this was my chance, and I nailed him as hard and as many times as I could with both fists. I was scared stiff and I gave it everything I had. All of a sudden, he just went limp and his friends jumped right in, grabbed him, and hauled him away.

I was lucky, lucky. The Matlock boys came over, and we talked the whole thing over. They were behind me all the way, but they couldn't believe I had come out on top. I couldn't either. There was only one reason. The guy was big, but he wasn't hard. He was just a big college kid that wasn't really the mean, tough kind. But the facts were that I was the winner, and word got around. It did me more harm than good. By this time, I had really gone off the deep end. I was walking that very thin line that leads to destruction and was actually doing things that were causing physical damage to myself, and all just to enhance this bad guy image. I had one friend besides Dave Sutter that could still put up with me. His name was Jim Byrnes. He was not that big a guy, kind of on the quiet side with a slow, easy grin. But he could be a real scrapper, and if he didn't agree with you, he let you know it. He would drink, but kept it pretty much under control. He had a '57 Ford and kept it in top shape.

A few weekends after Clam Beach, we were out cruising in his car, and the cops pulled us over. I don't really remember where we were going that night, but we had 3 guys in the front, and 3 or 4 in the back seat. I was sitting right behind the drivers' seat with a case of beer under my feet, and an open one in my hand when they pulled us over. I knew for sure this was the end for me. We were all underage, and I knew if they hauled me in again, I wouldn't be breathing free air again for a good long time. When they told me to roll the back window down, I knew it was game over. The fumes that came out of that window must have smelled like the Olympia Brewing Company. There I sat with an open beer between my knees, and the cops' flashlight shining right on it! The cop shined his light around, asked us a few questions, told us to take it easy, and just walked away! We couldn't believe it. This just didn't happen! It was more than a close call, I had reached the end of the line.

Oregon Reunion

It was time to say good-bye to California. I decided to go up to Oregon to visit my cousins, so I talked my friend Jim Byrnes into joining the adventure. That was a fairly bright move as he had that nice '57 Ford and we could arrive in style. One thing I decided to take along was my Colt Buntline Special .22 revolver. I know that to most law abiding Canadians, the idea of heading off down the highway on your holidays with a Colt revolver laying in full view in the middle of the front seat may seem a bit bizarre. In Oregon at that time if you had a hand gun that is exactly where you wanted it to be, right out in the open in plain sight, where John Law could see it if he happened to stop you. If you had it hidden away somewhere and he found it, you were in big trouble because it would be considered a concealed weapon.

I thought that Buntline Special was a pretty neat gun, the most outstanding feature was the 16 inch barrel. It was a copy of the .45 calibre Colt single action, which had a 7 inch barrel. A 7 inch barrel was really a whole lot more practical than this hog leg, because they could get it out of the holster in half the time. But to the old western lawmen like Wyatt Earp, who was the proud owner of a Buntline Special, that long barrel was real handy in a situation that hadn't got to the shooting stage yet. You could just reach over and conk the bad guy over the head before he got too belligerent.

I was looking forward to meeting my cousins, the Jones' family again. We made it up to Sweet Home, Oregon, without a hitch. They had moved from McDowell Creek to Crawfordsville, a few miles west of Sweet Home on the road to Eugene. We had a good re-union get together and I soon realized they had a lot of other interests besides trying to drink the town dry. Their lifestyle was quite a bit different from mine.

———

Jim and I cruised around for a couple of days trying to scare up a job. We finally found a logging outfit out of Cottage Grove that needed a couple of choker setters. Cottage Grove was a neat little sawmill town south of Eugene and Springfield. It was an hour or so drive from Crawfordsville. We got the job, rented a hotel room, had lunches made, and snagged our workpants off so we at least looked like loggers. I don't think either of us slept much that night as I had never set a choker in my life, didn't know the knob from the bell, and neither did Jim. Morning finally came and we got in the crummy with the real loggers and headed for the woods. They started quizzing us right away about where we were from, and when we told them California, they promptly called us "the California Sunshine Loggers". It was all in good fun, of course, but there was no doubt we were on trial and under the gun. I don't remember where Jim got his cork boots from, but mine were an old pair of my Dads' that were a size 8 or 9, and I wore a size 11. We both had a tin hat, raincoat, hickory shirts, but no long johns to wear. This was in the last part of March or early April and the weather was exactly like I remembered from my Milo Academy construction days. First the sun would come out for 5 minutes and then it would pour rain by the bucket. Then to increase the variety, it would dump wet snow the size of silver dollars for half an hour, then more rain, and then it would do it all over again.

My job was slinging beads behind a D7 or D8 that was flying 6 or 8, 1 inch by 25 foot chokers. I'm guessing at the size because that was a long time ago; but it was big timber and they were big chokers. The hooker looked like something that had just escaped from the gorilla cage at the zoo. He was 5 foot 10 inches tall and about as broad. Half the time he didn't wear a hard hat, and with his close cut black hair, 3 day beard stubble, and low forehead, he looked mighty close to his Neanderthal cousins. His job was to tell us, or rather me, as Jim was setting chokers behind another cat, what trees to set the chokers on. He would squat down on a big Fir stump, rain running off his head and dripping off his chin, a big chew of Choke'em Gag'em (logger term for Copenhagen) in his lip, and point and grunt toward the logs he wanted me to snare. I would wrap a choker around myself enough times to keep it from getting hung up, and head off to try and get them all set before the cat came back. When the cat started skidding it tore open a bunch of springs in the ground. The country was fairly flat and by noon the ice cold spring water was running down the skid trail half way to my knees. With my too small cork boots, it wasn't long before I couldn't feel a thing from my knees down. It was a long day, and when it was finally over and we crawled into the crummy that night, Jim and I were pretty sad looking loggers. But we had toughed it out. By the time we hit the sack that night after a huge supper at the hotel, and getting our boots half dried, we didn't have much trouble going to sleep.

The next day was a repeat of the first, only a little bit longer and a little bit worse. It was a complete mess of a day, and about 10 a.m. I decided I'd had enough. When 12 noon rolled around this California Sunshine Logger was going to pack it in. It turned out, the Oregon loggers had enough as well, and at 12 noon they shut the whole operation down. Whooee! Was that a close one! I hadn't told anyone of my plans to quit, so when we stopped and got a case of beer on the way home, Jim and I celebrated right along with the Oregon boys, just like we were as tough as they were. They accepted us right into the logger clan but that was the end of our Oregon logging career.

I've been through Cottage Grove many times since then and every time I do, I think of those tough old loggers that logged the west coast from California to Alaska. My Dad was a faller and bucker for 35 years, and my brother Ron worked the rigging for many years. One thing that would have been a big help to Jim and I would have been a good pair of long handled wool underwear. As one old Oregon Moss Back logger told me, "Son, if ya got a good pair of them woollies on, no matter how cold and wet ya git, yer always warm and dry!"

When we got back to Sweet Home, Jim decided his future lay back in California so he took off. I really was sad to see him go, as he was a good friend and besides, he had that nice '57 Ford I could ride around in and impress the local girls.

Life with the Cousins

The Jones family were a lot of fun to be around. Every weekend there was a party at their house, and it would be full of people. Noel Richards and some of his family would be there, or more likely Butch & Doris Nieman and family, who owned the tavern in Crawfordsville, along with a few other locals. It was like the old McDowell Creek days. There was a lot of laughing and music and goofing around. The Jones boys, Ed, Dick, Dwayne, Donnie, sister Carma, and mother Maxine all had a great sense of humour, and when he was in the right mood, Red did too.

Ed & Bob in Crawfordsville, Oregon

For some reason, it seemed like every dog and cat they ever owned was an eccentric of some kind. The cat they had at that time would stroll around until the party really got into high gear, and then it would start running around in circles in the middle of the living room floor, gaining speed until it actually had built up enough momentum to where it would go right up and run around the sides of the living room wall! It couldn't go too far so it would hit the floor again until it got enough rpm's built up, and up on the wall it would go again! This caused real chaos among the people sitting around because it would run across your lap or over your head, or wherever until it could hit the wall again! But it was a real conversation piece if nothing else. The cat was also a very good hunter and one time it brought in a full grown Cottontail rabbit.

Dick and Ed were opposites in a lot of ways. Dick was more interested in electronics, mechanics, and doing things like wood carving, at which he became very good. Ed was more athletic. Ed was on the tumbling team at their high school. He was a natural. About five foot ten inches tall, broad shouldered, with a real swimmer's build from all the summers they had spent in the Calapooya River. He was still having a little trouble talking when Jim and I arrived because of an acrobatic miscalculation he had made. He was practicing doing a standing full forward front flip, and somehow, when he landed, his chin came down and hit his knee. Now that was bad enough, but he had his tongue between his teeth when he hit and promptly bit his tongue in half, just a bit forward from being right in the middle! As luck would have it, there was still a little piece attached to each side so it didn't fall off and they sewed it together again. He was on a liquid diet for quite a spell and not ready for any long winded arguments. He was starting to get back in the talking business when we showed up, but was still fairly quiet.

I'm not sure now where it came from, but somehow we got our hands on a motorcycle. It was just a small thing about half the size of a real bike. It was a single cylinder called a "putt and a quarter". I think it was a Harley Davidson, the "putt and a quarter" referred to the size of the engine. It was a wore out piece of junk, but we had no end of fun running it through the brush and bog holes of somebody's property across the road from Jones'. We spent a lot more time monkey wrenching it than riding it, but it awakened a burning desire in me to have the real thing.

A month or so after the Cottage Grove logging experience, both Dick and I got a swing shift job at Santiam Plywood in Sweet Home. It was a good job and the money just started rolling in. So as quick as I could, I bought a real bike. It was a sharp looking metallic blue 2 cylinder Triumph, and when you cracked the throttle, it wasn't "a putt and a quarter". It was a British bike similar to the bikes that James Dean and Marlon Brando rode in their movies, but without the high front forks and steer horn handle bars. It was still an impressive machine.

I had a couple of experiences on that bike that left a lasting impression on me. A neighbour up the road had put in a few acres of green beans. He would hire a lot of the local kids for picking, hauling them back and forth to work on a school bus that came right by the Jones' place and into Crawfordville. Dick & I were working swing shift and didn't start until late afternoon; I had the whole day free. It was a hot day and I had decided to whip down to the Crawfordville Store on the bike to get something. I was about a quarter of a mile from home, and on the way back, when coming up over the top of a sharp outside corner in the road, I got into trouble. Helmets weren't mandatory in those days, but anyone with a wee bit of common sense should never ride a motorcycle without a helmet, goggles, leather coat, leather boots, leather pants, and leather gloves. All I was wearing that day was my good 501 Levis and a pair of slip on shoes. No gloves, no hat, not even a tee shirt; bare hide from the waist up. Gravel roads and bikes aren't the best combination, and when I came up over that hill and into the corner, the law of gravity quit working. The bike went sideways on the gravel and hit the ground, and I sailed right straight out over the handle bars. It must have looked quite graceful to the busload of bean pickers that came along about then. I hit the ground on my hands and knees, and the hide just flew. When I stopped skidding, the bean picker bus pulled up beside me. The kids rolled the windows down and kindly asked how I was doing... they were howling with laughter! It was quite a sight I'm sure, but I didn't really think it was all that funny. I had lost quite a bit of hide, especially on the heel of my left hand, but that was the worst. I wasn't going all that fast when I lost it, but even going down the road on your hands and knees at 20 miles an hour isn't a good practice. There were control wires hanging off the handle bars all over the place. I managed to get it up on its' wheels and started pushing it home. It was still in one of the high gears, and as I started pushing it, all of a sudden it fired! So I jumped on it and rode it the rest of the way home, got out the Iodine and gauze repair kit and patched up the damage. In a way, landing on my hands and knees kept the personal damage to a minimum, and the gravel didn't wear through the knees of those Levi 501's, but it was still not the best way to dismount from a motorcycle.

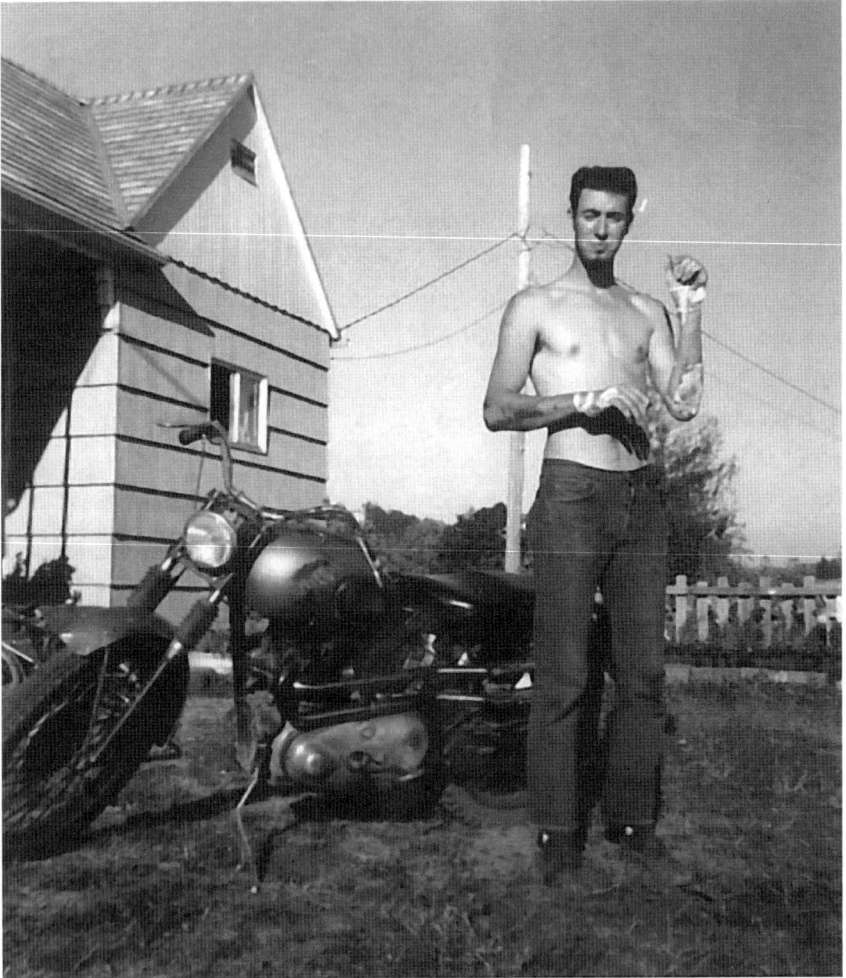

Bob after his wreck

Ever since I had arrived the talk around the Jones' house had been about moving to Vanderhoof, British Columbia, Canada. Red was getting a tandem trailer all rigged up and painted a nice, light, grey with red trim, to pull behind his grey 1952 Jeep pick up; the excitement was building. The plan was for Ed to go up in his car in the middle of the summer and build a rough lumber, single bedroom house, with a steep roof pitch, so it would have a big attic where the boys could sleep. Ed had a white and light tan Pontiac that he kept in top shape, so he headed north about the middle of the summer of 1960 to begin the great adventure. He was really chomping at the bit to go, as he was right into building, and a pretty good carpenter even then, so he was really eager to take on the challenge.

Red & Maxine Jones

While Ed was off to adventures in the north, Dick and I were getting broken into life in the real world with our jobs at Santiam Plywood. Dick ended up in the dry end grading plywood; I was put in the green end, pulling veneer off the green chain behind the clipper. The clipper was a machine that cut the eight foot veneer, that had been peeled off the rotating log by the lathe, into four foot wide sheets. It also cut the filler strips which were used for the cross strip fillers in a sheet of plywood. The dry end building was the best place to work in winter as it was warm. The green end building was best in the summer because of big open doors and good air flow, but it could still get plenty hot in there on a warm day. Our crew was a bunch of young guys on the green chain, with either 3 or 4 to the side. There were guys on both sides pulling veneer off the big flat table, with the moving chains carrying the veneer along. There were two clippers that fed the green chain, one on the ground level, and one directly above it. When both those clippers were going, it really kept us jumping to keep up.

Our foreman was a big, easy going, overweight older man named Ed, with receding wavy blonde hair and rimless glasses who aged a week for every day he had to spend around us. He was very safety conscious, and I'm sure lived in a state of continual nightmare, both for our safety and his job.

———

We had a new man start work after I hired on, who we nick named "Lightning". I don't remember his real name, but I will never forget him. He was the perfect image of a bad guy out of a western movie. He wore a dirty, slouchy, old cowboy hat, always seemed to have a three day growth of beard, expressionless eyes, and a gaunt, sallow face with a thin lipped snaggle toothed smile. He mostly kept to himself, did his job, but nothing extra. I guess that is part of the reason we called him "Lightning." But the other reason was when you did manage to get into a conversation with him, it always seemed to drift to what a good shot he was, and how fast he could quick draw a handgun. Well, this interested me no end because I had done quite a bit of practicing quick drawing with my trusty Colt .22 Buntline Special with the 16" barrel, and I figured I was pretty fast. After a few weeks on the job, and getting a little better acquainted, I asked him if he would like to take a trip out to the local dump, shoot a few rats, and pop off a pop bottle or two. He seemed more than willing to take me up on this invitation, so one weekend we headed out.

Red Jones had made a set of oak handgrips for my gun on his shop smith to replace the standard black ones, and with these all oiled and polished up, it was a pretty sharp looking shootin' iron. I had a belt and holster made for it, and when I had that thing buckled on and the holster end tied down to my leg, it looked mighty impressive. I'm sure it would have made the bad guys of Deadwood City and Tombstone shiver in their boots, but it didn't seem to impress "Lightning."

When we got to the dump, we got out of the car and strolled over to see if there were any rats running for their holes that we could dust off, and since there weren't, I suggested we have a little quick draw contest. I had thrown down the glove! This would be the test. We would see if this guy was really as good as he said he was! It wasn't even close, his hand was just a blur. He had his gun out and was breaking bottles before I even cleared leather. He looked over at me with expressionless gun fighter eyes and a smirk on his face, and never said a word. He didn't have to. We didn't stick around the dump too long after that because all of a sudden, I had some important things to get done back home. It was a pretty quiet ride back to town. But from then on, whenever I talked to "Lightning", I tried to steer the conversation away from guns and quick drawing, and none of us ever gave him much of a hard time about anything after that.

———

Our coffee breaks were always lively times where we all smoked and cussed up a storm, and bragged about our latest performances. The main guy everyone gathered around at coffee breaks was Jerry; tall, curly headed with glasses, a weight lifters build, and one of the lathe operators. We really looked up to him, because a lathe operator was the production man, and had to really know his stuff. When the big fir logs came up the chain to the lathe, they were kicked into position with hydraulic arms so they could sock the dogs in the end of them, get them rotating and start peeling the veneer off onto the trays. But it was more than this, he was a natural leader. He would sit with his smoke in his hand on the edge of this piece of round concrete culvert, and in an easy going way, would hold court. He could tell the best ribald, drinking stories of anyone, and was really one of the boys.

Then all of a sudden, there was a change…no more smoking, no more ribald jokes, no more cursing and crude drinking stories. He was a totally different person. What was wrong with this guy? Had he swallowed a purity pill? It turned out he had gotten married and became a Christian.

Oh yeah, whatever it takes to make the little woman happy, we all thought. We watched him like a hawk. Nobody gave him a hard time about it, maybe a sly dig or two, but we didn't want to push him too far in case he had a relapse and mopped the pavement with us. After keeping an eye on him for two or three weeks, it became pretty clear this was the real thing. He was a changed man. He didn't beat us over the head with it, but you could see he was a different guy and just not interested in the garbage any more. He had to relearn the English language again, I'm sure, because like most of us, when we talked, the swear words poured out like water out of a boot, maybe that's why he was so quiet. But he managed. Secretly, I admired him for the stand he had taken, and although deep inside I wasn't really happy with my prodigal ways, I was a long way from any change.

Easy Rider

After a couple of months on the job the work started to become a bit monotonous. A few of us fell into the routine of stopping off for a few beers at the local bar, The Pastime, in Sweet Home. I remembered the place from when I was a kid at McDowell Creek, and never imagined I would ever step through its' doors. We had about an hour between the time our shift ended, and when the bar closed. If we hustled right down after work, we would have roughly 45 minutes to sit at the bar, drink and shoot the breeze with the barmaids, and each other, before the doors closed.

It was a relaxing time when you could soak up a few, listen to good country music on the Jukebox, and if you were in the right mood, and hit the right song, blubber in your beer. The one barmaid was a middle aged motherly type you could tell your troubles to. The other was a slender, attractive younger lady with short blonde hair and a quick friendly smile that I found quite interesting. We seemed to hit it off pretty good and I was developing more than a passing interest when I discovered much to my surprise that she already had a husband. Well, this rang all the alarm bells those old German preachers from the McDowell Creek days had instilled, and I quickly decided it was no doubt best to leave well enough alone, and to stick with blubbering in my beer, and listening to the Jukebox.

It was during one of these bar room reminiscing periods that I decided to jump on my bike and take a run back to California. It was a spur of the moment decision people tend to make when their brain is a little fuzzy, and off I went. I had probably gotten up around noon the day before, and by the time I got out to Jones' after putting in the shift at the mill, stopping at the bar, and a few other diversions, it was around six o'clock in the morning. But I was young and restless and ready for a break. I let Red and Maxine know my plans, took a short leave of absence from the job, put on my leather coat, jumped on the trusty Triumph and we were California bound. It was a ball. I was still not completely in the real world because of the influence from the night before, but the cool wind blowing in my face at 60 or 70 miles an hour soon brought me around. By the time I got to Eugene and headed south on the freeway, I was definitely wide awake. It was an exciting adventure as I cruised along on the freeway and thought of seeing old friends and catching up on the action. But I had two things that were not in my favour. The first was my bike didn't have a windshield. The second was that I didn't have enough common sense to stop and buy some goggles, or at least some sun glasses to protect my eyes from the wind, dust, and bugs. But there was an image to maintain, that of the "Rebel Without a Cause", and "Easy Rider", the James Dean, Marlon Brando type in the movies! I roared down the freeway living the role. When I got south of Roseburg and headed toward Grants' Pass, it started to get pretty warm and I began to get a little drowsy, so I pulled off into a small town and managed to buy some no-Doze pills. This was the first time I had ever taken anything like that. I was determined to make it home that day before dark, so I probably followed the trend of the day and washed the pills down with a bottle of Coke. Oh, was I ever awake then!

It's hard to imagine in the world we live in now, where every kind of dope from pills to pot are so prevalent, that for myself and my friends, taking dope or drugs wasn't even something we considered. The way we saw it, booze was legal (if you were old enough), and in a totally different category than drugs. Drugs were something they used in Los Angeles or San Francisco, but I didn't know of anyone who would have even thought of smoking pot or shooting up with anything. So to take even these seemingly innocent No Doze pills was a big step for me.

When I was droning along the freeway, I just kept up with the traffic. After I branched off at Grants Pass to head over to Crescent City on the coast, I was more in my element. And when I hit Oregon Mountain, I was in Motorcycle Heaven. It is a very scenic drive, and I was out to make up for lost time. It is an ugly, slow piece of road in a car, but with that bike I just gobbled it up. It was just one corner after another, and you could lay that thing over and pass everything you came to.

It cooled off a lot as I got toward the coast, and by the time I got south of Orick on Highway 101, it was starting to get fairly dark. I knew then the most I could make was Trinidad, a few miles north of where my folks lived at McKinleyville. The headlight on my bike wasn't working due to a simple lack of maintenance that I was later to find out was a matter of twisting two wires together. I finally decided it was too dark to be riding without a headlight, so I got behind a semi freight truck with big clearance lights. I must have followed him for the last ten or fifteen miles along that crooked coast highway into Trinidad, where I pulled off into a gas station and phoned our old friend Wes Hale. He was back from the Air Force and had moved up there with his little wife Emma who he had married while stationed in Germany. He kindly came down and I followed his tail lights a couple of miles to their place. By then, I was one thoroughly wore out easy rider. I went into the bathroom to have a shower, looked in the mirror, and instead of eyes, it looked like two solid red marbles looking back at me!

I went on home the next morning, but my eyes wouldn't clear up for a week although they didn't really hurt much. A day or so after I got there, I went to work with Dad and his partner. Then I came down with a real classic case of the flu, and was flat in bed for three or four days so I didn't get to see many of my old friends. By the time the bout with the flu bug was over, I was ready to head back to Oregon.

Before I took off, we went to a motorcycle shop and Dad bought me a white motorcycle helmet and a good pair of goggles. It was a real nice going away present, and he probably figured it would improve the chances of seeing me again. I was more than glad to slip them on, and it proved to be a smart move on the way back, as somewhere in southern Oregon, I got hit right square between the eyes with a big water beetle while doing about 60 miles an hour. I had to pull off and clean water beetle innards and juice off my goggles and forehead. Other than the head on collision with the water beetle, the trip back was uneventful and I was soon back at the mill pulling veneer.

Cousins on the Move

The Jones' family immigration to Canada was getting closer. Ed had been in Canada the last few months, and was building the house on the quarter section Red had purchased in the Lakes District, south of Vanderhoof. He had been living with Tom & Inez Curl since his arrival, and also had helped fight a forest fire at Tatuk Lake, south of the community. He was getting acquainted with the neighbours and really liked the country.

Jess & Rosalie Brown with daughters Pam and Julie

While he was getting acquainted up north, I was getting acquainted down south. I met Jess and Rosalie Brown and their two daughters, Pam and Julie. The Browns would become close friends, and their friendship would mean a lot to me later on in Canada. The Browns' and the Jones' had become good friends while tipping back a few together in Butch Niemans' tavern, in Crawfordsville. While they were visiting, the stories of the last frontier up in Canada stirred the sense of adventure in Jess, and he began to think of heading north. This was his idea, not Rosalie's. She was convinced Crawfordsville, Oregon, thank you, was just the place to stay!

Jess was a natural for the north. He was a real outdoorsman and crack shot with a rifle. He had grown up in the outdoors, and joined the U.S. Navy during the Second World War at a young age. He lost a very close friend on their second round of combat, and had seen some pretty tough times during his tour of duty. After he married Rosalie, and while still a young man, he was working on a log yard cold deck when he was hit right in the face with a big haul back line that either broke or came loose. His tin hard hat was probably what saved him, as it took a lot of the blow. The line hit so hard it threw him through the air and he landed on a log with a limb sticking up, badly injuring his back. After surgery, it took him a good two years or more to recover.

He had done a lot of boxing in his younger days, and was always more than ready to go a round with anyone. We made a point of steering clear of him because it was pretty plain he was in a different class than we were. I think his nose had been punched a few times before he got hit with the haul back line, but that really finished it off, and he looked like a lighter version of Rocky Marciano with glasses. After becoming friends, they agreed to let me board with them for a couple of months after my cousins left for Canada.

The going away party for the Jones family was quite a blow-out if I remember correctly. I think at one point, I did a few Elvis songs as my contribution. That part of the country had been home to the Jones' for a lot of years, so there was a big crowd of friends to see them off. It was held in a Community Hall in Crawfordsville just off the edge of the highway.

———

It was a major move for the family, especially the older kids, Ed, Dick, and Carma, to leave behind their whole world of friends and community at that time of their life, and be plopped down in the backwoods of central B.C. For whatever reasons, Carma didn't come up in the initial move, but stayed with Elma Jean Lovely, a friend who was closer to her than a sister. She didn't come up until the following summer, which was just as well, because it was pretty basic for a while.

The Jones' trip to Canada was quite a journey, Ed came down from Canada with his car to help with the move. They had every nook and cranny in the car, the pickup, and the trailer crammed to the limit. The bumpers were just about dragging on the ground. It was the first of November, 1960, when they pulled out, not the best time of year to move to the frozen north.

It took them twenty-four hours of straight driving to get there. I don't remember what time in the morning they left, but they got to the Canadian border at midnight. Red drove the pickup and trailer, and Ed drove his Pontiac.

The Fraser Canyon above Hope was definitely not the road it is today. A lot of the road was held in place by wooden cribbing filled with rock, that hung out over the edge of nothing. The Ferrabee Tunnel was still a one way traffic project, and there were a lot of places where there was nothing beyond the edge of a narrow gravel road but the mighty Fraser River, hundreds of feet below! Maybe it was just as well they travelled that part by night.

It was a long, long journey, and what waited at the end wasn't exactly the Taj Mahal. But still, compared to what the early settlers had, it was a palace. They had left a fairly nice 3 bedroom home, and now, here they were. Ed had done a good job on the house, but hadn't been able to get it completely finished, but at least there was a roof over their heads. The view from the huge front window he had put in looking south was unbelievable.

———

Meanwhile back in the lower 48, I was adapting to new landlords. In all truth, Jess and Rosalie took me in like one of their own. They had actually moved into Red and Maxine's house when they left for Canada. I'm not sure if they rented it or what the deal was. I boarded with them for 2 months, and then decided to head north to Canada to pay my cousins, the Jones', a visit.

Pam was a nice girl. Both her and Julie, who was a little beanpole blonde headed kid, had quick smiles, twinkles in their eyes, and lots of personality. They also had minds of their own. A trait I think they inherited from both Mom and Dad. By the time I left, Pam and I had become good friends. Hopefully, if and when they moved north, it could be resumed.

Welcome to Canada

It was the first of January 1961, when I stepped on that bus in Springfield, Oregon, with the warm rain coming down, and headed for Vanderhoof, British Columbia. Little did I know of the completely new world and way of life I was about to enter. I never was the type to waste a lot of time in preparation, my philosophy was, "Don't sweat it, somehow it'll all work out!". So, with a poorly packed suitcase, and 400 or so good American dollars in my pocket, I was on my way.

Strangely enough, I found the Canadian border crossing just south of Vancouver B.C. had a slightly different philosophy than mine. When we got there, they asked me where I was going, and I told them. They asked me if I was coming to visit or if I would like to come in as a landed immigrant. Well now! I thought that to be given a choice was pretty novel, so I decided to be a landed immigrant. That sounded a lot more stable, and the price seemed to be about the same. Their next directions were to grab a taxi and get down to the Immigration Office in Vancouver B.C. and get myself immigrated. If I got it done fast enough, I could catch the next bus north. I got down there as quick as possible, and the Immigration Officer pulled out a piece of paper about two feet long, and quickly ran through the questions. The questions were things like, "Do you, or have you ever had this or that, and have you ever had any kind of mental problems?". Well, since I was in a hurry and wanted to catch the next bus north and didn't want to get into a long confession, I told him "No". When the next bus pulled out, I was on it.

That's how long it took to become a landed immigrant in Canada in 1961. At that time, they were looking for young guys to come in and help open up the country, so if you looked like you could handle a shovel and swing an axe, they hustled you right in.

When I got off the bus in Vanderhoof, my cousins were there to pick me up. I was now a landed immigrant, and gave my $400 to Maxine to throw in the family pot.

There was a large influx of Americans into the Vanderhoof area over a period of roughly 10 years beginning in the mid to late 1950's. A lot of the interest in the interior, from Williams Lake to Smithers, no doubt came from the books written by the well-known local author, Richmond P. Hobson Jr. He wrote three books, Grass Beyond The Mountains, Nothing Too Good For A Cowboy, and The Rancher Takes A Wife. I think anyone who had an ounce of pioneering blood in their veins, and read any of his books, came to some part of central B.C. to check out the last Frontier. Time was to prove they could take the hardships, because a lot of their families are still there, and have helped to make the country what it is today.

At one time Vanderhoof was known as "Little Oregon", due to the number of people who came from there. They were ranchers and farmers, homesteaders and free loaders, you name it. It was almost like a minor Gold Rush. Only, instead of gold, it was land.

At first you could homestead it, then pre-empt it, but you could still get a quarter section covered with timber for under two thousand dollars, and the timber would far more than pay for it. It was a new country and yet an old country. The settlers in the early 1900's naturally took the prime flat agricultural land on the north side of the Nechako River, and gave their districts names like Prairiedale and Braeside. But there was still a lot of good land left.

There have been a lot of excellent books written about the history of the Nechako Valley. But suffice to say, that the history of the white man, this side of Alexander Mackenzie and Simon Fraser, included the Nor-West Company establishing a trading post at Fort Fraser, 20 miles or so west of Vanderhoof around 1806. They joined with the Hudson's Bay Company in 1824, by which time Fort Fraser and Fort St. James were well established.

For us newcomers, seeing the natives from the Stoney Creek Indian Reserve, located a few miles southwest of town, routinely coming to Vanderhoof in a team and wagon was quite an eye-opener. We felt like we were part of living history. This wasn't a wild west movie, this was the real thing!

Grizzly Bears, Sawmills, & Groundhog Gravy

Another thing that happened not too long after we arrived that made us realize we weren't living in downtown Portland, was what happened to Orin Kennel, who had moved up from Lebanon, Oregon, several miles west of Sweet Home. Orin had lived a pretty tame life working in a feed store in Lebanon, before he heard the stories and bought a ranch just east of us in the Mapes district. It was a scenic area with a lot of rolling pine and poplar country, and quite a bit of natural swampy meadow land. The good meadows that could be drained were what the early settlers went after. With a minimum of work they made good hay land. His ranch was one of the nicest places in the area, and located a mile or so down what was called the Stump Road. It branched off to the east from the Mapes Road which ran south off Highway 16. The elementary school was only a mile away, and there were a number of farms in that area, so it was fairly well settled.

One early spring day, Orin went for a walk in the meadow that was just across the road from his house. This meadow was a main hayfield that ran off into willows and standing timber. It bordered the edge of endless miles of wilderness on the east side of Sinkut Mountain. As he walked along, a moose suddenly burst out of the willows at the edge of the hayfield, and right on its heels was a big Grizzly Bear. If you have ever seen a Grizzly lounging around in a zoo, that is not the kind of bear that Orin Kennel saw that day. The raw power of a Grizzly in action is a frightening thing. The minute he spotted Orin, the bear left the moose and came after him. I only met Orin a time or two, but he didn't strike me as the backwoods "Grizzly Adams" type, so this must have seemed like the worst kind of nightmare. He turned and ran for his life, looking for a tree of some kind to climb. The bear finally got so close he didn't have a choice, so he went up the closest thing he could find. It was a small Lodge Pole pine, so small that when he got up as high as he could the tree started to bend over. The bear stood on its back legs below him, roaring and trying to reach him, just missing the soles of his boots with its' great curved claws. It was nothing short of a miracle that saved him that day, and the fact that the tree was still frozen in the ground, because the bear actually tried to push it over and shake him out. After a while, it finally gave up and wandered far enough away that Orin made another run for it. The bear was watching and came after him again. This time he was able to get up a bigger tree, and the Grizzly finally gave up and left. After a long wait, he ran to the home of Matt Goodland, a neighbour, and passed out on the porch. That's where Matt found him. He was completely finished. Orin sold out not long after that, and went back to Oregon. I sure couldn't blame him. But he had a bear story that most people wouldn't believe, and one he would probably just as soon forget.

———

The Jones family had been more than busy since their arrival. Red had made a deal with a neighbour, George Tee, a dyed in the wool, "Old Chum" smoking, cockney Englishman, to bring his sawmill over and cut lumber on his place. Every Mennonite and backwoods stump farmer had a sawmill in their backyard in those days. There was one enterprising Mennonite by the name of Bill Martens, from Swift Current, Saskatchewan, who had set up his own mill and planer on the north side of the Nechako river at Vanderhoof. He would buy all the rough lumber people brought in. Having this local market brought an income to a lot of small sawmill operators and homesteaders who were trying to get started.

Red bought a little John Deere 420 Cat for skidding, and with that he was in the lumber business! He did the falling, Ed or Dick the skidding, and I worked packing slabs and stacking lumber at the mill. It wasn't really what you would call a high production operation, as George wasn't an overly early riser, and by the time everything got started in the morning and we cut a few boards, it was time for lunch. Then when you got to the house and ate, and everyone had a couple of roll-your-owns, and listened to a few of George's stories, (which he never seemed to be short of) and got back to work, it could be 2:00 o'clock. When everything was rolling again and we cut a few boards, it was 4 o'clock and starting to get dark so we had to shut it down. But we were self-employed and that was what mattered.

Georges' sawmill was quite a contraption. It was powered by a long, flat belt that ran off the side pulley on either a Massey 44 or 55 tractor. It was pretty badly under powered, so eventually he got a stationary Dodge Power unit from a neighbour, George Evans. For a number of reasons, the boards coming off the mill always seemed to be a little over or under the two inches they were supposed to be. As well, one end of the board was thicker or thinner, than the other. So, the Jones boys named the operation the "Thick and Thin" Lumber Company, and then added, "Custom Made Wedges and Shims". George thought that was pretty comical.

He was quite the guy. You never saw him anywhere without a can of Old Chum tobacco tucked under his left arm. He could whip a cigarette paper out of its' pack, and make up a roll-your-own, and be puffing on it almost as fast as most people could dig out a tailor made and get it lit. He was a heavy smoker, even when he was running the mill. A lot of the time, he would be squinting through a haze of smoke and flying sawdust. But it was when you were sitting around visiting that he really hit his stride. He liked to talk, and unless there was something pushing him, could carry on for hours. We were all fascinated by his ability to converse intelligently on just about any subject that came up.

George had the most astounding circulation I have ever seen. He very seldom wore mitts, even at twenty degrees (F) below zero. When he was sawing, he held the feed rod with bare hands. The only person I ever saw that even came close to his ability to stand the cold was my cousin Dick. When George was sawing, he was really in his element. He wore a pair of regular black summer gum boots 12 months of the year. The only concession he made for winter was he would either stuff straw or newspaper in them.

George and his family spent a lot of time visiting the Jones family. His wife, Rene, was a short, stout, jovial lady that followed in Georges wake. She was well liked in the community and famous for her talent and skill at decorating wedding cakes. They had three girls. The oldest, Gwen, was about 12, a tall, quiet girl. The next two, Shirley, a couple of years younger, and the youngest, Jacqueline, about six. The two younger ones were as aggressive and ornery as their older sister was quiet and reserved, and were always punching each other.

———

We suffered that first winter. We weren't even remotely ready for that kind of cold. Worse yet we were as unprepared physically as we were mentally. To begin with we had thought that U.S. surplus combat boots and blue jeans would do the job, for winter wear, along with a fairly heavy pair of leather gloves. But that didn't work!

We tried to live off the land as much as possible, but since we arrived after hunting season, it was too late to shoot a moose or deer, even though there were plenty around. We didn't think it would look too good to be deported two months after we got there, for shooting a moose out of season. But there were snowshoe rabbits everywhere, likely at the peak of their cycle, and we ate rabbits until we began to hop! The only thing that broke the monotony of rabbit was ling fish, an ugly but good tasting fresh water cod, we caught with set lines out of Sinkut Lake. The ling fish, along with a few nice rainbow trout were a big part of our diet. Then toward spring we really hit the jackpot! Ground hogs! The windrows of brush piled along the side of the Sinkut Lake road were loaded with them! Talk about high class grub! Nothing quite like ground hogs and gravy! The hardest part to get by when you were skinning them was that buck toothed smile. Another problem was that they were crawling with fleas. But they never bothered us. The fact that we didn't have a bath very often probably helped, but they must have been a different kind than an Oregon flea or they would have eaten us alive.

One day Maxine had completely ran out of anything to make for dinner, but she hadn't told anyone. Although she didn't attend a church, she always had a deep faith, a faith that would be severely tested before too many years went by. She prayed that morning that there would be something on the set lines, and when she went down and pulled them up, there was a big fish on each line. It seems like a simple thing now, looking back, but it made a very deep impression on her.

There was no electrical power at the Jones' place when we arrived and that's a luxury you can live without. But there's one thing you've got to have, and that's water. Maxine had bought a huge black iron pot at a second hand store in Oregon, that she used for everything from washing clothes to making soap! I don't remember how many gallons it held, but filling it made the water detail a never ending chore. Because of the cold, it wasn't practical to haul it from the neighbours. We couldn't store it outside anyway as it would freeze solid. Besides, it would be a constant bother to the neighbours. But there was a whole lake full about 300 feet down a steep hill, just waiting to be hauled up in 5 gallon buckets. We would take one in each hand, and head down the hill. Going down was easy, especially in the winter, when the trail was a sheet of ice. Going down, as the old saying goes, is no problem, it's the sudden stop at the bottom! But, oh! The trip back up! A full 5 gallon bucket of water isn't light, especially when you're going up a steep hill on an icy trail with a bucket in each hand. The real difficulty was when you slipped. If you held on to the buckets, you would land on your face. If you let them go, they spilled, and you had to start all over again.

It wasn't a popular chore. The cardinal rule in the house was that the one who used the last water in the bucket had to head down the hill and fill the buckets. This was bad enough in the daytime, but at night it was a catastrophe. We used every devious method we could to make sure we weren't the one to empty the bucket. It ranged from outright stealth and deception to shriveling slowly from dehydration; but eventually somebody would have to give in, and down the hill they would go.

After they got established Red started digging a well in late winter. He wasn't a big man, probably 5 foot 10 inches tall, but he was solid built and as tough a Welshman as they come. His plan was to dig one foot a day. He joked that in one hundred days he would be down a hundred feet. He dug and cribbed the well with one inch Spruce lumber completely by himself. He made a windlass to haul up the bucket when it was full, then back down he went, filled it again, crawled up the ladder, and cranked the bucket up again. The digging had been through solid hardpan, and was a long, tough job. The windlass he made was like all things he built, a work of art. He hit water at 35 feet. It wasn't a big amount, but at least it supplied the house.

·

The Lakes District – Kind People, Good Neighbours

It was early February that my stay at my cousins ended. It was bound to happen and it was my fault. I can't recall now if I had heard Red mention that he was thinking of cleaning out a small patch of young poplars by the road or if it was my idea of being helpful, but that's beside the point. I took his power saw and cut them down. I also sawed a couple of rocks in half in the process which didn't really improve the sharpness of the chain, and when he realized what I had done, it didn't improve our relationship. First of all, his power saw was something that was, in the main, never touched by anyone but him, and for sure never by a greenhorn like me. Secondly, the trees were his to cut down, not mine. He was more than right, and I was more than wrong. It was in the evening, and fully dark when he called me outside to get things straightened out. The end result was he told me to find another place to live, and I told him I was on my way.

I stomped off down the road to the Curl's home, and Tom and his wife Inez were kind enough to take me in. I stayed with them for about a week then found a job working for Mel Lynum, a neighbour, who owned a small dairy, and he offered his cabin for me to live in.

Mel and his wife, Kristine, were some of the people who went out of their way to make us feel welcome when we first arrived. It's hard to explain how generous and helpful the people in the Lakes District were to us. The Jones' home was right beside the road on the way to town where it was easy to drop in for a visit. Their home, although it was pretty rough at that time, had a special combination of open friendliness, humour, and personalities that made visitors feel at home. When people stopped by, they found it hard to leave. I think a lot of that came from Maxine's old down home country style, Midwest upbringing, that really made you feel welcome. But it came from the whole family. I'm not sure now if that's the way we got to know

Mel and Kristine, but there's a good chance it was, as he had to go by on regular trips hauling milk to town. Mel was a tall, raw boned Norwegian with a strong Scandinavian accent. He was probably over 60 when we knew him, and I would soon find out what a rugged old farmer he was. I think his wife, Kristine, was a few years older. She was a short, heavy set, grey haired little lady who always seemed short of breath. But she wasn't the least bit short of breath when letting you know her opinion on things. Melvin would stand beside her when she was giving her views, with a twinkle in his eye and a little grin on his face. Every once in a while, he would add, "yaw shore, yaw shore", like he was really enjoying it. In a lot of ways, Kristine reminded me of my Grandma Batman with her outspoken ways. But the biggest similarity was in her cooking! When you sat down at their table, there was always twice as much as you could eat. When I came into the house early in the morning for breakfast, there was oatmeal porridge, with milk and brown sugar, bacon and eggs, potatoes with toast and jam. It was endless, and almost enough to make you forget about groundhogs and gravy!

Mel had a big black German Shepherd named Thunder, (he pronounced it "Tonder"). Every morning after breakfast when we were sitting at the table, he would call him over and tell him to "Sit". The dog would quietly sit down, and Mel would carefully balance a cube of sugar right on the top of the dog's nose. Thunder would sit without moving a muscle. Mel would sit back in his chair, and for a minute just look at him. The dog would sit like he was carved in stone, with his eyes zeroed in on the sugar cube. Then suddenly Mel would say, "Okay!" and the dog would jerk his nose back and have the sugar cube in his mouth so fast you couldn't see it.

When we stepped out of the utility porch on the back of the house, there was a big, black Smith's anvil setting just outside the door. Mel would stop for a minute and look at it, then he would reach down and grab it in his big hands, lift it up over his head and press it 3 or 4 times like a barbell, set it back down and look over at you with a grin. I could hardly lift it.

He had a dozen big Holstein cows that he milked with a milking machine. My job while he was doing this was to milk Snowdrop, a gentle brown and white Guernsey cow. I had never milked a cow, but caught on fairly quick as she was a quiet, easy milker. One morning, just as we were getting started, the power went off, so we had to milk them all by hand. I finished Snowdrop in good time, emptied the bucket, and moved my stool up beside the first cow at the end of the main milking line. She had legs as long as a giraffe, and teats as big as a water bottle. She knew right off that I was an amateur, and began to look back at me and fidget around as I began to milk. I tried to sweet talk her with words like "Good boss, easy boss", and every other sweet word I could think of, but she wasn't impressed. I could feel the tension building until finally, in a move so fast I hardly knew it happened, she whipped her hind foot clear up behind her ear and let me have it. She kicked me, the stool, and the milk bucket, which was about a quarter full, clean across the barn. To prove to her I wasn't a quitter, I got up, cleaned the milk bucket off, and started again. She turned her head, lined me up, and once more kicked me, bucket, and stool across the barn. This was getting to be fun! By this time, Melvin could see it was a losing cause, so he took over and finished the milking, but from then on I just stuck with my old friend, Snowdrop.

There was only one time I saw an animal get the best of Mel. He had bought a little Jersey bull to use on some first calf heifers. Dairy bulls tend to have a meaner disposition than beef bulls, and Jerseys are one of the meanest. A few months later, when I was working in the area, I stopped in at his place, and he was standing by the corral with a broken fence post in his hands, and a sheepish look on his face. In the corral was the pawing, snorting Jersey bull. He had tried to move him into another pen and the bull had turned on him and put him over the fence. Mel had a terrible, fiery temper, so he grabbed a fence post and jumped back in the corral. When the bull charged him again, he broke that one over its head, but then had to jump the fence for the second time. Finally, he said, "Vel, I yost taught he had enawf." Melvin and Kristine kept an immaculate farmstead. Farmsteads like Mel Lynum's, with their painted buildings and yard fences, were few and far between in those days.

Slim Evan's ranch, next to Mel Lynum's farm, bordered the edge of wilderness country. More than once he had to shoot grizzlies that were getting into his cattle herd. Slim was one of the first people the Jones family met after they arrived. He was hauling hay, and Red's tandem trailer caught his eye, so after borrowing it a few times, he bought it. The name "Slim" (his actual name was William Robert) was a misnomer. He was a man of medium height, but powerfully built, much like his father, Bill Evans. He was a driver, a hard working rancher, and sawmill operator, who along with his wife Lil, tended to keep to themselves. They had a very nice ranch with good buildings and a nice herd of commercial cattle. His goal in life from a young age must have been to be a cowboy, because, instead of the usual style of Canadian speech with its "Eh? this and Eh? that", Slim perfected a real west Texas drawl.

Their children, Clifford and Linda, were complete social opposites to their parents, while Lois, the youngest, was more reserved like Slim. Clifford was a black haired, long geared extrovert with a crew cut, who had the same sharp featured, sharp eyed look as his Dad. Linda was a cutie. Small and dainty, with snappy eyes, she always seemed to be laughing and giggling. Whenever you dropped by, Slim and Lil were always hospitable, and made you feel welcome.

———

His brother, George Evans, wife Anne and their 4 kids, were some of the closest neighbours to the Jones', and certainly some of the most helpful. Their farm, like Red's had an ideal south slope location which allowed for good drainage, and early warming and drying in the spring. George had a nice herd of Hereford cattle, and a big chunk of good bottomland that was part of what had once been a big willow flat between Nulki Lake to the west and Sinkut Lake to the east. With Sinkut Creek now running through part of it the whole flat was ideal sub-irrigated hay land. Al Simrose, George Simrose, Jimmy Castle, Slim Evans, Mel Lynum, Harold Bradley, and George Evans, had farms or ranches all located in this big flat.

The George Evan's house, like most of the others in the country, was still in the finishing stage. Built to last for the north country, with 6 inch studding, sheeted with one by six shiplap, inside and out, and tamped in dry shavings for insulation. With a wood cook stove and heater, they were warm and comfortable.

It was always fun to visit the Evans family. They all had a good, if not more reserved sense of humour than our bunch. Their son, Jim and his cousin

Clifford, became real buddies with the Jones' boys. There were three girls in the family. Sheila, an attractive girl with light brown hair; Betty Anne, a kick up your heels, dark haired tomboy with glasses; and Lynn, a cute little dark haired busybody, who was a lot younger than the rest.

George & Anne

George, Slim, and their sister Edith (married to Ed Dickson), were all children of early Vanderhoof area pioneer settlers. Their parents, Bill Evans and Florrie (Hargreaves) Evans, were united in marriage on May 31, 1913, the first white couple to be married in the Nechako Valley. Slim's wife, Lil was one of the Schultz family who came from, I believe, northern Saskatchewan, and settled in the Mapes, Sob Lake district. Anne Evans,

George's wife was born in the Vanderhoof area in 1925. She was the daughter of Robert and Laura Collins, who were school teachers, and came in 1923 from New York City! They settled on Greer Creek, which in 1923 had to be in the middle of the middle of nowhere! It was a place about 20 miles or so south west of Vanderhoof that was in the same area as Rich Hobson's famous "Rim Rock Ranch", a unique and beautiful part of the country. Anne was typical of the wives and mothers who added that extra touch of class to what could have been a rough edged society.

—————

The Women's Institutes were very beneficial to the early communities. Not only for the projects they were involved in, but also to encourage and provide social contact and support for the women in the community.

The majority of people living in the Lakes District were solid, down to earth, common sense people. Some, but not all of them, would have a social drink or two, but that's where it ended. Of course, there's always an exception, but the majority had more important things to do. Houses to build, land to clear, farms to develop, and families to raise. Not every district was that way, but even though there may not have been a lot of people that attended church, there was still a definite influence from conservative Scottish and English backgrounds that influenced the community. This was especially evident at social occasions like the New Years dance at the Lakes District Hall. It was a family affair where they had a lot of fun, but no liquor was allowed in the hall, no roughhousing was tolerated, and there was a definite time to wind it up and go home.

There were still a lot of the old timers around when we first came to Vanderhoof. Bill and Florrie (Granny) Evans, (she lived to be 97 years old); Little Joe Murray, famous survivor of the Tatuk Lake Grizzly attack, described in Rich Hobson's book, "The Rancher Takes A Wife"; George Ogston, realtor and businessman; the Smedleys; the Hargreaves; the list was long. I never had the opportunity to meet Pan Phillips, who was obviously one of the more famous (or notorious) characters in the country. But in spite of human short comings, one thing I would certainly grant Pan Phillips, Rich Hobson and all the others that took on the dream, is they had to be tough men and women. We were to find out, if you play by the rules, the north can be a giving land, if you don't, you will pay the price.

I saw Rich Hobson one time, and always wished I had made his acquaintance. He was getting up in years, and you could see they had taken their toll. He was pretty broken down, but still a big, square jawed, ruggedly good looking man. The day I saw him he was wearing a fringed buck skin coat and a big black well used Stetson hat. Right by each side, as he walked down the street, were two huge shaggy dogs that looked like they were half wolf. Maybe that's part of the reason I didn't just charge up to him, stick out my hand and say "Hi, Rich, my name is Bob"! I think he was living on his River Ranch along the Nechako at that time, finishing up his last book.

Shot Rocks & Hockey Pucks

In February 1961 when I started working for Mel Lynum, he asked if I would like to be on his curling team. The community had built a single sheet curling rink, close to Harold Bradley's farm, next to the road that went up to Sinkut Mountain, and south to Sam Goodland's ranch. It wasn't fancy. Tin roof, double lapped rough lumber on the sides to keep out the sun, a nice big room on the east end for spectators, and a wood cook stove for making coffee and keeping the crowd warm.

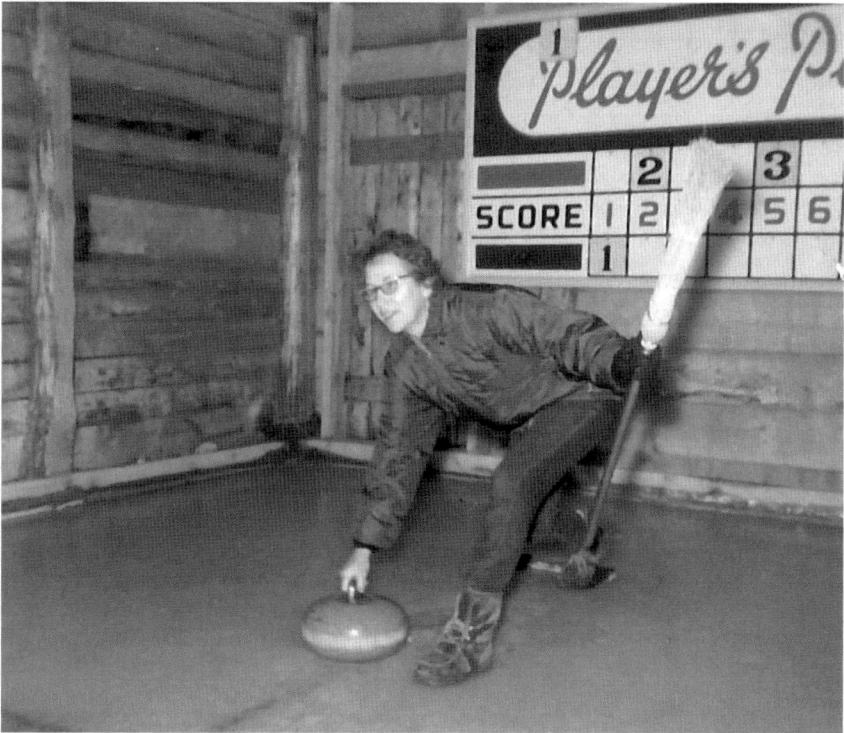

Inez Curl at Lakes District Curling Rink

We had five or six teams, all from the community, with a game every night or so. Curling was a whole new game for me. I not only had to learn the rules, but a whole new list of words and their meaning; words like "shot rock", "in turn", and "out turn", and "House", and when to sweep and when not to sweep. I had to learn what a "skip" was, and what was meant by a "third or fourth end". I was to play "First" because that didn't require any skill or finesse, just hopefully getting a rock somewhere in the "House". It was also a position where you could do the least damage.

The community decided along toward Spring, to have a "Bonspiel". The only word I knew that came close to that was a "bonfire". I think it was to be a three day, around the clock affair with different teams playing different hours. It was a great idea, especially when it came down to the last game, because then everybody, including all the cute girls in the district, showed up to see who would win the final game and be the local champions. I don't remember now who played second and third on our team, but Mel was the skip. George Evans, our neighbour, was an excellent curler. Under normal conditions he was a very congenial type of person who had a good sense of humour, but was inclined to just chuckle at a good joke, rather than really laugh out loud. He was lighter built than his brother Slim, probably taking more after his mother's side. But George was tough as nails, and when it came to curling, it was serious business, with no quarter given. Mel Lynum was the same. He had that fierce Viking temper, and when you were curling, you only played for one reason, and that was to win. As luck would have it, you don't have to guess who faced each other in the final game. George vs. Melvin, the Anglo Saxon Englishman versus the Norwegian Viking! That may be stretching it a little, but there was no doubt at all, it was serious. It was a tied game, with only one or two ends left to play, with one rock left for Melvin to throw, and that's when I made the mistake that was to guarantee my place in local sports history, and ban me from the game of curling forever!

I guess young men's minds have always been prone to wander when pretty young girls are around. The problem was that this was neither the time, nor the place to let your mind wander. I must have started losing concentration somewhere in the third or fourth end. Every time I went down to throw a rock, all those teenage girls had their noses and smiling faces pressed up against the glass in the spectator room. I lost it a little more each end, until finally I wasn't even in the game! The mistake I made was simple. Somehow I thought the last rock had been thrown! I thought the end was over. So I strolled out into the House and started kicking the rocks out of the House. Even now I can see the dedicated curlers passing out in disbelief! But that's what happened. The result was about two seconds of total silence and then the thunder struck. I think the explosion that came from Melvin would have even sent his Jersey bull running for cover, and I was sure glad there weren't any fence posts around! I won't repeat what his first dozen words were, but as he stood there with his grey hair sticking straight out in every direction from under his Tam, his jaw jutting out, and his red eyes flashing fire, I was reminded very much of a mad porcupine. Then he roared at me at the top of his lungs, "Vots da matter vit you? Vot are you doink? Are you craassee!!"

I don't remember now how they solved the problem, but I kept a pretty low profile for a few days, and stayed away from the fence post pile. I guess he eventually forgave me, but after that, no one seemed to be interested in having me on their curling team.

———

Speaking of sporting events, it was in the late winter of 1961 that I unwillingly ended up in an American versus Canadian confrontation outside the back door of the Vanderhoof Hockey Arena. Hockey games in the small towns of the Interior were a major event in the whole area at that time. People came from everywhere. There were 4 teams in the Cariboo Hockey League, the Vanderhoof Bears, the Prince George Mohawks, the Quesnel Kangaroos, and the Williams Lake Stampeders.

Big crowd entertainment at that time was more or less limited to hockey games, curling bonspiels, and local dances. A winter that was close to six months long could get pretty boring, creating a mental condition only half jokingly referred to as "cabin fever". It was a raw, hard drinking, frontier country in those days, so the attitude toward a lot of things was "the rougher, the better". This mentality could get pretty wild at a hockey game. I loved Football, the slam bang of the game, the thrill of making a big catch, the blocking, the tackling, the roughness, but still, because of the tightly enforced rules, it was a fair game. Hockey was football at 30 miles an hour with no helmet and most of the rules thrown out, with only a two minute penalty for an all-out brawl! To increase the hazards to life and limb, each player had a hard wood stick four or five feet long which (in spite of the rules) was used to spear your opponent in the belly, crack him over the head, or trip him. The stick was also used to shoot a frozen, rock hard piece of rubber called a "puck" that was half the size of your fist, at close to a hundred miles an hour. This missile was fired at some poor guy called a "goalie", who was standing in front of a net. The puck, along with the stick, could do considerable damage to spectators as well, especially those who hung too far over the boards! But I loved it!

Our biggest rival was the Prince George Mohawks. They were the "Big Town Boys" from the metropolis of Prince George sixty miles east. The population at that time in Prince was roughly fifty thousand. In the sawmill, logging, and cow towns of Vanderhoof, Quesnel, and Williams Lake, population ranged anywhere from two to four thousand. Prince George having more job opportunities, had a wider choice of players.

I had developed a talent, if you can call it that, of drawing cartoons or caricatures of people during my high-school days. This was perfected at the expense of more serious subjects like Math, Science, etc. Eventually I did some cartoon work for a couple of local guys, Ken Koreen and Julian Riggs, who ran a Chevron Service Station in town. The cartoons were usually of Clifford Evans who worked for them. He was a walking cartoon to begin with, so it didn't take much imagination to come up with one.

A few years later my cartoon fame had spread to the point that someone asked me to draw a group caricature cartoon of the whole Vanderhoof Bears hockey team. At that time I was a fan of "Mad Magazine", and their premise that "no matter how often you cultivate people, you are bound to turn up a few clods", intrigued me. From then on I signed my cartoon "Clod". It's a fine line in the cartoon world between making people laugh, and being sued for defamation of character. By some fluke, and hours of labour, and a whole box full of top quality erasers, I hit it right on. At least they all got a real laugh out of it, and it was put in the local paper, The Nechako Chronicle, in February 1966.

OUR TEAM

Bob's cartoon of the Vanderhoof Bears

Everyone had their favourite players on the team. Mine were Dave Wall, who played center on their first line, and Ken Clay on defence. I believe Dave had played in the N.H.L. or in the next league just below it, but was injured and that ended his career in the big time. When I knew him, he looked like he was doing most of his practice and training in the pub at the local hotel, but he could still bring the crowd to its feet when he wound up behind the net, and came huffing and puffing down center ice with Donnie Finney on the right wing, big Jim Silver on the left, and neatly stick handled his way through the opposition defence and popped one in the net. It was no trouble seeing what Dave had been in his prime, and Ken Clay was the perfect picture of a defensive hockey player.

I don't think hockey helmets had even been thought of at that time, so the defence and especially the goalie were quite commonly knocked cold or badly cut when they caught a puck in the head. Ken Clay had blond, close cut hair and a face that looked like it had caught a few pucks. With his square jaw, high cheek bones, and a solid build, he was the epitome of "drop the gloves, not give an inch" defence. On top of that, he had a blistering slapshot. I'm not sure now if it was the end of a stick, or a puck that cost him his one eye, but, he was right back on the ice with a flimsy Industrial grinding mask for a face shield. I have since heard that this mask was the first face guard and led to the hockey helmets and face guards used today.

———

My part in this whole hockey thing was as a rabid spectator. If I was there by myself, or with the boys from Sinkut Lake, we would try to get right down along the boards so we could shake our fists and explain to the opposition players as they whizzed by, that they should go back where they came from. On this particular evening, I was in more sophisticated company as I was with my girl friend, Lynn Curl, who is probably still embarrassed at what happened. We were out on a seemingly peaceful double date with David Smith and his girlfriend. Dave was a big soft muscled type who would not be much help in a tight spot. We were cheering our guys on, and the girls were snuggled up nice and close to keep warm, which we didn't mind at all because it was probably 20 below (F) outside and 30 below (F) inside, typical hockey spectator conditions in those days of unheated arenas.

It was just before the end of a period when I looked across the arena and couldn't believe what I saw. Standing just across the ice from us on the second or 3rd row of seats was a guy with a girl sitting on his shoulders! He was swaying around like a tree in the wind and no one around them even seemed concerned. I was sober as a judge that night, and though it was probably none of my business, it was plain to see this was a disaster waiting to happen. He was clearly drunk and if he lost his balance and fell forward, (which could happen any second), his friend on his shoulders would have her head split wide open when it hit the boards or the ice, many feet below. So, like the Lone Ranger, I jumped up and headed over to correct the situation. When I got there, I kindly suggested he put her down because of the danger, but as I looked into his glazed eyes, I knew it was a lost cause. When I made my suggestion, he returned the favour by asking me to step outside and settle the question about interfering with the fun he was having.

I had no choice. By this time, the period had ended and the whole arena was aware of what was going on. So out the door we went.

It's funny how fast the word can travel in a small community. It didn't take long after we got there until the whole country knew there were some new Yankee boys around. My cousins and I had been harassed by a carload of local guys one night when we were going home after the game. Now this little sideshow between periods would be a perfect way to see one of these newcomers get his tail kicked! I felt very alone when I followed him out the back door of the arena. I was clearly in the minority. Suddenly I had a whole new appreciation for the way hockey players must feel when they step on the ice in an opposing town. It was a mob that followed us out. My friend David Smith bravely stuck right with me, so that helped, but I sorely wished I had my old "Okie" coon hunting buddies, the Matlock brothers from Clam Beach, California, to back me up!

My adversary, the guy with the girl on board, was from Fort St. James, and a pretty husky boy. He was probably a year or two younger than I was, and I'm guessing around six feet tall, with an attitude that night like he was seven. I hated to disappoint the crowd, after all the hoopla, but when I got my coat off and turned around and popped him in the jaw, he was off to Dream Land without a whimper. The real truth was that he was so far gone that a ten year old kid could have pushed him over with a feather. That was the one and only time I ever saw him that I know of, in all the years I lived in Vanderhoof, and the years I worked out of Fort St. James. There was no animosity intended, but as the crowd dispersed that night, more than one person stopped and warned me that his Dad, who apparently was a well known and respected machinist and welder in the Fort, would soon be down to tune me up. Thankfully he never bothered, and let his kid fight his own battles.

Nulki Lake and Racetrack Bill

During the early spring of 1961 I became engaged to Lynn Curl, daughter of Inez Curl, from a first marriage. Forrest and Susan, the younger son and daughter, were Tom & Inez's children. Lynn was not very tall, a little on the bashful side, and a very nice girl. Fortunately, for her sake and mine, we realized that I wasn't ready to settle down, so we ended our engagement. Lynn later married Bob Stewart, a reliable, local young man, and things turned out well for them.

In June of 1961, I got a job at Nulki Lake Resort. By this time, I had more or less got back on track with a normal life. The reasons for this were simple. I didn't have any money to buy booze, and no way to get it. On top of that, it wasn't the lifestyle of the people I worked for, or the community I was living in.

I would miss working for Mel & Christine Lynum on their farm, and will always remember and appreciate their kindness, but it was time to move on. Besides, I was quite sure he had found someone with better ability to concentrate on playing on his Curling team. I would also miss the smiling face of their granddaughter, Caren, who had almost become like a younger sister to me.

Nulki Lake Resort is in a beautiful spot. Located a couple of miles southwest of the Stoney Creek Indian Village Reserve, and a quarter of a mile or so on the east side of the Kenny Dam Road, it is a one of a kind setting. A few miles straight south, the Nulki Hills stand high above the surrounding interior plateau. A bit lower than Sinkut Mountain, they are a distant timber covered range of high, rounded hills that run for several miles east and west. To the southeast and noticeably closer, Sinkut Mountain rises in a long sloping climb to it's perfect 4,000 foot summit. It is pure Vista Vision, with nothing in the way to block the view. Nulki is one of two lakes that lie in an almost direct east to west direction, a position that is common for many interior lakes. Its' sister lake, Tachick, is a short distance to the northwest, and somewhat smaller. Surprisingly, both lakes, when it comes to fishing, are quite different. Tachick has larger trout, but they are harder to catch and not as numerous, and Nulki trout, though smaller, (up to 4 pounds), are more plentiful and easier to catch. Both lakes are relatively small compared to Stuart and Babine, the first two major lakes to the north, which each exceed 50 miles in length, and are much deeper. But all lakes can be dangerous, especially those running east and west. This is because of the prevailing west wind from the coast, which in a matter of minutes can turn a relaxed fishing or boating trip into a battle for survival.

Nulki Lake Resort was owned by Bill Wineberg. He also owned the Portland Meadows Racetrack in Portland, Oregon, so he was fairly well off and obviously didn't have to worry about where his next meal was coming from. This was fine with me, as long as I got mine! The deal was, I would be on duty 24 hours a day, seven days a week plus room and board, for the staggering sum of one hundred Canadian dollars a month! Not a bad deal for Bill, even back in 1961! I could see why he owned the Portland Race Track and I didn't! One little carrot dangled before my nose was that if I hung around long enough, he would clear the land and start a ranch and I could be the manager! Wow! I could hardly wait! Ah well, depending on how they fed, it was better than ground hogs and gravy!

The main Lodge at Nulki, surrounded by a few poplar trees, was a straight forward rectangular log building. They had added a frame structure, sided with rough lumber, on the east end for storage and a little more space. The inside of the huge living room, with its round log walls and rock fireplace on the north wall was comfortably rustic. The Lodge had originally been a grocery store, which along with a post office, was located somewhere between the Stoney Creek Reserve and where it is now. Anne Evan's father, Robert Collins, had moved it to Nulki Lake. He and his wife, Laura, had only stayed a short while at Greer Creek when they arrived from New York City, and then moved to the site where Nulki Lake Resort is today. He acquired the store after it closed down, skidded the logs to the lake, and re-assembled it there.

Robert & Laura Collins eventually sold the place to Tom Moran, who rented out a few boats and cabins, then sold it to Bill Wineberg. Bill turned it into a resort business, with the new restaurant, boat and cabin rentals, as well as campsites. The new restaurant was a large, airy, frame building a couple of hundred feet west of the Lodge, with the whole south wall from four feet up completely covered with windows. The panoramic view of lake and distant mountains was impressive. This is where the hired help ate, as well as any guests, but some of the time we were the only ones there. Between the Lodge and the restaurant was the boat dock. On a bench to the east, away from the Lodge, was a good big shop with east facing windows along a back wall. There, amid the dust, tools, discarded plywood and junk was my humble bunk! It was perfect. I felt right at home. Move over pack rats, the competition's movin' in!

There was a small trailer like building just across the driveway, between the dock and the restaurant, where Louis and Mary Kohse lived. Louis was the real thing, a legendary old north country trapper. Louis, his wife Mary, and his brother Ed, had ran a trap line and packing business for years in the Mt. Baldy – Pinchi Lake area, north of Ft. St. James. This was in the days when an Indian would slowly walk by him in the Fort, and quietly say, "If white man go out to trap, maybe he not come back." Louis would tell him, "Maybe Indian not come back either!" This was no joke. There were still some tensions just under the surface at that time.

Louis wasn't a big man. Surprisingly, a lot of the old trappers and bush-whackers were not big men. There were exceptions of course, like Skook Davidson, the legendary northern packer. It is only possible to use the word "legendary" so many times, but it could be fittingly used to describe a long list of the people who opened up and developed the country. Among them would be the early explorers, traders, missionaries, trappers, and surveyors.

Mary Kohse was a good cook. And just like in a logging camp, the cook is the most important person on the job! She was a kind hearted woman if you were on her right side. I made it a point to stay on that side. She was tough, and once told me how they coughed blood one morning on the trap line at Mt. Baldy, before they realized it was 60 degrees below zero (F). She was from Estonia, a small country along the border of Russia. Her full name was Maria Nilk Severt, and she married Louis Kohse on June 7, 1928, in Vanderhoof. They never had any children. She was medium height, with a solid, stocky peasant build. Her face was flat and heavy, with wide set Mongolian eyes that usually held very little expression. But they would light right up when she was laughing at a joke. She had a good sense of humour, and was usually easy to be around. When she talked, she spoke in a high, flat monotone. If she was mad, it could get pretty loud. But I got along well with Mary and Louis. Maybe it was because I wasn't afraid to get at it and earn my high salary. Louis was the boss, and I enjoyed working for him. They had recently sold their mink ranch on Tatuk Lake, about 40 miles south of Nulki, to Bill Wineberg for hunting territory. Part of the deal was that they work at Nulki Resort during the summer and fall for 3 or 4 years, as Louis had the guiding license for that territory.

My job really started off with a bang. I had only worked there for a few days mowing lawns, painting, building, clearing new campsites, and keeping an eye out for any cute girls that came along. Suddenly there was a big panic. Someone up on the top bench had spotted a boat with 2 people on board that had turned over. It was about 200 yards offshore on the east side of the upper bench, in what was usually an area protected from the west wind. Louis was working down at the dock, so I ran down and told him. We jumped in a big, stable, twenty foot boat, with a 30 horse kicker, that he kept on hand for this kind of thing, and headed out.

It took 5-10 minutes to get to the overturned boat. When we did, it wasn't hard to tell why the men had tipped over. They were pretty well soused, and it wasn't with just water. Booze and boats are a bad combination. They were right on the verge of going under, and didn't seem to realize what was happening. They had life jackets on, but they were too small to do any good. The one guy was a big man and had already taken on a lot of water, but we managed to get them both in our boat. Hypothermia was the big concern. The ice hadn't been off the lake long, so it was straight ice water, another half hour and they would have been goners. It was quite an eye opener.

The shallow lakes of the interior go through an interesting cycle of change from spring to fall, depending a certain amount on how cold or hot the summer is. From the time the ice goes off until roughly the end of June, the water is cold and clear. As the days lengthen and heat up, a green algae begins to appear in the water. Some lakes seem to be worse than others, and Nulki, being quite a shallow lake, could get pretty bad. The summer I was there, July and August were scorchers. The resort was located on the north side of the lake in a shallow bay protected from the prevailing wind. It was a perfect spot for a boat dock and resort. The problem was that without the wind to stir up the water, the algae built up around the dock into a blue green scum about two inches deep, and soon had a flower blooming on top of it! The fish in the lake were mostly beautiful solid silver, excellent tasting Rainbow trout, but there were also scrap fish like Squawfish, Suckers, and Red Mouth.

I was standing on the dock one hot afternoon, when I noticed the water stirring a few feet out from the beach. As I stood there, the head and top part of what I think was a Red Mouth suddenly popped up through the scum and started gasping for air! I can only assume it had came in too close to shore where the scum was so thick it couldn't breathe, and was suffocating!

As a rule, the grub we got at our end was pretty good, and that was important, because that's basically what I was working for. Mary Kohse was not only a good cook, she was a fussy cook, and simply wouldn't throw just any kind of slop on a plate and stick it in front of you. I enjoy fish for a meal once in a while, if it's the right kind and cooked right. In the early part of the summer, those Nulki Rainbows were the right kind, and Mary knew how to fry them! We had trout for supper a couple of times a week and they were top of the line.

I don't know what happened over at the Lodge with Bill and the boys. Maybe his horses weren't doing too well down at the racetrack, but whatever the reason, suddenly we were put on an austerity program, and went on a "living off the land" diet. When I walked through the restaurant door one evening for supper and took a breath, my nose plugged solid. Mary was trying to fry some trout they couldn't hack over at the Lodge, so they sent them over to us. On a year like we were having, even the Rainbows developed a distinct musty smell and taste from the algae bloom, and weren't any good to eat for a while.

Mary had a distinct style; you never saw her without a scarf on her head. It was wrapped around her head from the back, came up over the top of her ears so it covered both the top and sides of her head, and was tied, or rolled in a knot at the top of her forehead. When Mary came out of the kitchen door that evening with her scarf all tied up, she reminded me very much of how Mel Lynum looked wearing his Scottish tam the night I prematurely kicked the rocks out of the house at the Bonspiel! Her Mongolian eyes were flashing fire, and she was as unstoppable as a D8 Cat. With her old fashioned, flour sack country dress, and a full length apron flapping in the breeze, she headed for the Lodge. That was the place where the more prosperous folks were eatin' good, and livin' high. From what I heard later, when she came through the door, the higher society folks ran for cover! She told Bill loud and clear in her flat, high pitched monotone voice, what she thought of those who were too cheap to supply decent food for the workers. Then she literally cleaned house! There was a huge fridge and deep freeze, in the add on section of the porch where they kept the fancy grub, and she took a big part of it. Oowhee! Did we ever eat good for a while! It was the finest money could buy! Bill seemed to get the message after that, as we ate pretty good from then on.

There was one other time I saw Mary take things in hand. She was, like Louis, a real bush whacker, and if things started getting out of line, be it people or animals, they weren't long getting them straightened out again. Somewhere along the line they had teamed up with a well-known character named Roy "Father" Hughes. He was a dapper looking little Irishman, about medium height, with straight, slicked back, dark hair, narrow face, and a thin moustache, who looked and acted more like a card shark gambler than a beaver trapper. Roy was a likeable guy, a smooth voiced con man if there ever was one. The name "Father" Hughes seemed to come from his habit of preaching, or trying to preach to his partners when he reached a high state of intoxication. He was down on the dock one day, helping put motors on boats and getting tourists rigged up with rented boats and fishing gear. Unfortunately, he was nipping a little on the side, and starting to argue with the customers. Mary spotted what was going on from her cabin across the road, and in her slow, purposeful way, headed over to see what was taking place. When she got there and confronted Hughes, he was standing about halfway out on the dock and a couple of feet from the edge. When she got right in front of him and demanded to know what was going on, he started mouthing off at her. He was holding a little outboard motor with both hands, and when she hit him both feet came right off the dock, and Hughes, motor and all sailed right over the edge into four feet of lake water. For the astounded tourists standing by, it was a lesson in northern style public relations! Mary stalked off back to her cabin, muttering to herself, and a much subdued Hughes waded to shore packing his motor.

In later years, I was to learn that Roy Hughes had come to B.C. with my wife's step grandfather, a little Englishman named Ed Fisher. They were the most unlikely partners you could imagine. Apparently, they came down through the McBride-upper Fraser country working in sawmills along the way, until they ended up in Prince George in the 1930's, where at some point, they went their separate ways.

———

Nulki Lake resort was located a mile or so south of the Stoney Creek Indian Reserve. At one time it was an ideal spot to net fish out of the small creek running through from Nulki to Tachick. There were more than a few interesting people in Stoney Creek, and it was inevitable that we get a visit because of the candy bars and pop etc. that we sold at the restaurant. One day we heard the sound of a tractor coming down the driveway at high speed, and suddenly out from beside the restaurant flew a little red Massey 35 tractor with a farm wagon hitched on behind. For a minute, I thought it was going to be "Custer's Last Stand" all over again. The wagon was loaded with whooping, hollering Indian kids. It came to a screeching, skidding halt in front of our bait shop, and all the kids jumped off and headed to the restaurant. The driver, a high cheek boned, young native guy, with a mop of jet black hair, hopped off the tractor with a big grin on his face. It was a nice warm day, and he was wearing jeans and a white T shirt; but the most noticeable thing about him was that he only had one arm. There was just a stump from below his shoulder. As soon as they had their candy bars, they jumped on the wagon, Smokey jumped back on the Massey, shifted it in gear, opened the throttle wide open, dropped the clutch, and away they went. I don't know how he ever shifted gears and kept that thing on the road at the same time, unless he used his knee to hold the steering wheel. They flew past the Lodge, up the hill to the top bench and around it, then back down past the Lodge. Those of us who were standing by with our mouths hanging open heard one final whoop and war cry, then they were gone. We had just been invaded by the "One Armed Bandit" Smokey Quaw and the kids from

Stoney Creek. Thankfully this only happened a couple of times during the summer, but it left everybody with frazzled nerves for a day or two.

Smokey was quite a drinker and one cold winter night when my cousin Dick Jones was going out to Jess Brown's, on the road that led to Stoney Creek from town, he saw a snow covered figure lying beside the road. He stopped to see if he could help, and the minute he stooped down and tried to pick him up, he knew who it was. He had grabbed the side with no arm!

———

Girls at Nulki were a problem. There just weren't any. The majority of tourists who came from the States were older, and the locals who showed up didn't have older teen age girls who were into trout fishing! Then one day, a car with California license plates pulled in, and guess who stepped out of the car! A tall, blonde haired beauty! Well, I may be stretching it a bit, but she WAS tall, with long blonde hair, and when you haven't seen any girls for a while, it doesn't take much to be good looking! The truth was, she might not have won a beauty contest, but she wasn't bad looking, not bad at all! I made myself and my magnetic personality available to their slightest whim and got them all settled in and rigged for fishing. Later that evening, I dropped by, mentioned I had grown up in California, and tried to get acquainted. I hit a brick wall. The attraction seemed to have gone out of my magnetic personality. But I kept up my attentions, and after a couple of days she began to respond (who could resist!). On the third day, she agreed to go on what I viewed as a romantic canoe trip to the big island down the lake. It was a real success. By the time we got back, she thought I had been part of Alexander MacKenzie's party that discovered B.C.

The romance deepened until by the time she had to leave a couple of days later, we were ready to exchange wedding vows! I promised to be down to see her as soon as she got home, and she promised to faithfully send a letter covered with kisses every single day in the meantime. I couldn't wait. When I finally got a letter 10 days later, it seemed she had run across someone with a little more personal magnetism, so this was goodbye. I moped around for about 5 minutes, and then started checking out the incoming cars again.

Somewhere along the line of swapping guns for guitars, and guitars for guns, I had ended up with a nice sounding little Martin guitar. Someone heard me singing to myself and the pack rats up in the shop, and invited me down to entertain the big boys and their wives at the Lodge. They didn't look like the "You Ain't Nuthin' but ah Houn' Dog" types, so I did some Sons of the Pioneers songs, and a few of the other old tunes. One guy there, who looked like Colonel Saunders of Kentucky Fried Chicken fame, really seemed impressed, and wanted me to make a tape he could take back with him to the States.

I also met the Head Chef of the Vancouver Hotel and his girlfriend one night when they were camped up on the top bench. We sat around their campfire and sang a few songs and got acquainted. He invited me to stop in and see him sometime when I was in Vancouver. He was a big, tall, wavy haired, middle aged man, and his much younger companion, with her burnt blonde hair, and tanned outdoor look, was a nice looking lady. They were both very friendly people.

Part way through the summer another young guy showed up. I think he was a nephew to either Bill Wineberg, or his girlfriend, Joyce. He was a couple of years younger than I was, a little shorter and lighter, with a crew cut, and had an answer for most everything before you asked him! He was a real city boy, but after we got a couple of things straightened out, we became good friends. I liked Lex. I think someone had sent him up to learn how to work and he didn't mind learning. Somehow, he came into possession of a 6 pack of beer, most likely donated unknowingly from his relatives, and as we sat around and polished that off, it seemed to cement the friendship, and helped break the monotony.

———

When fall came, Bill Wineberg would bring out his shot gun and stand on the dock in his sport slacks and shirt, and shoot a few ducks. It was clearly a gentleman's sport, as he would be puffing on an expensive cigar, and had his full size black poodle, Nicky, along to do the retrieving. Bill was a nice enough guy in a master/servant way, but he plainly had an aura of the "Big Dealer" about him. He radiated that sense of power and control that men in his position have, but was friendly enough. I loved that black poodle. He was a real slam bang ruffian and a first class retriever. Although it was apparent with his neatly clipped hair that he was a high class dog, he loved to dig up the most stinking mess he could find, have a good, long, squirming roll in it until you couldn't stand to be near him. Then he would head for the Lodge as fast as he could go. There he would strut around like he had just doused himself with Old Spice, and expect everyone to let him know how good he smelled.

Trapper In Tennis Shoes

Back in a far corner, away from everything, was the smoke house. It was located in such a way that the wind carried the smoke away from the Lodge and campsites. A lot of the guests wanted their fish smoked, and Louis was the man. He would split the trout down the middle, sprinkle a little salt on it, and then rub in the brown sugar. There was no alder in that part of the country, so he would use diamond willow, or, as a last resort, poplar, for a smoking fire. Once in a while you would get a whiff of smoking trout that would make you drool. A lot of the old timers had the smoking art all figured out, and when they pulled the trays out, broke one open, it was done to perfection.

In the last part of August, we started getting things ready for the big moose and grizzly hunt at Tatuk Lake, that had been booked by three Washington hunters. This is where I really got a glimpse into what the old trappers and bushwhackers had to deal with. It also helped me understand the saying "the north is a giving land, but it can also be unforgiving". The most important word in their vocabulary was "preparation". Louis told me there was one time he was in the bush for 6 months, and never saw or heard the voice of another human being, so you had better make sure you brought enough matches along.

We spent a lot of time getting ready, checking over and over again, and this was only for a few days hunting trip! What if you were headed out for the whole winter? I was really looking forward to it. It's been almost 60 years ago, so details get a little fuzzy. The main plan was to go out to Louis' former mink ranch at the west end of Tatuk Lake, a week ahead of time, with a team and wagon, and saddle horse, to get things set up. Then we would come down with the big boat to the east end where the main road came in from town. There they would pick us up and take us back to the Lodge, where we would meet the hunters, then go back out and up the lake in the boat. Early one morning we were on our way with nothing left behind (I hoped); Louis driving the team, with me on the saddle horse.

Louis Kohse was one of the last of the pioneers. Born on July 16, 1902, to Ludwig and Auguste Kohse in Franzdorf, Germany, his parents came to Ellis Island, New York in October 1909. He became a Canadian citizen on Sept. 13, 1926 in Ft. St. James, B.C., and lived to be 98 years old. To watch him drive that team was to watch history in motion. Louis, like any good teamster, knew and looked after his horses, "Babe" and "Baldy", a mare and a big bald faced gelding. I'm not a horseman, so I'm not sure what breed they were. They were a dark bay with black manes, and not much feathering on their legs, and were round as barrels from lazing around on good feed. It was quite a sight, Louis holding the reins and slouched down in the wagon seat, rocking along, talking to Babe and Baldy. He was a man in his element.

Louis had a full head of iron grey hair, bushy eyebrows, and a thin face with a small chin and sharp, steady eyes. He was medium height, and light framed, with big hands. His shirts, with the sleeves always rolled up to the elbows, hung on him like a scare crow. He usually had on a pair of light khaki coloured cotton pants, held up by a good set of heavy-duty suspenders. These suspenders always kept his pant cuffs about 6 inches higher than the top of the black and white tennis shoes he always wore. This wasn't quite the image I had of a northern trapper, but there were surprises yet to come. Louis always wore an old, green, mashed down, flat topped baseball cap that was, like all comfortable caps, grease stained and worn. But he was always clean and freshly shaven. There were two things that were his trademarks. The first was "Old Betsy", his curved stem pipe, that was always clenched in the corner of his mouth, and the other was his stammer. It never really seemed to bother him, but during a conversation, and especially if he got a little excited, or if he was meeting someone for the first time, his chin would drop down on his chest, he would grab "Old Betsy" out of the corner of his mouth and give a few gasping, snorting, snuffing sounds through his nose and mouth until a word or two popped out. That seemed to clear the way, and out the words would come! It was quite a performance.

When he was driving the team, especially going up a steep hill, he would be slapping their backs with the reins, and then with "Old Betsy" sticking out of the side of his jaw, jumping up and down, he would yell at them to "Git up B-B-B-Babe!! Git up B-B-B-Baldy! Whada ya th-th-think yer doin'!" While this was going on, I was trailing behind in the dust.

The road to Tatuk Lake had been in for many years to Sam Goodland's place. Sam had a small ranch a few miles north of the east end of Tatuk. This was the road that Rich Hobson took to his Batnuni Ranch, and from there it eventually found its way south into the Chilcotin country. The whole length of the road had been upgraded the summer before, when they had the fire on the north side of Tatuk Lake that my cousin Ed had worked on. I'm not sure how far we travelled that first day, less than 20 miles I'm sure. But by the time we had gone 10, I was remembering how comfortable the seat on that Triumph motorcycle had felt, and by the time we reached the first cabin where we camped that night, I had invented ways to sit on a saddle horse that trick riders had never heard of. By the time I got off, or fell off, I was more than ready to let Roy, Gene, Hobson, and Phillips, be the cowboys; I would be the biker!

The next day wasn't much better, but after we turned off the road past "44 Cabin", we had to bail off and cut quite a bit of wind fall that blocked the road, so that helped. About half way to the west end of the lake, where the house was, Louis had an interesting story to tell. Years before, they had been to Vanderhoof for supplies, and on the way home, right where we were, they ran into three big grizzlies. The wind was blowing toward the bears, so he coolly stuffed "Old Betsy" full of fresh tobacco and started puffing. When the bears caught the full brunt of the smoke from the old pipe, they took one whiff and tore out of the country. Louis still got a big chuckle out of that.

––––––

It was hard to comprehend the scope of this country. There were endless miles of Jack pine timber, Spruce swamps, and slough grass meadows. The spruce swamps were the places that made the hair stick up on the back of your neck. It was dark, spooky kind of country with little creeks and scattered meadows and willows running through them. But that's where the moose hung out.

When we finally got to the old mink ranch, I was impressed. I don't know who first owned the place, and built the log house, but it was another of those perfect settings. It was situated on a bench above a protected bay on the northwest side of the lake, with a small hayfield just east of the house, and Finger Creek meandering along the base of the hill in front.

I didn't know it then, but there was a ton of history here. The Finger-Tatuk Lake area had been occupied and used by the Carrier Indians to hunt, and also to fish the Kokanee runs, until late 1890. The village site at the mouth of Finger Creek, where it ran into Tatuk Lake, had several "pit house" depressions where they lived in the winter. This same area was the site of a mink ranch in the 1930's run by Louis Kohse, who also trapped in the area. Other early pioneers included trappers Joe Murray, who was badly mauled by a grizzly on the south-east of Finger Lake, and Joe Lavoie, who is buried southwest of Tatuk Hill.

What a spot! To the southwest, across the lake, a long, timbered ridge ran off to the east, and there was an unobstructed view across and down the lake. We didn't waste time; there was a lot of cleaning up and getting ready to get done.

———

My first job was getting some grass down for horse hay. The weather was perfect that week, and as I swished away in the boiling sun with the old scythe, head shaded by a dilapidated straw cowboy hat, I couldn't help but think. Where I was, and the work I was doing, was very conducive to thinking. When I stopped to have a drink of water or a smoke, there was not a sound. All you could hear was your ears ringing. Oh yes, once in a while you might hear a far off raven, or a bird chirp, but mostly it was total, dead, suffocating silence. There would be a time in later years when I would bask in the wilderness quiet, but at this point I found it hard to handle. This was a long, long way from rock and roll and Triumph motorcycles.

Toward the end of the week, we were getting things in pretty good shape, so I decided to take the rifle and go for a little walk. It was a nice afternoon. I thought I would go up the wagon road that went west from the house to Finger Lake, and when I hit the trail that bent off to the left, I would follow Finger Creek back to the house on Tatuk. It was a long loop that would take about an hour. I didn't really have anything specific in mind, but I wasn't about to go wandering around without a rifle, because this was real grizzly country. Right close by at Finger Lake was where the famous grizzly attack, and mauling, of little Joe Murray had taken place. Bear stories about this place weren't hard to come by. When I left the wagon road and started back along Finger Creek, I suddenly realized I might not have made the brightest move. The creek was loaded with kokanee, a small landlocked salmon......and bears like kokanee! I forget the size of rifle I had that day. It was one of Louis', probably his old Winchester 30-30. He had told me of a time when he first came out there, that he had shot a grizzly on this same creek, with a 25-20, which is not a very big gun. He got the job done by shooting it through the ear into the brain.

As I slowly walked down the trail along the creek, I didn't make a sound. It was a clean trail, and the boots I had on were good for quiet walking. I was getting close to the opening that led to the house, when just around the corner I heard a loud scratching, scraping sound. Every grizzly bear story I had ever heard started running through my mind. I knew that just around the corner where I couldn't see him was a huge grizzly standing on his hind legs and reaching up 15 feet to sharpen his claws on a tree, and I had to get past him to get home! To say I had a bad case of buck fever (or better, bear fever), was an understatement! Slowly I pulled the hammer back, eased the gun to my shoulder, and began to edge around the big pine that was blocking my view, expecting any second to come face to face with a huge Interior Silver Tip Grizzly. Inch by inch, I moved around the tree until everything was in full view. There was nothing there. Not a thing. Then, from half way up a dead jack pine, 30 feet ahead, came the same loud scraping, scratching sound. I looked up, and there, industriously working away, was a big Pileated Woodpecker! Talk about an overactive imagination! I was quite glad no one was nearby or they might have picked up sunburn from my red face. I eased the hammer back on half cock, and quietly walked on to the house, but never bothered telling Louis about the ten foot woodpecker I had almost shot.

When we finished up that week, and got the horses set up for a couple of days, we jumped in the big, wide beamed, wooden boat and headed down Tatuk Lake to meet the pickup man, then back to Nulki Lake to meet the great white hunters!

The Great White Hunters

I can't really recall now, but I think there were 3 men in the party. One would have been enough. I also don't remember any of their names, which is also just as well. But they were all old; old and in very precarious, physical health. One thing I do remember very clearly is that their biggest ambition, and their greatest goal in life, was for one to outlive the other, so they could pee on his grave! This was a main topic of conversation the whole time they were there! I have to confess, even in my few years of being around some fairly odd people, this was a new one for me! We got them loaded up and headed for Tatuk Lake.

On the way we stopped to have a look at some meadows along the road that were ideal moose hang-outs. The first one was by the cabin where we camped when Louis and I brought the team and wagon out. We stopped, got out, and while the three great white hunters were loading their rifles, I lit up a smoke. I thought doing this, along with pulling down the front brim of my dilapidated cowboy hat, would give a nice John Wayne atmosphere to the beginning of the expedition. Louis thought different. Even before the match had gone out, he whirled around with an angry look, and hissed at me to "put that thing out!" He meant it, and he never stuttered once! We never saw any moose there and I learned right quick that lighting up a smoke before you check out a moose pasture wasn't the way to hunt moose.

The weather got progressively worse that day. By the time we reached Tatuk Lake, loaded the boat, and headed out, we were in some bad stuff. The wind was coming straight out of the west, so it was really piling things up at the east end. We had a good, deep, wide beamed boat, and plenty of power and freeboard for the load, but once we cleared the islands that protect the bay at the east end, we were in trouble. I was in the bow to keep an eye out for any logs or rocks. Louis, an experienced lake and river man, was in the stern running the motor. The three hunters were in between and balanced out good with the cargo, but after we passed the islands and hit the open water, it was plain to see we had a problem. We had good rain gear on, and the supplies were tarped down, but we weren't making any headway. We were creeping up the north side of the lake and Louis was trying to use every bit of cover without getting close to the shore and grounding the prop. He finally found a spot in a small protected bay, and we pulled in and waited it out. We must have been there a couple of hours before things settled down enough to take off again. The rest of the trip was no problem. I did notice, at least, that this small diversion gave our guests something to talk about besides their favourite topic.

It was quite a trip. Two of the hunters I will never forget. The first was a fairly short, dumpy built guy, with rimless glasses and a round, saggy, face that was always as white as a sheet. He's the one that had to keep popping nitro-glycerin pills to keep the old ticker working, and was always on the defensive. I spent most of my time with him. The other hunter was the very epitome of what I think many people view as a typical American. Tall, white haired, with glasses, and an over-bearing personality, constantly griping about everything, knew everything, told you how to do everything, and never shut up! Oh great! And we get to spend seven days trying to keep him happy!

Louis was good at it, far better than I was. Once in awhile he would slip up beside me, "Old Betsy" puffing smoke, lean over and confidentially say to me out of the corner of his mouth, "-i-i-if we get these old g-g-geezers outta here alive, we're gonna be l-l-lucky!"

The weather that week was as bad as it was good the week before. We had three days that were fairly good; the rest of them, it poured rain. Early fall can be a spectacular time in the north, with frosty nights and warm, blue sky days, with the yellow of the poplars against the dark green of the conifers. But not that week! We hunted our tails off, Louis and I, and not a single moose or bear of any description was to be found. Years later, when my parents came up, I brought Dad out to the east end of the lake and 15 minutes later he had a nice bull moose. The truth was, I don't think these old gentlemen ever planned to do any serious hunting; they couldn't. It was impossible for any of them to walk more than 200 feet at one stretch without stopping to huff and puff, discuss their favourite topic, and pop a couple of nitro pills to get their heart going again. They seemed to be more than content to set back in their easy chairs, play cards, belly ache about how there were no moose in the country, and argue about whose grave would get irrigated first. While they relaxed by the fire, Louis and I hunted. From morning to night, we hunted. It was terrible weather, nothing but wind and rain. We checked out every moose pasture and spruce swamp he knew of for miles, and never saw a fresh track. Looking back, I'm sure that it was too early in the season and the bulls hadn't started moving. But one thing I got was exercise. Louis had a quick, short stepped way of walking, that he had perfected over the years. Although he was 60 years old at the time, and I was 20, he ran the wheels off me. By the time we got in at night, I was wore out and we, (mostly he), had to get things cleaned up, make supper for everyone, and get things ready for the next day, as well as listening to the complaints of our wanna be hunters.

The day before we had to leave was nice. The plan was to load the wagon half full of hay, get everyone on board, and take the trail over to Finger Lake. There Louis would take the tall, white haired American, and his friend, around Finger Lake to look over some good moose spots, using the boat we had stashed there. I would take the nitro popper back in the wagon to the house. He had mainly just wanted to come along for the ride anyway. We got everything unloaded and Louis turned the wagon around towards the house at Tatuk, then he headed up the lake in the boat with the two hunters.

I had never driven a team of horses. Babe and Baldy turned their heads and checked me out with a very skeptical look. They knew right off there was a greenhorn at the wheel. I slacked off on the lines a bit, gave a little cluck and said, "All right, let's go". They knew of course, that they were headed back to the barn where the rigging would all come off, and they would get a handful of oats, so I didn't really need to say anything. The wagon road wasn't exactly the 401, or the I-5, but the first quarter mile we covered in 10 seconds flat with me hauling back on the reins, yelling, "Whoa Baldy, whoa Babe"! at every jump. My nitro-glycerin imbibing hunter spent most of that time doing handstands on the edge of the wagon box and asking me if I had ever drove a team before. When we finally came to a panting, sweating stop, I assured him this was my first time, so he volunteered to take over. I had liked this guy right from the start, he seemed like a real down to earth farmer type, and always seemed to be on the losing end, so to speak, when it came to the favourite topic. After popping a couple of nitro pills to get things firing properly again, we headed out once more. He was a real old mule skinner. Those horses knew right off their fun day was over. Every time one twitched an ear the wrong way, he let him or her know it. The rest of the ride was pure, slow, back-in-time enjoyment as we relived the days of the wagon trains.

We got skunked on our hunt. Not a moose was seen, not a bear, nothing bigger than a grouse and a pine squirrel. It reminded me in a way of when my brother and Melvin Holden and I went on our survival camping trip in California. The only difference was this time we didn't even have a pair of rabbit ears for a trophy. But they didn't seem to really mind, and in spite of the complaining and the one topic of conversation, they were a pretty good bunch. Bill and the crew at the lodge threw a big party for them when we got back and they were happy when they left.

When the Party's Over

That was the only hunt Louis had booked that fall, so it was back to work. I was starting to get restless again and it was about time for them to close the resort down for the winter. I forget now what the occasion was, but they had one more, big blow out party before they finished up, and asked if I would bring my guitar down and help entertain the crowd. Joyce, Bill Wineberg's girlfriend, had always been nice to me, so I was more than happy to go down. I didn't know it then, but that night was the start of a chain of events that would bring things to a conclusion that had been building for years. There were quite a few big time guests there that night, and there was no shortage of liquid refreshments. I quickly fortified my self-confidence, and when I should have quit, I didn't. I got through the entertaining part all right, but things fell apart pretty bad after that.

At some point I bumped into Colonel Saunders, the guy who had asked me to make the music tape for him and thought I might have a chance at the big time. He took me over in a corner and informed me that the guy he gave the tape to, said I wouldn't make the grade in the recording industry. I was disappointed, but not really surprised. I knew I wasn't Jim Reeves, but I guess I had gotten my hopes up. I picked up the little Martin guitar and headed up to where I lived in the shop. As I went past a power pole along the way, I took my nice little Martin guitar by the neck, and smashed it into a hundred pieces. That was an expensive little temper tantrum that didn't solve anything!

We had just got paid, so when I reached the shop, I packed my stuff into my duffel bag and decided to leave. As I went by the big window that faced to the east, I stopped for a minute and looked out. It was a moonlight night, and as I looked out that window, a text from the Bible, of all things, came to my mind. It said, "As the lightning comes from the east, and shines even to the west, so shall the coming of the Son of Man be". (Matt.24:27.) I stood there in a drunken haze, looking out that window, and the thought came

149

to me, "Where are you headed with your life? What if He were to come now? With the knowledge you've been given in the past, by good Christian people, what excuse would you have to not be ready?" Forget it, I thought. I'm headed for town, and from town I'm headed to good old California; I've had enough of B.C. I'm going on a good drunk, and forget this Bible stuff.

I managed to get a ride to town, spent a little while in the Vanderhoof Hotel pub, then bought a bus ticket to Vancouver, crawled on, and passed out. When I woke up, we were close to the big city.

It was a major change from the total silence at Tatuk. Traveling the last few miles into the metropolis I decided to drop in and see my chef friend at the Hotel Vancouver. I grabbed a taxi when we arrived at the bus depot, and was dropped off at the Hotel. When I crawled out, and looked up at the Hotel, I suddenly realized that I was clearly out of my class, and a long way from sitting around a campfire at Nulki Lake.

Cranking up my courage, I walked in and asked if I could speak to the Head Chef. They told me what floor he was working on, so I jumped on the elevator and up I went. When I stepped off, I was very tempted to step right back on again. This wasn't roasting a trout over the campfire at Nulki Lake, this was Big Time. They were preparing a banquet. The endless tables were set fit for a Queen; and situated among all this finery were a number of huge, perfectly carved, ice sculpture swans with their long, gracefully curved necks. Well, here I was; and soon found my friend The Chef. Amid all the chaos of preparation, he welcomed me like an old friend, and gave me the address of his mother's house, where I could go and freshen up, (which I badly needed). His mother, a very kind lady with a definite air of English aristocracy about her, welcomed me like a long, lost son. That night we had a party at her house. It was all singing, laughing, telling stories, and drinking. They found a guitar and I gave it the full shot. After the party was over, I spent the rest of the night there, with plans to take off in the morning.

Amazing Grace

When I got out on the freeway the next morning and started hitch hiking to California, I felt, like the old saying goes, that I had been pulled through a knot hole, backwards. Once my foggy brain cleared, I did some serious thinking about where I was headed in life. I was 20 years old, and what had I accomplished besides supporting the brewing industry? Now I understood what was on the other side of the billboards, with the cool, smiling party people holding up their bottles. Now I was beginning to get the real picture, and it wasn't pretty. I had seen what booze had done to my brother's life, his wife and children. My mind went back to Mack and Effie McTimmonds on McDowell creek, and the pointless suffering and sadness it caused them. I thought, (maybe selfishly), of my good plaid Pendleton coat that my old logger buddy, Stan Robson, was likely wearing somewhere right now, and how he probably couldn't even remember where he got it. I thought of the skid row world where talented, brilliant people took their last breath, lying in some garbage filled back alley, or stinking gutter, and those who loved them didn't even know where they were.

As the cars whizzed by my out stretched thumb, I remembered people like those old, hard line, German preachers at the Berlin Church, who didn't mince words when it came to right and wrong. To the kind, patient Sunday School teachers, to Albert Swink who raised those good tasting turkeys and faithfully hauled us backwoods hicks to Sunday School. I thought of Gray Banta, my Grade 9 teacher, with his cowboy shirts and boots, and endless patience; the look of sadness on his face when we failed him with our drinking spree. I thought of Paul Fleming, the Pathfinder leader, of Elder Schoepflin, our Bible teacher at Milo Academy, and my roommate there, Gordon Klein. There was no end to the pictures of good solid, caring, giving Christian people who make the world a better place; people like the Lakes District community that had been so helpful and welcomed us in. But most of all I thought of my Mother. Like all of us, she wasn't perfect.

But there was one thing I knew for sure. She would never stop praying for me, and in the end, I believe that's what made the difference.

When I got home to Arcata, California, I spent some time alone, reading and studying the Bible, and thought it through. Any of my old drinking buddies seeing me sitting there, with a Bible in my hand would have thought it was a joke, but I was serious. At the end of three days, I made the decision. I knelt down and committed my life to God. I almost hesitate to use the words, because they have been used by some less than reputable ministries, even to the point where they have lost credibility. But to millions of people who have been delivered from a life that has no meaning into a life that, in the blink of an eye, is changed, there are only two words that describe it. Those words are "Born Again". No, I wasn't perfect. I'm still not perfect, only in one way. When I made that decision, and accepted the sacrifice Jesus Christ made for me, when He died on the Cross of Calvary, I became a different person. Every cuss word, every bottle of booze, all the wrong things I had ever done were forgiven, and the perfect life He lived, now stood in the place of my life. Just like that! I'm aware that not everyone who is converted has the same experience I had, but the promise is there. I had learned it from those Sunday School teachers at Berlin, "Believe in the Lord Jesus Christ, and you will be saved", Act 16:31. "Born Again", now that's a little awkward. One of the rulers of Israel, named Nicodemus, way back in Jesus' time, tried to corner Him on that one. It's a mystery, Jesus told him, it's like the wind. It's a spiritual experience that takes place where God, in the person of His Spirit, comes into your life. It's something that changes you. One minute you hate God, you curse His name, and laugh in His face. The next minute you bow down and worship Him, to the point where millions of people have given their lives, rather than deny Him as their Saviour. Suddenly the things you once loved, you now hate; the things you once hated, you now love. Overcoming some of my bad habits took some time but now I was on the right track.

I had a pack of Luckies that I struggled with, and my beloved old Snoose box took a while to get rid of, but the craving for booze was gone. Gone! Just like that! I couldn't believe it, there was just nothing there! But the thing I remember the most was the incredible feeling of freedom and release, and not being a slave to that stuff anymore. It was like the feeling I had when they let me out of that little 6' by 12' cell at the Detention Centre, only a thousand times more. I could understand to some degree, how those who had been enslaved felt when they were set free; and what John Newton, the hardened captain of a slave ship experienced, when he was converted, and wrote the famous song, Amazing Grace.

I stopped by a few days later to visit my old coon hunting buddy and best friend, Dave Sutter, who was now a married man. He invited me in and offered me a beer. When I told him "No thanks, I quit", he fell off his chair backwards! Well not quite, but he couldn't believe it. I couldn't either. Before, I had not only liked booze to get drunk, but I had also liked the taste of it. Now even that was gone. We had a good visit, and I left.

———

I didn't know it then, because I was flying pretty high, but the big test was yet to come. I went to work with Dad for a couple of days just to get out in the big timber again and wear off some steam. I still had a can of Skoal snoose in my pocket, that I was trying to wean myself off of, and wasn't having much luck. You would think I would have counted it a privilege to quit that awful habit, but that wasn't the case. I'm not sure why, maybe it was the he-man image, along with the habit and addiction, but it was a battle.

I was walking down a sharp ridge that fell off into a deep canyon quite a ways from where Dad and his partner were working, when I got the urge to stuff my lip full. That's when I decided this was it. I told this decision to God, hooked my finger around the can like you would a skipping rock, then hauled back and fired that can of Skoal as high and far as I could throw it. The urge to smoke only hit about once a day. The urge to chew even came in my dreams!

With all the bad stuff out of the way, life was taking on a more positive tone, though chewing licorice flavoured gum drops was quite a change from chewing snoose! But there was still one thing that was perfectly natural and legal, and added some "zing" to life. That was checking out the girls!

When I broke my collarbone playing football in my Grade 9 year at the McKinleyville Church School, I was in love with all three available girls, (sometimes one more than the other!) One of my favourite sweethearts had grown into a tall, slender, very pretty young lady with (you guessed it) short, dark blonde, naturally curly hair! I just had to stop by and see how she had ever managed to survive in my absence. Strangely enough, she hadn't even noticed I was gone! I had a lot of respect for her; she was really a nice girl, but in spite of this I was ready to move on.

The Big Test

It was time to head back north. When I left Canada, I never planned on going back; but the pull of the north was strong. In the States, it seemed like it had all been done. Up there, it was still waiting to be done. It was a new frontier, a new country, where you could start a new life. This Canadian landed immigrant was a lot different guy than the one who crawled on the Greyhound bus only 10 months earlier, and had become a lot more Canadian than he realized.

Dad decided to drive me up to Sweet Home, Oregon, and look things over again while he was there. He was really happy about my decision to join the flock again, even though at that time he wasn't a Christian. Looking back, I think part of the reason he drove me up was to give me a running start on the journey, and make sure I didn't stray off the path before I got out of California! As it turned out, it was providential that he did. We really had a good trip. I could see that at least he didn't seem to think I was a complete write-off now, and there might be some hope. We relived a lot of old duck and deer hunting stories, and Iowa and McDowell Creek history on that trip.

We stayed with Noel Richards', Dad's old logging partner. We visited around for a day or two and met some old friends. The plan on Sunday morning was for him to go back to California, and I would head north. On Saturday night a bunch of his old logging pals got together at Noel's and had a real old time McDowell Creek blow-out and hoe-down. Dad had brought his fiddle along and they really cut loose. I don't remember now if Dad drank at all that night, but if he did, it was next to nothing. Somehow, I ended up sitting between Noel and Dad. I was in a real awkward position, on my right was my Pa, sawing off those old knee slappin', hand clappin', hootin', hollerin' fiddle tunes, I had grown up with. On the left was Noel, one of my Dad's best friends, a generous, straight forward, honest, hardworking timber faller, that the booze was doing bad things to. Sitting right between them was this lily white, prim and proper newly converted Christian with his hands tightly folded in his lap, and an out-of-place look on his face. Every once in a while, Noel would turn to me with his heavy lidded, blood shot eyes and offer me a beer. I would graciously thank him, and tell him "No thanks, I don't drink anymore". He would look at me in blurred disbelief, and say with his slurred speech, "Oh, come on boy, have ah beer, one won't hurt ya".

This went on hour after hour, with him getting a little more insistent each time. Out of the corner of his eye, Dad was keeping track of this whole operation. The longer I sat there, the more the pressure built up. These were people I had been taught to respect and admire ever since I was a kid. They were part of the culture and history of my family. Noel was being friendly in the only way he knew how; this was logger hospitality. I finally caved in. When he turned and again offered me a beer, I told him "OK, I'll have one". Again, I don't want to over dramatize what took place then, but I have re-lived it a lot of times over the past 55 years. As I reached over to take that can of beer from Noel's hand, Dad stopped playing, put down his fiddle, turned around and said to me "Don't do it, boy, don't do it. You've stuck with it this far, stay with it".

Those words saved my life, plain and simple. If I had taken that one, it would have been the end of me, but thankfully Dad stepped in. Over the next few years, I would see the real life evidence of what drinking can do; the sadness, sorrow, and suffering, the ruined lives among family and friends, and people I worked with. Some would happen because of being completely drunk, some from just enough to alter good judgment. But the results were all the same; once you're dead, you're dead! How much is too much? You never know how well you can handle it until you drink the first one; and when you drink the first one, it can be too late. What kind of example do you set for others? If my simple story can save one person from the tragedies that can come from drinking, it will be worth the time I took to write it.

———

We left the next morning. There was a whole new frontier opening up in B.C., and if I was going to be a part of what happened, I'd better get at it. I don't think I told Dad the next morning when we parted company, out on the freeway, how much I appreciated what he had done at Noel's the night before, but I did tell him many times before he passed away in August 2014, 7 months short of his 100th birthday.

Dad took a picture of me, before he left me on Interstate 5 to hitchhike north, and he returned to California. It wasn't the kind of picture you looked back on in later years and thought of how much you accomplished, because, like most people, I've lived a fairly ordinary life. But to me, that picture is the black and white image of a water shed time in my life. I didn't have any glorious vision of what I was going to do when I got back to Canada. I just knew one thing, the north is where I wanted to be, not the south.

After I hitchhiked to Vancouver, I decided to take the train to Prince George. It was early November 1961, and you could feel winter in the air. The one thing I clearly remember that first night was crossing a long, wood, railroad trestle. I don't remember where it was, or have any idea how long, or how high it was, but it was an absolute marvel of engineering. It was a brilliant moonlight night, and as we left solid ground and moved out onto the trestle, It was like we were suspended in space. Far below, and all around I could see the country spread out below me. It was a unique experience that felt like a dream.

One thing that didn't feel like a dream was the cold I had picked up on my journey from Oregon. By the time I got to Prince George and into a hotel room, I was in a bad way. I was worn out, and my vision and courage had begun to sag a little. I knelt down beside the bed that night and prayed. This whole Christian thing was pretty new to me, and like Jerry, the lathe operator at Santiam Plywood, I would have to be careful with words. I've prayed a lot over the years. Some prayers, on the surface, seem to be a waste of breath, or weren't answered the way I wanted or expected. The only answer I have is that God knows what He is doing, and I don't; so just trust Him. But that night He answered, as I had never before or since, had a cold that bad, clear up overnight. That time I believe God answered the prayer of a greenhorn Christian, just because I needed it.

I was starting a new way of life. In the next month I would be meeting many people, from my cousins to people I didn't know, who would offer me a drink, or a smoke, or a dip out of their Snoose can, and I would have to have the guts to say "No".

A New Beginning

I arrived back in Vanderhoof the next morning, and caught a ride out to the Jones' home at Sinkut Lake. When I told my cousins they would no longer have to share their booze and tobacco with me, they were ecstatic, and welcomed me with open arms, handshakes, and slaps on the back. Red was the most supportive, not just then, but all through the years on my decision to quit drinking.

Now I needed a job and a place to stay. I got a job right away for Al Simrose, who had a dairy and beef operation at the east end of Nulki Lake, and was building a barn. It was the first ranch on the big flat bottom land, that ran from the east end of Nulki Lake, to the west end of Sinkut Lake. George Tee's parents, an older, kind hearted couple, offered me a room and board situation as they were just up the road from the Al Simrose place.

Al Simrose was one of the ranch hands mentioned in Rich Hobson's book, 'Nothing Too Good For A Cowboy'. Al came to B.C. in the early days, from Saskatchewan, working on farms and ranches until settling on the property south of Vanderhoof in the 1940's. Al wasn't a big man, but along with his wife Annie they were hard workers, raising 7 kids, and struggling to get the ranch established. Al was a reserved man and sort of chuckled instead of outright laughing. He had a rusty, taciturn way of talking, and you had to listen close to catch what he was saying.

The construction project was a loafing barn for his dairy cows. It was a pretty straight forward, 2" X 4" frame building, sheeted with 1" X 6" shiplap inside and out. The roof with a 6" roof pitch, was sheeted with metal roofing. It was a slow job as we were building it out of lumber that had been scavenged from half a dozen other old buildings, to save material costs. A very common practice at that time. This involved nail pulling, re-cutting long boards, etc., so took a lot of labour time.

My partner, Jasper Thomas, a big, square built Carrier Indian from Stoney Creek was really a nice guy. But when you worked with him, you worked!

There was no standing around discussing how it should be done. That was just as well, because carpentering at 20 degrees below zero (F), is not the warmest job. If we could have gotten some sun, it would have helped. Outside there was lots of it, because it was clear and cold, but inside the shed it was just plain cold. I had worked enough with Ed, my cousin, to at least know which end of a hammer to pick up, so that part wasn't too bad, but Jasper knew the trade. I've worked with quite a few natives over the years and have come to the conclusion that if they have a problem its not in the area of talent or ability.

Man, how glad I was when dinnertime rolled around and we could get out of the cold. The thought did enter my mind as I was working, that maybe this great urge to pioneer in the north wasn't quite what it was cracked up to be. But you adapt, and the minute you stepped through the door and smelled what Annie had for dinner, you forgot the cold.

Al & Annie Simrose and family

159

Their house wasn't anything elaborate, it was a working farmhouse, and it was warm and it was happy. The grub was good, and there was plenty of it. Annie was a tall, slender, work worn woman, with red hair and glasses, a ready laugh, and she knew how to cook!

She was the perfect picture of a pioneer woman. In her younger years you could envision her at a community dance, kicking up her heels and being the life of the party. Now she was surrounded by a bunch of kids, and like all pioneer women just took it in stride.

After we ate, we would sit around and visit for awhile, trying to think of some excuse to stay in where it was warm. One day I noticed a rifle over in the corner and asked Al about it. He dug it out and handed it to me. It was a long barrelled Winchester lever action 38-55. I had never heard of one, but I was interested. I managed to convince Al that I needed this gun more than he did and bought it from him. That took care of most of my wages on the barn, but I was happy. A short barrelled rifle is much handier in bush country than a "Long Tom" like this one, but I was fascinated by long barrels. I guess it went back to the pictures I remembered as a kid of those long barrelled squirrel rifles, and coonskin caps, from the hills of Kentucky and Tennessee. Because of the heavy calibre, it was a good bush gun, and because of that I decided to call my new gun the 'punkin slinger'! I really enjoyed working for Al Simrose, and working with Jasper Thomas, and was sorry to see the job end, but after about 2 weeks we had finished the job.

A Christmas to Remember

At the end of November 1961, I got a job, including room and board, working for Harold Bradley in his sawmill. One of the more prominent families in the Lakes District, Harold & Amy Bradley, were very involved in all the activities of the community. Harold in 4-H, Amy in the Women's Institute, along with community dances and curling. Their farm was bordered by Mel Lynums on the west, and George Evans on the east. The majority of their farmland was also part of the rich bottom land that lay between Nulki and Sinkut Lake. Sinkut Creek, a beautiful, clear mountain stream, came out of the hills onto the flat just a few hundred feet east of their buildings. The road beside their farm led to Sinkut Mountain, Sam Goodland's ranch, and Tatuk Lake. The curling rink where, the previous winter, I had performed my famous premature rock kicking blunder, was close to the Bradley property.

Harold & Amy Bradley were generous people. There aren't many, with a young family of their own, who would take a tall, lanky, foot loose itinerant worker, with no greater vision than the next meal, into their home. I know that beyond needing someone to help in his mill, there was a kinder purpose. They were interested in helping someone who was trying to do better. Besides the mill tailing job, keeping the wood box full, and other odd jobs, I helped feed his small herd of Hereford cattle.

Harold had his sawmill set up across Sinkut Creek, at the east end of a big willow flat that he wanted to clear to add onto his hay field. There were a lot of big spruce in this willow flat, covered with limbs. By the time the trees were felled and skidded to the mill there was hardly a limb left on them, thanks to the cold weather. But man, was it ever cold where that mill sat. It was right on the edge of the field, and wide open to the north wind. Harold had a little Cle-Trac cat that he did the skidding with. It was a funny looking thing but sure beat a scoop shovel for plowing snow.

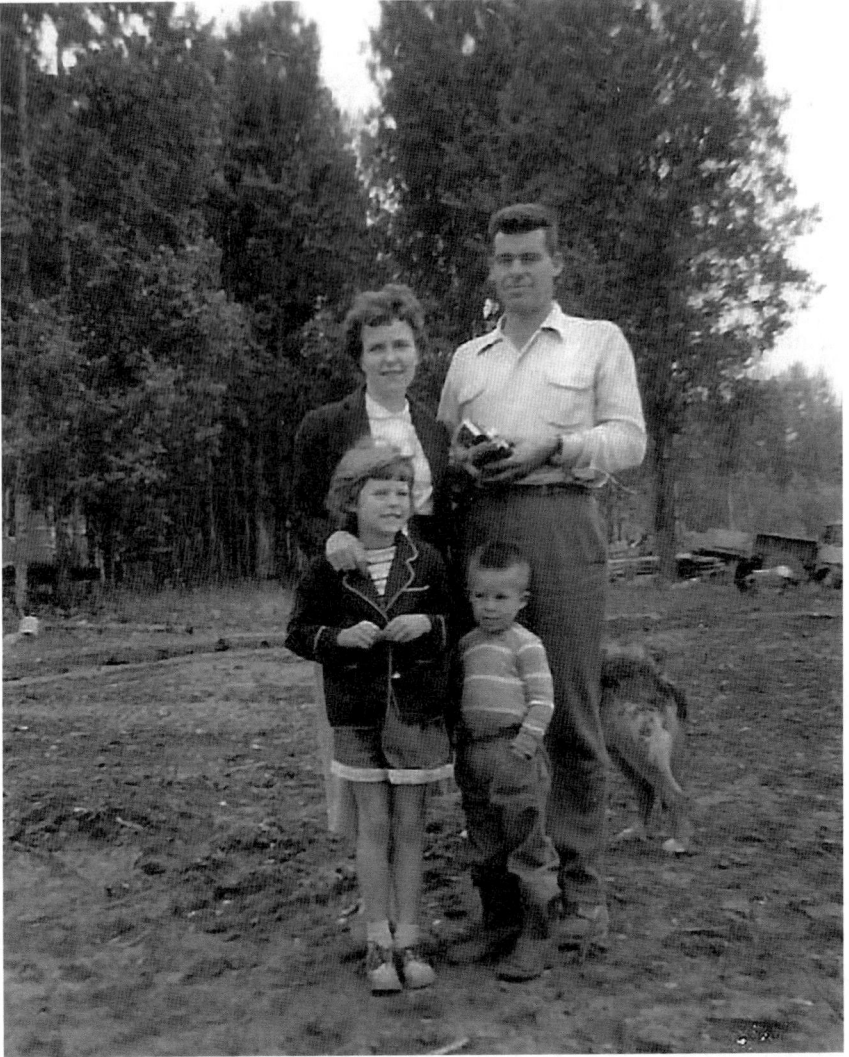

Harold & Amy Bradley with children Kathy & Larry

Along with his sawmill operation and looking after his herd of beef cattle, he also grew a few acres of potatoes. He had a good local market, supplying his brother Charles with potatoes for his grocery store in town, as well as customers on the Stoney Creek Indian Reserve. When it was too cold to operate the sawmill we would work in the big root cellar on the back of his shop sorting potatoes.

162

One thing I was really taken with the winter I worked for Harold, was his hard hat. I was really impressed with that hard hat! I had never seen one like it. That hat had style! The hard hats I had seen all my life that Dad, and the California & Oregon loggers wore, were a dull aluminum colour and had a wide, three inch brim, all the way around, to help deflect falling limbs. My Dad, who always had a flair for style, stuck the front couple of inches of his hat in a vice and bent it down a little, to give it class. But this lid of Harold's topped them all. It was so shiny it looked like it was chrome plated, and had a low crown. There were a lot more reinforcing ribs that came down to the edges of the brim. But what I really liked was that it only had a quarter brim that covered your eyes and forehead, just like a baseball cap. Best of all, it was light as a feather.

There was a store in Vanderhoof called Lenny's B.A., in the same area as Charles Bradley's grocery store, near the Co-op Elevator. Lenny's B.A. sold hard hats. But there was someone there that was a lot more interesting than hard hats! There was one good looking salesgirl! I could tell right off that she was tuned to a different channel than I was in my reformed condition, but I could still look and admire. It didn't take her long to sell me a hard hat, although I stalled it off as long as possible. She was a lot more pleasant to look at than spruce slabs and boards.

There was just one problem. I bought the wrong hard hat. I had to buy one for safety regulations; unfortunately, they didn't have one like Harold's. I had bought an ugly, red, fibreglass hard hat, that had all the personality of an egg. It probably wouldn't have mattered anyway, as I was so dazzled by the salesgirl that I didn't even know what I had on my head until two days later. Before I left Lenny's B.A., the smiling salesgirl had convinced me I also needed a red & black, checkered, wool bush coat, to match the new, red hard hat. Now I was colour co-ordinated. When I got back to the mill, Harold was more interested in me getting the slabs and boards pulled, than the colour co-ordination of my new outfit.

Harold & Amy's house was still in the finishing stages, with only one bathroom. For some reason the door on the bathroom didn't lock. That's fine when only the family was there, but when a twenty year old male moves in, it can cause no end of problems. I don't know why Harold didn't put a lock on that door; instead there was supposed to be some kind of notice system to let you know when someone was in the bathroom. This whole thing became very awkward. The second time I tapped on the door, with my teeth floating, and asked if anyone was in the bathroom, Amy came storming out and it was very clear she was not happy.

The final straw came when Amy had a Women's Institute meeting one night, and all the local ladies were visiting, teacups in hand. One lady suddenly felt the call of nature and headed for the bathroom. I guess no one had told her about the "system" because she barged right in without knocking. That was fine, except I was in the middle of having a bath. I wasn't aware that Amy was hosting a meeting, so there I was, trapped in the tub. Suddenly this lady realized there was a head of hair, with a pair of big eyes, staring at her over the edge of the tub. She made her exit in a hurry, and quickly told the other tea drinkers of her run in with the young man in the bathtub. Soon after, Harold installed the lock on the bathroom door, but I'm sure this story circulated for weeks throughout the community.

––––––––––

When we logged farther along the back edge of the willow flat, we began to see moose tracks on the skid road in the morning. It was right at the end of moose season and I had never shot a bull moose, so I asked Harold if he would mind if I came out early and checked it out. He had a lot of freezer room and figured it might be a cheaper way of feeding me, instead of using his beef, so he agreed. The next morning, I crept out nice and early with my old 38.55 Punkin Slinger, loaded right to the hilt with those big artillery sized shells. I was at the start of the skid road when it was just light enough to see. I walked real slow along the road, the willow bottom on my right, and the base of the hill on my left. You couldn't be quiet because it was 20 degrees below zero F. and the snow squeaked with every step. I had almost reached the end of the skid trail when a young bull moose jumped up and took off through the willows. He wasn't over a hundred feet away, and moving fast. Those willow tangles and deep snow didn't slow him down a bit, with that straight up and down, piston like gait and long legs, he was on the run. I jerked up the old Winchester and started shooting. The second shot, down he went. I wallowed over to him through the deep snow and bled him out, then took off to tell Harold that he could sell two more steers, as we now had a moose to eat. He was a prime bull. We skidded him out with the cat and hung him in the shop for a couple of days, then put him in the freezer. I don't think we ate beef the rest of the winter!

———

Christmas that year I will always remember; it was a real family day. Harold and Amy had three kids. Kathy, the oldest, was around 12. She was a tall, pretty girl, with short, dark brown hair, blue eyes, and favoured the Bradley side of the family, but she had her Mom's quick, warm smile, and laughing eyes. Larry, who was 4 or 5, always reminded me of a chipmunk. He was never still. He was a small, bright eyed, high speed kid, who made up with energy what he lacked in size. His hair was always cut short and when he looked at you, his bright little eyes said he was ready to take you on. Kenny, the youngest at 2, a good looking kid with curly blond hair, had a mind of his own. At mealtimes he was always standing up and jumping around on the tray of his highchair. Harold and Amy were constantly after him to sit down. The longer he was up there, the wilder he would get, until, finally, he would fall off head first. Harold would reach out and casually grab him by the ankle, just before his head hit the floor, and plunk him back in his chair, without missing a beat in the conversation.

Margaret (Grandma) Bradley came out, of course, for Christmas dinner. She was a short, plump, quietly reserved lady, with glasses and short, wavy, snow white hair; a real grandmotherly type with a warm, friendly disposition. That Christmas we had an absolute banquet of a meal. Everyone dressed in their finest, the best white, lace tablecloth on the table, and after the blessing was said, I ate until I couldn't breathe. Later on that evening, as we stood around the piano and sang the old Christmas songs, about the three wise me, and the Christ Child born in the stable, it had new meaning to me and brought back a lot of memories. This brought a perfect end to a perfect Christmas.

———

I wasn't aware of it at the time, but during the winter I worked for Harold, an idea of what I wanted to do in life began to take shape. It didn't suddenly pop into my head, but as we fed the cows, sorted spuds on the days it was too cold to sawmill, sat around the table at mealtime and talked about what was going on in the community, it began to take shape. This is what I wanted. Bradleys', to me, were an ideal Canadian farm family. Harold, with his rugged good looks and easy going personality; Amy, the perfect match, very attractive, and a good sense of humour; three nice kids; what more could you ask for? I didn't envy them but I did appreciate them, and decided that at some point in time this is what I also wanted to have. A wife and kids around the table (preferably ones that stayed sitting in their highchairs), a good piece of land and a small herd of cows. A farm and someone to share it with.

As this whole new vision for my direction in life began to take shape, I realized there were two very important items I would need to make it all work. The first, from a practical point of view, was a wife. (Two people can pick more roots than one!) The second, of course, was land.

———

Well, first things first. The top priority was to find a wife. The Lakes District hall was the center of community activities and held dances for the teenagers. The community dances were the old pioneer kind where everyone came, but these teenage get-togethers were just for the kids. Although I could play music, I had never learned to dance, so whether teen dances for the kids, or community dances, I would just set on the sidelines and keep an eye on the young ladies and visit with everyone.

There was one couple at the New Year's community dance I really enjoyed watching, Don and Marjorie Weaver. Don was a big, tall, raw boned Englishman, and Marjorie was just a little short gal of good Scottish heritage. She was one of the older children in the big family of Cal and Irma Stewart who lived at the east end of Tachick Lake. Marjorie didn't take a back seat to anyone when it came to having and raising kids, running a ranch or a business, or out on the dance floor. Their place was on the west end of Nulki Lake, and between sawing lumber and calving cows, they made a living. They were both business types, involved in community organizations, and everyone liked them. When they hit the dance floor, Don would set course right down the middle of the hall, with his eye zeroed in on the ceiling at the far end, and taking six foot strides while poor little Marjorie's feet only hit the floor about every third step. But she had a smile a mile wide. They were in time with the music and having fun, and that was what was important. Who needs those fancy spins and twirls anyway? Up and down the hall he would march, with what appeared to be grim determination. But that wasn't the case, that's just the way Don danced. Just don't make the mistake of getting in his way, because he's got his eye fixed on the far end of the hall, and it's your fault if you end up getting stomped on!

I only went to one teen dance that winter, but I saw two girls there I would remember for quite a while. One was a cute little blonde that I had heard about through the grapevine, the other was a fairly tall, slender girl with a real mop of rich, dark auburn hair who wore glasses and had a very nice smile. She was playing ping pong with another attractive girl who was a little taller.

The little blonde sitting on the west side of the hall had big blue eyes and knew how to use them. She was sitting by herself, wrapped up in a long, black winter coat with that pensive look on her face that makes boys want to come over and say, "Well, hello! Where have you been all my life!" Her name was Ginger Filan. I had heard she was going with one of the local Bronc and Bull riding Rodeo Stars, so I kept my distance as I wasn't too keen on getting a spur stuck in my hide.

The tall girl with the dark auburn hair wasn't interested in sitting around giving "pensive" looks, she was too busy playing ping pong and tearing up the dance floor! Her name was Joan Snyder from out in the backwoods Mapes District off to the east, where Orin Kennel was put up the tree by the Grizzly bear. Her dancing partner was Alec Dingwall, a fairly tall, thin faced guy with long stringy blond hair, and a goofy sense of humour and easy smile. He had more be-bop moves and flexibility than a Universal Joint.

I was more or less drifting along in neutral at that time, with no real promising root and rock picking girlfriends, or future wives in sight. There was also one more very important item in the grand plan that I should have given a lot more serious thought to. That item was money. If there is one thing you will need if you're going to take on a wife and farm, it's money! Lots of money!

Sure Cure For Blisters

When my job for Harold Bradley was finished in late February 1962, I moved back to the Jones household and went to work with them. Red had started logging for Nels Cruthers, who had bought a ranch not far from them. Red did the falling, Dick and I the limbing, and Ed, as the least prone to bucking rocks in half, did the bucking.

Nels Cruthers, and his family, came up from a little town a few miles north of Walla Walla, Washington, a major wheat farming area in the rolling hills of the Palouse country in the southeast part of the state. Nels and his wife, Midge, had 5 grown children; 2 boys, Charlie and Larry; 3 girls, Sally, Gale, and Irene. Midge was a short, plump, kind hearted lady, who always welcomed me into their home like one of her own kids. Nels, was a tall, strongly built man with long arms and sloped shoulders. He wore wire rimmed glasses, had a long, narrow, solemn face, and straight, thinning, slicked back hair. When he looked at you, everything seemed pretty serious. But, in fact, he was one of those straight faced, look you in the eye, old west kind that liked nothing more than a good joke.

One little stunt he liked to pull when meeting someone for the first time, was to act like he had a hearing problem. The small town they came from in eastern Washington was called Hay, (as in a bale of hay). The name of the town probably gave some indication of its size. When being asked by this unwary new acquaintance the name of the town he came from, he would turn his head a bit, lean toward them with a solemn, questioning look on his long face, and say, "Hey?" They would clear their throat and ask him again, this time a little louder. He would lean a little closer, and in a questioning voice once again say, "Hey?" but there was a twinkle in his eye. After they had asked him four or five times, he would finally grin and explain his little joke – that "Hay" was actually the name of the town they came from! Then he would have a good chuckle about his backwoods joke.

The old cowboys and farmers really enjoyed a good laugh, joke, or story. They could pack a lot of wisdom and good humour into a few words. A couple of these were: "Silence can be a speech", and "Never approach a bull from the front, a horse from the rear, or a fool from any direction"! But jokes aside, the main thing on the agenda was work. Nels must have been in his mid to late fifties when they came up to Vanderhoof in the summer of 1960 and bought their ranch. It was located a few miles south of town, and a mile or so down the Sinkut Lake/Blackwater Road from Highway 16. I think at that time, it consisted of a section of land, and was known as the McGeachy Meadows. They had also bought a quarter section of crown land at the corner of Highway 16 and the Sinkut Lake/Blackwater Road. This quarter section is the one they were logging.

I had never had the privilege of doing a lot of axe work before, as I was the slab packer at the mill when George Tee sawmilled on Red's place. When we went into town to get equipped for this attack on the local flatland conifers, I spotted an axe the minute we stepped through the door of Rich's Saw Sales, our local power saw sales and repair shop. It was a mean looking thing that resembled an early Nordic battle axe. It was a light weight single bit, with a long, narrow head that flared out to a wide curved blade at the bottom. It was called an "Iltis Ox Head", and was very lightly built. They tried to talk me into buying something with more weight and a more substantial, heavier head, but I was sold on that "Iltis Ox Head", and could already see the limbs flying.

Charlie, the oldest son, was probably about thirty at that time, with a wife and one child. He was the stable, "do everything right" type, as far as his lifestyle went, but when it came to running machinery, he was a wild man. They had an Allis-Chalmers HD7 Cat they had brought up with them from Washington, where they were used for farming, and pulling combines in the steep, rolling wheat country. They were more stable than the rubber tired farm tractors of the early days. It had a low slung cross spring which was good for a low center of gravity in the hills of Washington, but not great for getting over stumps in central B.C. I loved to listen to the motor on that Cat. It ran as smooth and quiet as a sewing machine.

The only time a good skid cat operator runs a cat full throttle is when he's on a good skid trail, in a low gear, pulling a full drag of logs behind him. Charlie had it in high gear and full throttle before he left the landing. His personality was the complete opposite of Nels'. He was always smiling and laughing, a bit on the chunky side, about 5'10" or so, with a round, beaming freckled face.

A lot of the timber on that quarter section was big, heavy limbed spruce scattered out through a fairly thick stand of poplar trees. There was no winch on the cat, so Charlie relied more on speed, dodging in and out through the poplars to pick up a drag. When he left the landing to start picking up a drag of logs, it sounded like a B-29 was coming. You could hear trees crashing down, loud laughter, the clattering of the tracks, roar of the motor, and then a loud bang, followed by complete silence, then hilarious laughter! Charlie had nailed another spruce stump with the cross spring. He skidded a lot of wood, but I don't know how that cat ever held together.

When it came to limbing those scattered, hairy spruce, it didn't take long for my treasured Ox Head axe to show its weakness. The spruce trees were limbs from the bottom to the top. Red had to cut his way into the trunk to even fall them. They were pretty ugly, with tough stringy limbs; you had to chop off every last fibre before a limb would come off. We found if we floundered through the snow along side the tree until we reached the middle, there was a place where the limbs opened up and half pointed toward the butt, and the other half toward the top. Then at least they were pointing away from you, and you could see the base of a limb to cut it off, but it was still hard work.

By the end of the first week, I had managed to accumulate a total of twenty blisters on my hands. That oxhead axe was the wrong tool. Every time you hit one of those tough spruce limbs, the vibration from that light springy axe head would come right up through the handle and into your hands. It was torture. I tried everything I could think of to heal those blisters, but nothing worked. Somehow Nels heard about my predicament, and offered a rather unorthodox solution. It was pretty simple – pee on your hands! It was a lesson he had learned from someone when he was a young kid shoveling wheat on a farm, and ended up with the same problem. Whenever you have to take a leak, he told me, and you can do it, pee on your hands! I was desperate enough by then to try anything. I couldn't afford to quit, or take any time off, and besides, I had to show my cousins I was as tough as they were, so I gave it a shot (so to speak)! Every chance I had, I applied the prescribed solution. Whatever the reason, they started to heal. After a few days, even if I didn't smell too great, the blisters toughened up and turned into calluses, and I was back in business. But I did one other thing that made all the difference. I retired that light, vibrating Ox Head axe into the junk pile, and got me a good, solid, heavy, double bitted Swedish steel axe that really made the spruce limbs fly. We had a good time working with Charlie and Nels, and were offered a job building snake fence after breakup.

Floating The Fraser

March 30, 1962, with breakup in full swing, Ed had a bright idea. He was always the adventurous one in the family, and had heard of the town of McBride, located in a logging and farming area on the Fraser River, east of Prince George. It sounded like an interesting place to do a little exploring, but we didn't take the time to do any research before we left. We just

Clod's cartoon of Bob & Ed

loaded up our Trapper Nelson packboards with grub, along with a little Marlin, break down lever action .22, that I had traded Ed in exchange for his guitar, and we took off. We decided the cheapest way to travel was by railroad boxcar. We sat in the weeds along the track in Vanderhoof until a train stopped that was headed east, found a boxcar, and crawled on. It was a novel way to travel; at least you didn't have to worry about forgetting your ticket! Our major concern was whether we had picked a train that would stop in Prince George, or one that was going straight through to Edmonton. As luck would have it, the train stopped, and we found a brakeman that told us which train was headed east and would stop in McBride. It was "All Aboard", even though we had to wait around quite awhile, and knew it would be in the middle of the night before we got there. But you can't be fussy when you're traveling "free". It was an exciting way to travel, standing in the open door of the boxcar watching the world whiz by; but you could see it would get old pretty fast. You couldn't help but think, as you rumbled along, of the old train wreck and hobo songs by Jimmy Rogers, Hank Williams, and Hank Snow; songs like The Last Ride, Hobo Bill, Waitin' for a Train, and The Wreck of the Old Ninety Seven.

Before it got dark, we were starting to get into some big mountain country, at least a lot bigger than Vanderhoof's Sinkut mountain. It was 1:30 a.m. and fairly cool when we rolled into McBride. You couldn't see a whole lot and we didn't have any idea where we were, so we stumbled down the road for a 1/2 mile or so, towards the west, found a patch of bush, rolled out our sleeping bags, and hit the sack.

We didn't think to bring a simple map of the area. That would have helped, but then again, Alexander MacKenzie didn't have one either. I did keep a diary, so at least we knew where we had been. But in this diary, I have the Rocky Mountains, which are a fairly sizable land mark, on the wrong side of the Fraser River! Its quite easy to see why I never went into exploring in a big way! But to us, this was just a fun trip, and after all, when it comes right down to it, mountain ranges are all pretty much the same.

The original plan when we arrived, was to check out the farming area around McBride. The next morning, after walking across the river on the ice, and talking to an older couple, we decided we would look at a couple of homesteads down the river. That's where the real adventure began to happen. What we didn't know was that the country down river was much different from the main agricultural area east of McBride. After staying in a dilapidated, leaky log shack, where the only dry spot was a platform in the middle, we found a nice log cabin farther down the river, and moved in for a couple of days.

The weather was lousy with rain and wet snow. As we lounged around in the warm cabin, Ed came up with the idea that to make this a real trip to remember, we should make ourselves a dugout canoe from one of the dry cedar snags near the cabin, and follow the ice out to Prince George. That was a typical Jones idea. Ed liked wood working and was good at it, so no sooner said, then started. We had the little axe, and an old double bit we found. Ed found an old buck saw, touched it up with a file we had, and patched up the handle with a piece of cowhide. The search was on for the perfect snag. The next morning we fell an old dry cedar snag, 28 inch in diameter. It was dry as a bone and hard to cut. We fell the old snag on a steep slope above the river, then chopped off a log 16 feet long and sloped both ends from the bottom up to a point at the top, so it would push us up if we got caught in the ice. Ed hollowed it out the full length, except for 2 feet on the ends. We patched the end that had a small rotten spot with some tar, cloth, nails, and brake fluid cans we found in the cabin. Then we nailed, and wired, a birch cross piece at each end, with a small dry cedar log attached to the ends of both birch cross pieces. The whole process took about 3 days and what we ended up with was a stable South Sea island type of canoe, with 2 outriggers. We named the canoe "The Flamer", a derogatory word George Tee used when irritated by something. We launched the Flamer out on the ice, shoved her in to try her out, and to our surprise, she floated like a cork! We would be ready to go after Ed shaped 2 paddles, one out of a fence post and the other out of a slab.

We couldn't have known less about the river, or the adventure we were starting out on. From McBride, the Fraser River winds through a180 mile or so, section of the Rocky Mountain Trench, to Prince George. The Rocky Mountain Trench is a well defined valley, from 2 to 10 miles wide, that runs northwest from the U.S. border in Montana along the west side of the Canadian Rockies, almost to the Yukon, a distance of roughly 900 miles.

The float trip on the river to Prince George would be a never forgotten, and somewhat risky undertaking. We were unaware that this unique stretch of wilderness was a goldmine of B.C. history, settled by a pioneer people of industry, ingenuity, and courage. It was one of the ill-fated routes chosen by some of the famous Overlanders, when they separated at Tete Juane Cache in the late fall of 1862. It was also the main, and most direct, access to the interior of the province from the east, before the railroads and highways were built. It was the hub of lumber production from the big mills we would pass by; mills that for years had cut big, clean, white spruce timber, into the best framing lumber you can buy, making Prince George the "Spruce Capital of the World". It was a very demanding land, a strange combination of small pockets of humming industry in a vast sea of wilderness.

When we were ready to go on April 9 we loaded the Flamer with our packs, extra wire and a grill we had found, as well as an old cowhide we dubbed "Old Filthy" to wrap around our sleeping bags to keep them dry, and launched into the Fraser River. We floated downriver for a mile or so, until we came to solid ice from bank to bank. We noticed a log cabin on a nice flat spot along the rail line side of the river, so we pulled in. The cabin was close to a little rail station called LeGrand, and had been long abandoned, but was still comfortable and dry, even with no doors or windows. We decided to hang out there for a couple of days to see if the ice would go.

By April 11 we were starting to run low on grub, and Ed was out of smokes, so we decided to hoof it back to McBride along the rail line. We saw our first moose then; it was a calf that tried to cross the Fraser on the ice and broke through. She was about 10 feet from the bank across the river and was real tired. Her forequarters, neck, and head were all that stuck up. We watched her for 5 or 10 minutes and she finally made it and crawled out. We had just got on the tracks when along came a work crew on their speeder. Talk about luck! They hauled us on board, a real friendly bunch, mostly Italians. One guy was smoking and Ed asked him if he would sell him a couple; the guy just gave him a few and wouldn't take a penny. They dropped us off just before we got to Lamming Mills as they had some work to do along that section. Lamming Mills was a small sawmill settlement a few miles downriver from McBride.

There were rail stations, small settlements, and sawmill towns, with names like Rider, LeGrand, Goat River, Crescent Spur, Loos, Dome Creek, Penny, Longworth, and Sinclair Mills. The rail line and river were their only connection to the outside world until 1968 when Highway 16 was finally pushed through to Prince George.

In 1943 the Lamming brothers, Oscar, Ernie, and Gordon, came to McBride and bought out a small local sawmill. A much larger, modern sawmill and planer were later built along the rail line a few miles from town. This was Lamming Mills, which eventually became a bustling community of mostly Seventh-day Adventist Christians, working in the bush, sawmill and planer, as well as the dairy farm which supplied the area with fresh pasteurized milk. Oscar, the eldest brother, ran the bush crew and helped with the sawmill and planer operation. At that time they were putting out 50 to 60 thousand board feet of finished framing lumber per shift. Ernie, next in line, ran the farm as well as helping out at the mill. Gordon, the youngest, was involved in the mill office and had a few projects of his own on the side.

When my cousin Ed, and I wandered into the Lamming Mills store that day, after leaving the rail crew, we were in for a surprise! Ed was a pretty heavy puffer and had polished off the smokes his Italian friend had given him, so was pretty wound up to get his hands on a can of Old Chum and roll-yer-own papers. When the tall, pleasant, white haired lady behind the counter told him, in a nice way, that they "didn't sell tobacco in their store", it set him back on his heels! He managed to make it the few miles into McBride without a nicotine breakdown, but we ran most of the way!

When Ed and I came back through Lamming Mills on our return to camp, we noticed a fairly large building with a sign, Oscar's Museum. Well! This looked interesting, so we knocked on the door. A middle-aged, averaged sized, thin faced man with greying hair opened the door. We introduced ourselves and asked if we could look around. He was more than willing and ushered us in with a friendly smile. This was Oscar Lamming, who along with running the logging and sawmill operation, also had a trap line, and kept snowfall records for the B.C. government. The number of interesting objects, tools, hides, and full life sized animal mounts he had put together in his museum, out in the middle of nowhere, was amazing. I had always been fascinated with taxidermy so was extremely interested. Oscar had taken a correspondence course in this demanding art, and his work was very well done. As he showed us through his museum, he fairly radiated enthusiasm and enjoyment for what he was doing. The animal that impressed us the most was a full life size mount of a huge grey, Northern Timber wolf. We had never, to that point, seen one and couldn't believe its size, especially the head.

After we thanked him for the tour, and headed down the tracks for camp, I noticed we would catch each other nervously checking back over our shoulders, as evening began to come on. It was most likely a good thing a coyote didn't howl about then, or we might have whistled back and spent the night in the McBride Hotel!

The ice had gone off the river by April 14 so we loaded our bedrolls and grub in the middle, wrapped Old Filthy around them, stood our packboards up, shoved out into the current, and began to drift. Downstream we hit a few small rapids and the Flamer took them in stride. We would get up around 5:00 every morning and this morning was no exception, with a beautiful sunrise, clear as a bell, but a little breezy. The mountain ranges were still covered with snow, and when the sun came up they shone with a beautiful pink glow. The Canadian geese and all kinds of ducks were coming up the river; Mallards, Widgeons, Teal, and Pintails by the hundreds. Spring was on its way!

We drifted past the railway station at Rider about 3:30 that afternoon, and downstream we saw a log house setting back from a bend in the river. We decided we would stop and see if they had a barn or shed we could stay in overnight, so we beached the Flamer and walked up to the house. When Ed knocked, we fully expected some dirty, grizzled, old trapper with a foot long beard to open the door. Instead, a cute little blonde haired, blue eyed girl and her tall, thin, work worn Mother answered our knock and asked if she could help us! Ed finally managed to get his tongue untied and explained our float trip adventure and asked if they had a shed or barn where we could spend the night. We had landed at the home of Mr. & Mrs. Bill Oliver and they were more excited about what we were doing than we were. Mrs. Oliver insisted we come right in, get warmed up, have tea and a bite to eat, and they would fix us up with a place to stay. She fussed over us like an old mother hen. They were extremely good to us and insisted we stay with them for a day or two, and let them show us around.

"Wild Bill" Oliver was a short, bald headed little Irishman with a black patch over one eye. He was a real spark plug with more energy than three ordinary people. His wife was a foot taller than him, but a wonderful, kind hearted, hard working, woman. She had made a very warm, comfortable home for the family in their log house beside the Fraser. I'm guessing they were in their mid to late forties at that time, but it was difficult to tell, pioneering can be a hard life. They had done an incredible amount of work on their place in the 2 years they had been there. There were three kids at home, one boy and two girls. The son, Bob, was about 14, and worked with his Dad like a grown man. They logged, sold cedar poles, and split shakes for a living. The next day they took us on a tour of a few old farm steads across the river, and showed how their pole and shake operation worked.

When we left on April 16, at 7:30 in the morning, Mrs. Oliver insisted on packing a full lunch for us to take along. When we pushed out into the river she took a picture of us in our canoe, and a few weeks later sent it to us in Vanderhoof, the only picture we have of that whole adventure.

Ed & Bob in the Flamer

We soon ran a couple of pretty fair rapids. The river at that time of year was low because spring runoff was just beginning. The Flamer was very stable, with the help of the outriggers, but not as manoeuvrable as a regular canoe. Because of this, and the water being low, we managed to hang one outrigger up on a rock as we went through one stretch of rapids. This threw us sideways to the current, which is not where you want to be. It was a bit dicey for a couple of minutes before we pried ourselves off, but that taught us to keep our eyes open.

The Olivers' had warned us about a place down the river called the Grand Canyon, where there was a bad spot, but we drifted all day and never saw anything to worry about. What we did start to see, when the river ran along the rail line, was dead moose. Later on, we were to learn that during the winter of 1961/62 there were 124 moose killed by the train between McBride and Prince George. During a deep snow winter this was very common. The moose would stumble onto the tracks and couldn't get back over the snowbank when the train came by. Once, as we quietly drifted along, we came around a bend in the river, and there was a big bull moose browsing on Saskatoon brush right along the bank. We very slowly drifted right up beside him, until we were just a few feet away, then quietly said, "Well! Hello there!" The moose jerked his head up, his eyes bugged out in total disbelief, and then took off in high gear with his peculiar high stepping gait. Looking back that was not the smartest thing to do!

———

On the evening of Wednesday, April 18, around 5:00, we came around a bend in the river, and there on the right was an unbelievable sight. A beautiful white stucco house! We couldn't believe our eyes! It was time to find a place to bunk for the night, so "nothing tried, nothing gained", we pulled in, tied up, and walked up to the house. It had not been our plan to stop at a homestead every night and ask for a barn or shed to throw our sleeping bags down, and we only did so at the Olivers' and now this place. Our appearance had not improved as the days went by, so it was a wonder anyone even came to the door. This time it was my turn to ask. Mrs. Elizabeth Winters, the attractive, dark haired lady who came to the door was very pleasant, and when I explained our float trip, she said we could bunk in the barn. There were four kids in the family, and they soon gathered around to check us out! The two boys, Jim, and Murray, or Moe as he was called, were a big help in showing us where to put our packs and bedrolls. Mrs. Winters had invited us in for supper as soon as we had our stuff stored in the barn for the night. It was pretty tough for Ed to compete with the meal she put on, although he was a good camp cook. We had been taken in again, just like at the Oliver home, and made to feel like family.

The next morning I got up when Jim and Moe came out to the barn to do the chores. While Jim milked the cow, I told Moe to roll Ed out of the sack, and he went right after him, pestering him until he got up. Jim, like Bob Oliver, seemed very grown up for a 13 year old kid. Moe was quite a bit younger and a real character. After chores and breakfast, Mrs. Winters had us in for coffee and gave us a tour of their very unique home. I say unique, because during the early years, most everything was built with logs. This two story, white stucco house, with the dormer in the roof, and arched porches extending out from the house, was built with lumber. It was built by Elizabeth Winters' parents, James Burton Hooker and his wife Adeline, who came from Minot, North Dakota, during the construction of the Grand Trunk Pacific Railroad. They were among the first settlers, reaching the end of the steel at Dome Creek in the early fall of 1913, with two loaded box cars, containing all the equipment and livestock needed to start a homestead. Jim Hooker must have been quite a guy. He was a railroad engineer when he arrived, but like most early settlers, did a lot of trapping to make a dollar. Over a period of years he developed a very successful hunting, guiding, and packing business in the Torpey River area that lay to the north west of Dome Creek.

The most impressive part of the house was Jim Hooker's den. The show-piece of the room, built into the east corner, was a beautiful curved fireplace made from round river stone. Mounted on each side was a full size Northern Timber wolf head, one black, the other grey. Jim and Adeline had hand picked all the stone from the river for the fireplace, and I'm sure the wolves came from his hunting trips.

Before we left that morning, April 19th, we walked across the railroad bridge and got a few supplies from the Dome Creek store. The store keeper told us that a few years back a bull moose with a monstrous set of horns broke through, and froze in the ice, with only his head sticking out. As the ice moved out in the spring the moose head went right with it! He also said we should be able to navigate the Canyon all right, but to be careful. Mrs.

Winters also warned us about the Grand Canyon, a twisting, rocky stretch of the Fraser River, with a series of rapids and whirlpools, that lay about 20 miles downstream. There was a reason for her concern; her youngest brother Ed had drowned there during a log drive a few years before. We were the first to come down the Fraser that spring. Everyone we met seemed to get a kick out of our big adventure.

————

Back on the river in the Flamer, we figured it had come up another 6 inches since the day before, and still had a lot of little ice bergs in it. The weather was warm, but cloudy, and a little breezy. We saw lots of ducks again but not close enough to get one. Right after our noon camp it got real windy and the water so rough we had to pull in. It started to rain hard so decided to camp in an old homestead we spied nearby, and dry out as even Old Filthy was damp! While Ed was cooking supper I shot a grouse, so we had some fresh meat. It got foggy that night so we hoped that meant an end to the rain.

In the morning it started to drizzle rain and the river was still rising. We got up early hoping the "April Showers" would be over. About 10:30 we floated past Penny so knew we were about halfway to Prince George. We had been told that the Canyon is supposed to be several miles below Penny, but no sign of it so far. We pulled in to shore and Ed decided to get out and walk to check things out and would meet me around the bend coming up. Ed found an old cabin back in the bush so we decided to pull in and hole up for the night. It was about 3:30 in the afternoon and the weather was lousy. When we came over to McBride in the boxcar, about 2 hours out of Prince George, we had looked out of the door and saw our first big mountain range. We realized that we were now camped at the base of it, but on the other side of the river. We later learned they were the Goat mountains.

It had rained most of the night and in the morning snowed a real sloppy, wet, spring snow. We decided to stay put and wait out the weather. About the only place that it didn't rain inside the cabin, as hard as it did outside, was about 6 feet square where our bedrolls were. We moved across the river and down a mile or so to a better cabin. There were 7 or 8 cabins there that had been a logging camp back in 1947. Everything was pretty busted up but much dryer. We discovered a big canvas laundry bag, with the name

O. J. Prather, in one of the old logging cabins. Ed thought it might make a good sail if we should need one. So we ripped out the seams on three sides, rigged up a sail pole, and installed it on the Flamer. The weather started to clear up in the evening and we made plans to pull out in the morning.

————

On the morning of April 22, by some strange fluke, we had a strong down river wind and our new sail just pushed us along. We made really good time but around noon the wind fizzled out and we took down the sail. We had just passed two big log cold decks when we could hear a real loud roar from around the bend in the river, and started to pick up speed. We realized that we were right at the head of the Grand Canyon of the upper Fraser. You could see at a glance that it would be wise to temper your bravery with a little caution. A lot of people didn't over the years and its estimated that over 200 had drowned in wrecks.

The river came around in a fairly long, sweeping bend, suddenly dropped over a ledge, then turned and roared off down through a narrow, steep sided, rock walled canyon. Our first instinct was self-preservation. We decided to pull in and lead the Flamer with 2 lines, in the current, until it reached a little back eddy, then climbed in and took off like a big bird. It was quite a thrill! The power of the current was incredible. It came up in big rolling heaves that boiled up from the bottom, and spun and threw you wherever. All you can do is keep her nose pointed downstream, and it was as rough as a cob!

There were three guys going up the rapids in a 25 foot river boat with a 35 h.p. motor, open to the max, yet hardly moving against the current. They told us that we were already through the worst, but couldn't believe the contraption we were traveling in! They said they would check on us on their way back, and took off. According to them the whirlpool ahead doesn't amount to much. Ed said we should call our expedition the "Loose and Cluck" rather than the "Lewis and Clark". Old Filthy has been worth her weight in gold as she keeps our bedrolls dry. Its been a long day and we're both so tired we can't even argue with each other. We noticed a cabin across the river where we decided to stay that night as it was starting to rain again.

We broke camp about 9:30 in the morning on April 23, jammed our gear in the Flamer with Old Filthy tucked tight around our bedrolls, jumped in, grabbed our paddles, and away we went. The Canyon, consists of the upper rapids, which we went through the previous day, a fairly placid, flat stretch where the cabin was, and then suddenly kicks into high gear into the lower rapids. This is where the river could open up from one bank to the other in a giant sucking whirlpool! Fortunately for us the water was low so the whirlpool wasn't active. We ran the lower rapids with all our gear in the Flamer; she shipped a little water, but made it through in good shape. Once we got into smooth water, we pulled in, bailed the water, and built a fire to dry out. But the fun wasn't over yet, Mother nature still had a couple of tricks up her sleeve.

After the Grand Canyon we had quite a few miles of good floating. When we got past where the McGregor River came in from the northeast, and down towards the Giscome rapids, where the Fraser begins its bend to the south, the country begins to change. Leaving the more scenic ranges of the Rockies to the right and the Cariboos to the left, it started to open up into the interior plateau.

When we crawled into the canoe in the morning of April 24, a stiff, ice cold wind was blowing right in our faces. Now cold is cold, but 30 degrees, or minus 40, can be downright balmy if you're dressed right, and there's no wind. But when you are paddling into a strong, cold head wind, it can chill you right through in a hurry.

After paddling for most of the morning, and not gaining a lot, we pulled into a logging camp that had been abandoned for break-up. As we wandered through the bunk houses trying to warm up, there on the wall of one bunk-house hung a mirror, and when we looked into it, what a sight! I knew that Ed looked bad, and I figured I looked bad, but I didn't realize I looked that bad! Month long beards, wind and sun burned faces which were the colour of well smoked beef jerky, skin peeling off the tops of our ears, and to top it off, a very bad case of B.O. We had a good rip-roaring laugh over the whole thing. At least it helped warm us up a little. Now I realized why some of those old trappers didn't look too sanitary when spring finally rolled around!

———

We continued on down the river because we hoped to get to Prince George the next day, and maybe even make it home to Vanderhoof, but it was miserable. How good a zip up, Pioneer Windbreaker would have felt out on that river. In the middle of the afternoon, far off to the west, we could see a thin, dark line of cloud. We were wondering what was up, when suddenly the wind switched and started blowing down the river! We dropped our paddles, threw up the sail, and in no time were plowing water like a jet boat! It was wild! We had to hang onto the sail pole to keep the whole thing from blowing away. We were right out of control! The Flamer wasn't meant for water skiing, and right then this sail idea didn't seem quite so bright.

Up to that point, it had been pretty slow, but now looked like we were going to end up in downtown Prince George in about 5 minutes! Then the wind suddenly switched and hit us from the side, and I thought for sure we were going for a swim. The wind practically ripped the sail right off, and almost flipped the canoe. One pontoon went clear under and the canoe tried to stand up on its side. We jumped up and managed to tear the sail down, then paddled for all we were worth toward the shore.

We managed to get the Flamer tied up in shallow water, and just got into the trees when the wind hit like a sledge hammer. It was mostly spruce and cedar in that area and they broke off, or were blown over by the hundreds. It looked like a giant mowing machine was knocking them down.

I would have to say this whole trip was introducing a little different spin on life to me; it made me realize how the people who lived, worked, and raised their families in a place like this had to keep on guard. Life out here wasn't a stroll in the park! It was a great life, and a great part of the country to live in, but there were these subtle little things you had to keep in mind until it became second nature to you, if you wanted to stay out of trouble. Watch for logs and dead heads when you were on the water, wind falls and hung up trees, and widow makers in the bush, a sharp dry limb that could poke out an eye, or puncture an ear drum, a sudden slip and fall that could break an arm or leg.

By a stroke of good fortune we had landed close to a plywood cabin that seemed to be a hunter's shack, as there was a moose hide from the previous fall, just outside the door. We had gotten into a habit of naming our camps so called this one Stink Camp, as the moose hide was smelling things up pretty bad.

When we hit the river again the next morning, April 25th, the paddling was good for a couple of hours, and then a headwind came up. But it wasn't long before the current picked up and we were into the Giscome Rapids. The rapids were straight forward fast water, with enough rocks sticking through to make them exciting. Ed always took the bow and I was the stern man. I liked that because if we piled up I could always blame him! We made this run with a full load, and ended up with six inches or so of water in the canoe, so had to stop and bail. We saw a steady run of moose through this section, so many in fact, that once it looked like a herd of beef cows browsing along the river. We also saw a lot of native people in river boats headed up the river. One guy hit a dead head when he was just opposite us. He hit it pretty hard, and it killed his motor, but he started it up again and took off. We were starting to get pretty antsy by now, to finish our trip and get home.

At 4 p.m., April 26, 1962, we paddled into Prince George. The Nechako River hits the Fraser to the west of where we came in, so it was a long haul of hard paddling across the current. When we pulled up on the bank of the Fraser just above the Hwy 16 bridge, a guy at a trailer court by the river said he would keep an eye on the Flamer for us. We hoofed it down the tracks to see if we could catch a "side-door Pullman", (hobo name for a freight car). We loafed around the freight yards for a half hour or so until we heard from a brakeman that the next train west didn't leave until 5 or 6 the next morning. We went up to the highway and found a telephone, called the Greyhound, and found there was a bus leaving for Vanderhoof in 5 minutes. We took off running as hard as we could right up the streets of Prince George. People looked at us a bit funny, but then again Prince George was a frontier town. A guy hollered at us, "where you going", we hollered back, "the bus depot". He said he would drive us up. He squealed around corners, drove through yellow lights, then came to a screeching halt at the bus depot. Just made it; then arrived back in Vanderhoof at 7:30 p.m.

A few days later we drove over to Prince George with an International one ton that Red had recently bought, to pick up the Flamer and our gear. The Flamer ended its days being used as a feed trough. An inglorious end for a canoe that brought us through our "epic" journey.

Gentlemen Prefer Blondes

Red had made arrangements with Nels Cruthers for all of us to work for Nels that spring. As soon as it dried up enough, we started to build a rail fence on the east side of his McGeachy place on the Sinkut Lake Road. Rail fences were a big deal then, because people thought it gave a place the "Ranch" look. It did, but it was a ton of work, and the first bull that got an itchy shoulder could tip over the kind we built. Another problem was that if you used rails that were too long, and didn't have a support in the middle, they eventually developed a bad sag. There was a lot of big poplar on Nels place, so that's what we used instead of pine or spruce.

Before we finished it, Red had to get back to his farm, and the other boys found jobs around the country. Nels asked me if I would be interested in working on his ranch for the summer, and I took him up on it. The deal was six days a week, 10 hours a day, for $200.00 a month. I would get Saturdays off, and could stay in the log house on the ranch to keep an eye on things, and he would supply the grub.

He probably wondered why I snapped up the deal before he finished offering it, but he wasn't aware of my former job with "Racetrack" Bill Wineberg, at Nulki Lake the summer before. Now, with this deal, not only had I doubled my wages, I also actually had a day off. But I had an even more ulterior motive in mind. I had been giving a lot of very serious thought to this homesteading, root picking, wife thing, and it had dawned on me that the cute little blonde haired girl with the "pensive" look I had seen at the Sinkut Lake Community Hall was his niece! If I worked hard, and made a good impression, word could eventually get around, and I might even get to meet her. Now, for a country boy, that was some real long distance thinking. But I have to admit I had some concerns. The biggest was that she didn't look like a root picker, but I figured there's always room to learn. Well, the whole scheme went off without a hitch. I'm sure Nels wondered who I was trying to impress when he came to the farm in the morning, and I already had a half day's work done. I do believe though, that he quickly realized he had made a serious mistake when he said he would supply my grub.

But I did earn my keep. The meadow on the place was a real bog hole when he bought it. The first summer he had managed to get a ditch of sorts pushed in around the inside edge of the high half circle shaped knob where the house sat. They had hayed some of the slough grass on the outside edges that first year, to help things dry up. He had picked up the hay with an Oliver 88 tractor, with a high lift, Farm Hand loader, and dumped it in a big rectangular log feed bunk with 10 inch spacing between the logs. The plan was to put a roof of some kind over it, pick up a few head of bred cows, and feed it out by poking the feed through the space between the logs.

Well, somehow the roof never got put on, and once it gets rained on once, it gets rained on twice, and finally there is more pressing things to be done. The top logs on this ingenious feed bunk were probably 12 feet or so from the ground, and they had filled it right to the top. A years worth of rain, plus the winter snow, had packed what had once been fairly good slough grass hay down to about 6 feet of something having the consistency of cow manure. The first foot wasn't bad, as I scooped it out. In fact, the brown tinged grass I poked out through the cracks had kind of a pleasant, roasted tobacco smell. But thats where it ended. As the day wore on, my apprenticeship as a B.C. ranch hand got worse, the sun got hotter, and the higher the pile got along the outsides, the deeper I went in on the inside. And the deeper I went, the worse the smell. They had left the HD-7 parked back in the shade, and the plan was for Charlie to shove the stuff away once it reached a certain height, so you didn't have to lift it much over waist high to poke it through the cracks. It didn't work out that way. Finally, it got to the point where I was having to lift this slop over shoulder high, and when you turned the fork over, it dumped it down your neck. By this time, it had reached about 120 degrees inside this airless hole, and I wasn't thinking too much about word getting out to the little blonde about what a great worker they had found. I was working hard, and not getting anything done. When it finally came to ground zero, where the stuff outside wouldn't let me shove anymore out from the inside, something had to give. So, I crawled out, fired up the cat, and started moving rotten hay. Charlie wasn't long in arriving and taking over as cat operator. It wasn't hard to see he had spent a lot more time on the seat of a machine than on the end of a pick and shovel, which was no doubt a sign of intelligence on his part. We got along pretty good most of the time, and I loved living and working on that ranch. The next project, before haying, was building a set of corrals.

Like most of us, Nels was chasing his dream. He had made a deal with the Forestry to get corral rails off a nice clean stand of Jackpine, about half way between the east end of Sinkut Lake and the junction of the Mapes/ Blackwater Road. He had bought an old white skid horse from somebody out in the Chilco district, a few miles northeast of Vanderhoof, and set things up to keep him out on the job.

I can't really remember now who did what in the logging operation, but I'm sure Charlie did the falling, and Nels the skidding. The horse didn't have a comfortable seat, hydraulics, or a gear shift, so that would have automatically disqualified it for Charlie! I seem to recall that I did the landing work. One interesting thing we saw in that nice clean stand of pine was a marten, a medium brown pine squirrel hunter, about the size of a big tomcat. He was a real acrobat when it came to chasing squirrels, and we saw him 2 or 3 times.

One thing we didn't see one morning was our skid horse. Nothing but a set of tire tracks where the horse tracks ended. Eventually we found out that somebody hadn't paid somebody back down the line in Chilco, so the former owner found out where the horse was at, and came out and hauled him off. Nels and Charlie had a Bill of Sale, and finally got him back, but it messed up our corral project for awhile.

The day the horse went missing, we were looking for tracks along the road when a teenage girl came by riding bareback on a big bay mare. She was headed for the annual Mapes Community picnic at the east end of Sinkut Lake. Nels asked her if she had seen anyone around the area and she politely said no, and rode on. As she rode off, I realized she was Joan Snyder, the same girl with the nice smile and dark auburn hair, that was dancing up a storm at the Lakes District Community Hall the winter before. I thought she had a pretty impressive mop of hair all right, and a very straight forward, direct look and way of answering questions, but there was the old saying "Gentlemen prefer blondes"!

By the time we got the corrals up, I was getting pretty well settled into the harness on the job, and Charlie had got to the point where he could at least tolerate me. It must have been somewhere around the first of June, because the leaves were out good, when they had a Sunday family dinner at the home of Albert and Bernie Filan, and invited me to come. Well, this was the chance I had been waiting for. Albert and Bernie were the little blonde's Mom and Dad! Ah! So Charlie and Nels must have been giving at least a few positive reports on the new ranch hand.

I managed to make myself presentable in a blue cowboy shirt and a pair of fairly clean Levis, but I had one problem. I had started to grow a debonair Clark Gable style mustache, and instead of coming in a striking dark brown or black, it looked a lot more like peach fuzz! Well, I didn't have any black shoe polish, so I lit up a couple of big wooden matches and let them burn for a bit, and then dipped the head in a cup of water. When I applied the nice black charcoal to the peach fuzz, I was even surprised at how good I looked. It must have been close to a 3 mile walk over to Filans' and I covered it in record time. I slowed down quite a bit the last mile or so because I didn't want to arrive all steamed up.

The get-together was a lot of fun. They all attended the Pentecostal Church in town and they made me feel welcome. I could see Ginger, the little blonde, and her mother were pretty nervous, because there was a lot of laughing and giggling, and looking my way. I made a couple of trips to the bathroom to make sure they weren't laughing at my mustache paint job dripping off my chin, but it held up surprisingly well. After dinner, I managed to meet Ginger and arrange to come over and listen to some Elvis Presley Gospel songs she had.

I was on Cloud Nine when I walked home that night, at least she hadn't ignored me. But then again, with a mustache like that, how could she? It wasn't long before it became a regular thing. Just friends at first, then invited to church, then finally there was no ignoring it! She finally had to tell me to get lost, or give the bad news to Toby Millard, the real, genuine Rodeo Star. Finally, I got the word – she had dropped the Rodeo cowboy! I couldn't believe it! I could only come to one conclusion: she couldn't resist that mustache! I was flying pretty high. I even thought of asking what size gloves she wore, and if she had ever done any root picking.

Albert & Bernie Filan and their daughter Ginger

Things were looking up. What I needed now was a set of wheels. There was a guy in town, Bud Lewis, a typical small town car dealer, who stocked used cars that had been recycled about six times. This put them in a price range that I could afford. I found a slightly used, medium blue 1956 Chev, two door sedan, hid away in a back corner. It had 3 unique features. First, I could afford it. Second, the door on the driver's side was a light, yellow green, so it was easy to identify if someone were to steal it. And the third feature, when you stepped on the gas, the front seat, not bolted down, tipped you and the seat on its back, and gave you the impression that it had more power than it did. I grabbed it on the spot.

In no time at all everybody in the country knew I had bought a car. The seat took a little getting used to, especially at the first few stop signs, but it discouraged your buddies from wanting to borrow it.

The high point of the summer, and my romance with Ginger, was when they celebrated the 4th of July with a big family picnic. Everybody was there, her family, Nels and Midge with their kids, and Charlie and his wife and little one. This was an All-American holiday, even though I was in the process of becoming a Canadian, I loved the 4th of July! It was a hot, lazy day, and after the picnic, while everyone else was visiting, Ginger and I went back to her place and washed my car. Needless to say, it was a pretty lame excuse, (it would have taken a lot more than a wash job to improve the looks of that car), but it gave us a chance to spend some time alone. It was fun, we did get the car washed, but spent most of the time spraying each other with the hose, and having a few hugs and a kiss or two (maybe three)! She liked the name Ginger, which was short for Virginia, because she felt it added a little "spice" to the name, and who was I to argue? But there was a problem. The difference in religion was very real, with all of her family being dyed-in-the-wool Pentecostals.

In the area the Filan family came from, Walla Walla, Washington, there was a Seventh-day Adventist behind every fence post. The college at Walla Walla, churches, schools, and businesses, the big Harris Pine mill just across the border in Pendleton, Oregon, farms and orchards, there were Adventists everywhere. Ginger's family had spent a lifetime around Seventh-day Adventists, and they weren't too keen on their youngest daughter marrying one! Later that summer, I did finally cave in and buy a cheap, blue spray can, and painted the door after my new sweetheart flatly refused to ride in the car, but she thought the seat thing was pretty cool, like going for a ride at the circus. I was progressing by leaps and bounds, and really on a roll, by the time haying season came around.

Sometime during that fall of 1962 the Lakes District community had a hayride for the young people. A perfect opportunity to take my blonde girl friend and maybe do a little snuggling in the hay!!! That hayride was a first for many of the young people to start the dating process that would end in long term marriages. Ed Jones and his new friend Carol Martin, Dick Jones on his first date with Pam Brown, Carma Jones on her first date with the cowboy, Toby Millard. In the confusion of activity in the dark, I even found myself mistakenly holding hands with Joan Snyder, the girl I had seen on the horse a few months back. I had to admit she had a very nice hand to hold, but for now I was totally in love with my little blonde.

———————

Right from the start, the hay meadows of the central interior fascinated me. It just looked so natural the way they were laying there with the dark green of the forest surrounding them. It also looked so easy, just put in a little ditch, sharpen up the old mower, and start knocking 'er down. If you ever talk to anyone who developed a meadow, you will find it wasn't quite so simple. Any kind of raw land clearing was brutal, hard work, especially in the old days. The wide bladed, sharp edged, native slough grass that grew in the boggy wet parts of a meadow was not top quality hay, but it would get an animal through the winter in surprisingly good shape. However, the tall, fine stemmed leafy grasses like Red Top and Blue Joint, that came in after a meadow was drained, would put weight on a cow. Some meadows were a lot easier than others to develop. A lot depended on how they were shaped, and how the water came in.

The MGeachy Meadow was fairly straight forward, and though it was postage stamp size compared to the huge meadows of the Chilcotin country, it became a good grass hay meadow. Nels knew something about hay. Custom haying had been his business. He told me that when you finished baling a field for a client, there had better not be a spear of grass or flake of alfalfa left on the field. That's how fussy they were. There it was baled alfalfa, here it was loose slough grass. All loose hay operations need a stack man. That's the poor idiot that has to spread the big wads of hay around with his trusty 3 tine pitchfork and get it all tromped down and form the stack before they dump the next load on him. It is one hot, heavy, sweat generating job, but there is an art to it, and a certain feeling of satisfaction when it's done right.

Bob stacking loose hay on the McGeachy Meadow

It was poetry in motion to watch Nels sweep up hay with that tractor and loader. They were like one machine, smooth as glass. The loader had a wide set of several tapered wooden teeth on the front, and a hydraulic push off frame that dumped the hay on the stack. Nels would head down the windrow, setting tall and straight in the seat, sweeping back and forth with those beautiful clear fir teeth until he had built up a nice even load, and then head for the stack. Charlie was mowing, raking, or doing some other job that required being in a setting position, and I was the stack man. Well, the first 3 or 4 feet of the stack went up fairly good, but you must remember that stacking rip-gut slough grass is not the same as stacking loose Alfalfa, or even native Red Top and Blue Joint. It would fit more in the category of stacking greased eels. The more you tried to keep it spread around and stomped down with the sides nice and straight, the more it bulged out, and the more you stomped, the more it fell apart. No one seemed too anxious to take my job away, and we finally finished, but the stacks weren't anything to brag about.

I pushed my luck a little too far one day. It was a nice dry morning, which wasn't really common, especially since it's usually into the middle of August when you're putting up swamp hay. I had been watching Nels as he smoothly swept up those windrows with that farm hand loader, and it looked pretty simple. So, I decided I would just fire that Oliver up and make a few sweeps before he got there, and get things on the move. What better way to impress him, and maybe strengthen my position with a good report to Ginger, or even more, her parents, who I was getting the feeling were not as taken with me as she was.

The first couple of sweeps went pretty good as I took it slow and easy, and just idled along and took my time. Then I started to build a little confidence and get the feeling that this was easier than it looked, so I cracked the throttle and kicked it up a gear. Within two minutes I snapped off three of those clear fir teeth! Oh boy! Now I was in big trouble. When Nels showed up, things really hit the fan! That was the only time I ever saw him really mad. He was normally the patient, long suffering kind, but after that incident, I stayed at the other end of the stack until he had cooled down. But the view and feeling from the seat of that Oliver 88 had been pretty exciting, and I was determined to someday have a tractor, and a ranch of my own.

Well, for the first few months, religion took a back seat to romance, and even though I let my Clark Gable Mustache fade into oblivion (no one even noticed), I could still dazzle her with my Elvis singing. But sadly, even that began to lose its appeal under the hard glare of reality. I was pretty set in my ways, and with the pressure from her Mom and Dad mounting, so was she. But love doesn't die easy, and I still had my plan.

A House of Cards

When winter set in for real in early December 1962, we got back into logging. By this time, I had learned which end of a power saw to pick up without cutting my finger, so Nels agreed to hire me to do the falling. I bought myself a brand new Pioneer 620 power saw with a 24" bar and chain from Rich's Saw Sales in Vanderhoof, and began my 25 year career as a timber faller, following in the footsteps of my Dad. Nels was still logging the quarter section of land that cornered on Highway 16 just a few miles east of town, and about a mile north of his ranch. It was real handy for me because it was only 5 minutes from where I was living in his log house. By this time, he realized that supplying my grub, even if he only paid me $200.00 a month, was definitely a losing proposition, so he put me on falling and bucking by contract, and I had to buy my own groceries. But he paid good, and we got started.

I had never made so much money in my life. But I worked like a wild man. I didn't walk from tree to tree, I ran! It was a nightmare of a place to learn how to fall. Like most of the good agriculture land in the valley, it was covered at that time in big poplars with stands of spruce and scattered jackpine mixed in with the poplar. The logging method then was to top skid the tree; you limbed and topped it right where it fell. A few years later, you just dumped them, and they butt skidded the whole tree to the landing where they limbed it with a rake skidder or flail limber.

The big problem with falling among the poplars was "hang ups." A lot of the spruce and pine weren't heavy enough to break their way through the poplars, so if you missed the hole you were shooting for, the tree would hang up in those poplars. What made this really exciting was when you fell another tree into the first one to knock it down, and it also hung up. By the time you had done this 5, or 6 times, the whole mess strongly resembled a native tepee, and you now had the opportunity to really test your courage. The real trick then was to creep in under this jackpot you had created, and fall the "trigger tree" (how I hated that word "trigger"), and be out of there before the whole works came crashing down around your ears! This operation could be a bit hazardous, but one thing it did was keep your arteries cleaned out with the big shots of adrenalin that surged through your veins! I got pretty good at falling these "tepees". The first month I put on endless extra miles because of these "hang ups", and "tepees", but gradually things improved.

My cousin, Dwayne Jones, also worked for Nels that winter, limbing trees and working on the landing. We stayed together in the old log ranch house where I had lived all summer. We got into a regular routine of making a huge moose meat stew on Sunday. It was made from big chunks of moose meat, we chopped off of a frozen portion of moose, that we had hanging on the back porch. First, we thawed them out, rolled them in flour and browned them good in a frying pan. We then chopped up big piles of potatoes, swede turnips, carrots, parsnips, onions and whatever else was laying around and set it to boil on top of the stove. It was good, but even better by the end of the week! After its nightly unthawing, (it went down to below zero on a daily basis in the ranch house), and heating up again, it was perfect. It no longer looked like something most people would eat, but that's when it tasted the best.

There was a 45 gallon barrel stove in the ranch house and even if it was thirty below it didn't take long to warm things up. But one morning we had a bad scare. We used a little can of white gas on the porch for the gas lamp, and a can of diesel fuel for getting the barrel stove going in the morning. Somehow, they got mixed up and one morning when it was Dwayne's turn to get the fire going he picked up the wrong can. There were still a few hot coals left in the stove and when the white gas hit those hot coals there was just one big KABOOM! A ball of fire came out of the end of the stove just like a cannon had gone off. Dwayne was never blessed with much hair at the best of times but he lost it all that morning!

Somehow, we managed to get the fire out without burning the house down, but he was a sad looking sight! Dwayne was a nice guy to be around. As mentioned earlier, he was a quiet guy, and a deep thinker. He was interested in studying the Bible and a lot of nights we would sit around and study together. Many years later he became a Christian and serves as a Deacon in the Vanderhoof Seventh-day Adventist Church. Fortunately, they have a natural gas heating system so he doesn't have to worry about lighting the fire!

———

Things were going pretty good when my house of cards began to fall apart. On the job, we had just finished lunch around the fire, where we all gathered at noon to shoot the breeze and warm up. There were a few, 20 to 30 foot tall spruce trees, along the edge of the landing that needed to be knocked over. That's where I headed, half dozy from the fire and lunch. I fell one tree, and hung it up in another one about the same height. That's when I made my mistake. Looking back, it was probably the best lesson I ever learned about working in the bush. The limbs on these trees were about the size of those on a big Christmas tree, and when I stepped in and started to fall the standing tree, the tree that was hung up came down. It happened so fast, and hit so hard, that for a few seconds I didn't even know what had happened. One minute I was falling the tree, the next I was standing there with the saw knocked out of my hand and looking at a tree top laying where the saw had been. The top of the tree that nailed me was only about 4 inches through, but it had fell from close to 30 feet up. It didn't do a lot of physical damage, only breaking the bone in my left hand, about an inch behind the knuckle on the first finger. I was wearing a heavy pair of mitts so that helped. I felt more embarrassed than hurt. But I was out of the falling business for a while! It never hurt that bad at the time, just kind of a dull ache, but I couldn't use it.

They ran me into the hospital, and Doc Mooney looked at it, then looked at me, shook his head, and put on a good solid cast that left the bottom half of my fingers and thumb sticking out. Everybody was very sympathetic, and went out of their way to be helpful, but I really felt dumb. One minute of pure carelessness had put me in an awkward spot.

My golden haired girlfriend was shocked and dismayed that this had happened, but I quickly assured her I could still drive my trusty blue Chev. The first week wasn't bad, as it was still pretty sore and I couldn't really use it. The second week, I began to get cabin fever, and it started to feel better. By the third week, I was ready to go back to work.

Nels had hired Ken Smithers, one of the local hockey heroes to come out and do the falling, so I dropped down to see how things were going. Ken was a tall, craggy faced, middle aged man that had grown up in Vanderhoof, and played defense for the Vanderhoof Bears. He was a rangy, reserved, hardworking family man who was one of my favourite hockey players. As I hung around the landing, helping out where I could (mainly getting in everyone's way), I strolled over to look at where my little mishap occurred. Someone had finished falling the tree I was working on when the other one came down. As I stood there, looking at the stump, I realized I was a fortunate young man. If I had been a few inches closer to the tree I was working on, the falling tree would have either hit me on top of the head, (and I would now be five toot ten instead of 6 foot 4), or if it had hit me behind my ears where I was bent over, I could now be 6 feet under. There hadn't been a lot of margin for error. In my new, reconditioned way of looking at life, I had already sent up a prayer of thanks. I now sent up a special delivery one that was a little more specific!

By now, my wounded wing, thanks to the supporting cast (literally), was feeling quite usable, so I decided to help Charlie set chokers. He could quickly see some advantage to that, as he might not have to leave the seat of the Cat quite as often, so he took me along. I couldn't wear a mitt over the cast of course, so opted for pulling a good big dirty wool sock over it. That worked like a charm, and we were back in business. This happy state of affairs lasted about 2 days until the moisture from the snow seeped through the sock and began to disintegrate Doc Mooney's good cast. When that cast started falling apart, so did my resolve to work. I quickly realized my hand was a long way from being ready to set chokers.

I went back to see Doc Mooney. He was not impressed. He was a short, solid built man with a stern face and sharp dark eyes. When I explained my peculiar predicament, all he said was "I'll fix you so you won't be setting anymore chokers" and when he said it, he never smiled once. When I came out of that office, I couldn't even lift my arm. He had put on a cast that went from my elbow to what looked like a white basketball around my hand. Now I really had a problem.

———

It was about this time that Ginger and I decided to try to find the middle ground in our religious differences, so we started going to the Gospel Chapel church. The Gospel Chapel was an Evangelical Christian Church with sincere, friendly, members. But it didn't work. One thing that didn't help was the disagreement over the sling. When we went to church, I always wore a suit. That's the way it was back then. But it was very difficult to get my Doc Mooney cast down the sleeve of my suit coat. The cast was heavy and cumbersome, and my hand would get pretty painful if I left it hanging straight down, so I had started wearing a sling to solve the weight problem. As well, it saved the 2 hours trying to wrestle my suit coat off with one hand when I got home. I'm not sure why, but Ginger was not happy when I wore that sling, and I wasn't when I didn't.

We had a little confrontation. It had been building for a while. It hadn't reached the point where her parents were hanging a "Get Lost, Bob" sign on the door, but it was getting close. They were nice people, and if I had been them, I would have felt the same. After all, I wasn't exactly a future Bill Gates dating their daughter. I called a little meeting with all concerned and told them what I thought, and they told me what they thought, and I left in a huff. At least I had left the ball in their court, and it wasn't long in coming back. Within 2 days, I got word that they were sorry, and Ginger wanted to see me again. I was getting pretty lonesome by then so when she apologized, we decided to try it again.

It was getting toward break-up by then, and I had been charging gas at a local gas station and needed to pay the bill. So, I sold my car. Then things really started going downhill. That's when my old friends, Jess and Rosalie Brown, who I had boarded with in Oregon, came to my rescue and took me in. Their farm was on the right hand fork of the road that went straight on south to where Ginger lived. I was on foot now, and break up had come, so even when my cast came off, there wasn't any work around. I caught a ride to their church a couple of times with them, and her folks were friendly enough, but there was a feeling of distance with her. One afternoon when I knew her folks were gone, I walked over to see her and that's when she gave me the word. An old boyfriend was coming to see her.

I was at Nels' and Midge's house in town, a few evenings later, and while I was sitting in the kitchen, she came in. Her new buddy was waiting outside. She didn't even look my way. Fair enough! Now I knew how the Rodeo Cowboy felt when I showed up and he got turned out to pasture! Somehow, even as slow as I was to catch on, I knew it was time to go. I had more important things in mind. I was headed for the local pub to drown my sorrows.

When I got outside, there sat the boyfriend in a shiny rented black Chrysler! This girl was blonde, but she sure wasn't dumb! I couldn't help but think the "pensive" look might better be classed as "expensive". I had to hand it to him, "All is fair in love and war". He hadn't done anything I hadn't done to the cowboy.

As I made my way to the bar a couple of blocks away, a rational thought somehow broke through the gloom. "What you are planning to do isn't going to solve a thing". Once again, I think there are times when God's spirit speaks to you. It may not be an audible voice. It wasn't then, but I didn't go to the bar. I was down, but not out. Somewhere, there must be a good dependable Canadian girl who could learn to pick roots!

I don't remember how long I stayed with Jess and Rosalie that spring, but I'm sure it was long enough that they were more than glad to see me go. By this time, their oldest daughter Pam, and my cousin Dick Jones, were getting serious. They had hit it off pretty good and I was happy for them. Dick could always spot a good deal when he saw one. They didn't know it then, but a few months down the road, they would do me a big favour.

Lamming Mills

With all the courting and boyfriend/girlfriend stuff going on, I just stayed back out of the way. I'd had enough for a while, and needed a little time to recuperate. But I hadn't been knocked around enough to completely swear off the girls. I remembered the little Adventist community, Lamming Mills, east of Prince George, and gave it some thought as a potential place to find a job, as the mill was owned by Adventists. I jumped on the train at Vanderhoof, going first class this time, not in a boxcar. That train trip was quite an experience. It was like a hotel, school bus, cookhouse, drunk tank, and gossip center all combined in one.

Until the highway was finally pushed through from McBride, the combination of wet cedar side hills, muskeg swamps, and skunk cabbage bear pasture, the river and the railroad were the only way to Prince George, and the west. I think they called this train a way freight because it stopped at every whistle stop along the way to drop off everything imaginable, from people to potatoes. But what it lacked in convenience, it certainly made up for in community. Everybody along the line got the news on who had caught a cold, and when, who had looked too long at whom, or who had smiled or not smiled. I was unfortunate enough to get a seat directly behind a local boy who had over imbibed in Prince, and now spent the whole trip passed out in his seat, ripping off high octane snores all the way to Lamming Mills. The trip was at night so I didn't get much sleep, and was getting a little woozy myself from the fumes!

When my friend, in the seat in front of me, and I were dropped off (him literally) at Lamming Mills, I went to the office and got a job right away. There were a whole bunch of young, single guys staying in the bunkhouse, and after I got situated, it was time for supper. I had never actually stayed in a camp bunkhouse before, but living in the dorm at Milo Academy was much the same. The big difference was the cookhouse where we ate. In later years, I stayed in a few camps, and eating time was serious business, and not the place you bragged about all your exploits over the last 10 years. This cookhouse was different, but mainly because of 2 big husky loudmouthed German boys. I tried to find a place to eat as far away from them as possible, and met some interesting people. One guy's name was Al Fedor, and as he was interested in the ranching business, we spent a lot of time talking about the merits of different parts of B.C. He had seen an aerial photo of an area located in the Coast Mountains, across the Fraser River from Lytton, where the clear waters of the South Thompson River meet the muddy waters of the mighty Fraser. This interested me, and we decided that sometime in early summer, we would check it out.

Meanwhile, I had a new job to break in on. As mentioned before, sawmill work was not what I viewed as my ultimate destiny in life, but right now I was desperate, with a capital "D"! The job I ended up doing was loading box cars. Now that didn't sound bad to me. In Vanderhoof, the lumber was loaded onto trucks at Blue Mountain Sawmills, across the river from the rail line, then hauled down to the tracks, parked beside a box car, and hand bombed through the open door where it was neatly stacked by the guy inside. I think this was all contract work, so the harder you worked, the richer you got. This was the vision I had in mind when we arrived. Finally, a mill job where you could set the pace.

I was in for a big surprise. Here the box cars were pulled off on a siding directly below the planer, where a live conveyor chain ran directly from the planer to the open door of the box car. If the lumber came down the live chain at a humane speed, it wasn't bad. But if they came in a pile you couldn't handle before the next ones came, you were in trouble. There were 2 of us in the box car. My working partner was an athletic young Mennonite boy around five feet ten inches tall. He was fast, and practically a magician at handling lumber. I was six foot four with the skills and speed of an uncoordinated giraffe.

With some lengths and sizes, it was a snap. With others, it was total chaos. You were ducking, dodging, and diving with lumber piling up against the far side of the box car, and the ends of incoming boards shoving against the butts of boards that were stuck against the far wall of the box car. It could finally get to the point where we were completely snowed under with boards folding and bending and breaking and the whole operation turning into a 3 ring circus. We usually hit the stop button on the conveyor before things reached this stage, but this didn't make the guys feeding the planer too happy.

I vowed at the end of every sweat drenched shift that it was my last. But desperation kept me coming back. I had arrived during the early part of the week, and they shut down at noon on Friday so people would have time to get ready for the Sabbath. Well, by noon on Friday, I was ready for a break. I really admired that young Mennonite boy. He was a real Christian, and could work the pants off me.

When Sabbath morning rolled around, I couldn't wait to get to church. First, it was a real treat for me to worship with fellow believers. And secondly (close priority) there was the possibility there might be some eligible young ladies in the group. But I was sadly disappointed, all the ones that had potential were already taken. After church I was invited home for dinner by Jess Spangler and his wife, a very pleasant couple in their mid 50's with an attractive young daughter (unfortunately a little too young), who made me feel welcome in their home. I met a lot of the people in the McBride Church who would later become good friends.

When the time for loading box cars came around again on Monday morning, I knew my days were numbered. This box car loading was too much of a nut house for me, so by the middle of the week, I gave them the word, pulled the pin, and caught a train back to Vanderhoof.

Before leaving I had made arrangements with Al Fedor to check out the potential ranch site he had seen on the aerial map of the Stein Valley. Sometime near the beginning of May 1963 he picked me up in Vanderhoof and we headed for Lytton.

Earlscourt Farms

The only thing I knew about Lytton was that it was located in the upper part of the Fraser Canyon, on the dry side of the Coast Range. The remarkable change of climate in this area was made plain to me years later as I drove up Hwy 97 from Vancouver. As I drove into the south end of one of the tunnels at the top of the canyon, it was pouring rain and wet snow, when I came out the north end, it was the most beautiful day imaginable! Hardly a cloud in the sky and looked like it hadn't rained for 6 months.

But I learned one thing about Lytton in a hurry. It can get hot! The month of May in central B.C. is one of the nicest times of the year. No bugs, and long days, with new leaves coming out on the trees. The 20th of May is garden planting time. At Lytton, it was already smoking hot when we arrived.

Al was a slope shouldered, barrel chested guy of medium height, close cut black hair, dark rimmed glasses, easy to get along with. Since we were ranch hunting, we had to be appropriately dressed. Al was wearing a medium brown, felt cowboy hat, and I had bought a solid black, full brimmed, flat crowned Stetson. These were the worst possible hats for a 100 degree in the shade back pack trip. I love cowboy hats, in the right place at the right time, such as a Cowboy Poetry Gathering, with no one sitting within six feet of you. But for a working hat, especially when it's hot, give me a full vent J.D. baseball cap anytime, (the older you get, the more comfort takes priority over image).

When we arrived at the town of Lytton, we had to follow a narrow winding road down to a small ferry to get across the Fraser. Al didn't seem to know a whole lot more about where we were headed than I did. There was one thing we sure didn't know; we were about to blunder into one of the most fascinating chapters on the history of B.C.

When we drove off the ferry with our 2 dogs and pack boards, we turned to the right, and drove up a gravel road for a short way where a driveway came in on the left. At the end of this long driveway were some farm buildings, so we decided to see if they could tell us how to get to the Stein River. We didn't know it yet, but we had just arrived at Earlscourt Farms, established in 1864. It was the first commercial apple orchard of any size in the history of B.C. but there was a lot more to it than that. There are a lot of unique micro-climates in British Columbia, that are created by a combination of mountain ranges, sun angles, air currents, and a few other odds and ends that come together. But what this place did have that most others didn't, was gravity fed water. There was no end of pure, ice cold, clear mountain water straight off the snow capped, coastal mountains. It was called Stryne Creek, and came roaring out of the mountains in just the perfect place to stick a wooden flume in and gravity irrigate the whole place. It also provided electrical power as well, via a Pelton Wheel, to what was now a self-contained paradise of 700 acres of Fraser River bench lands.

The first owner of this property, Thomas Gardner Earl, had originally come from New Jersey to try his hand in the Cariboo Gold Rush. But Earl discovered a different kind of gold – golden and delicious apples. After hearing of the first successful apple tree plantings in 1862 by a Secwepmec First Nation man, named Lorenzo, Thomas Earl settled on the land which now bears his name, Earlscourt, in 1864. By 1875 the Earls were considered to be one of the largest apple producers in British Columbia. In 1912 Earlscourt Farms was sold to David Spencer, owner of a chain of department stores. He died in 1920, and in 1948 his family sold the department stores to T. Eaton Co., but kept the farm in Lytton. In 1959 the Spencer family finally sold Earlscourt Farms to rancher Norman Gregory. Gregory's ownership was short and the property was bought by Raymond Mundall in 1962. Mundall was a medical doctor, and the owner of a 100 acre almond orchard in California, before buying Earlscourt Farms.

My friend Al and I came on the scene a year after Dr. Raymond V. Mundall had bought the place. The providential part for us, on meeting the Mundall family, was that they were Seventh-day Adventists. I've often wondered why Dr. Mundall moved his family to an out of the way place like Earlscourt. Coming from California, it must have been the idea of being self-sufficient. We never got well acquainted with him, but he must have been a person of remarkable talent, vision, and energy. His wife, Louise, was a tall, slender, attractive lady who managed her small bevy of kids and hired help, with an air of calm, almost regal, authority.

The Earlscourt mansion, which had been built around 1912, had to be seen to be believed. I don't have any idea how many square feet that house had in it, but it was huge, with a total of 22 rooms. After getting acquainted with the family, and telling them I was also a Seventh-day Adventist, and had grown up in California, we told them why we were there. They kindly invited us to stay in a cabin on the place.

Later Mrs. Mundall took us on a tour of the house. When they called it the Earlscourt Mansion, they were not exaggerating. After about the first half hour, I didn't have a clue where we were. There were at least 5 large fireplaces in the house, and so many bedrooms, bathrooms, dining rooms, and setting rooms, it made your head spin! The house was built on a wide knoll, on a river rock foundation. The terraced rock and flower gardens, manicured lawns, tennis courts, swimming pool, and outbuildings were all spread out below. This place was literally a world of its own, a self-contained paradise. What I found the most fascinating was the gravity feed irrigation system. There were endless rows of apple trees and fields of irrigated alfalfa. I didn't realize it then but these "Earlscourt" apples would play a very important role in my future. But for now, we had some exploring to do.

———

The Stein River was located on the north side of Earlscourt Farms. It came down out of the Coast Mountains, and hit the Fraser River above where the South Thompson came in on the opposite side. The Stein was more like a big oversized creek than a river, but what it lacked in size it made up for in velocity. There are no roads in the Stein Valley, which is approximately 60 km long. It would have been an absolute travesty to have put a road in and logged that valley. Thankfully, there were those who had the vision, foresight, and determination to prevent this. It wasn't until I had flown over the coast range, years later, that I began to realize what it meant when they said that the Stein was the last untouched valley. From the air, there truly is not any place that hasn't been logged. In valley after valley, as far as the eye can see, it's licked cleaner than a cat can lick a sardine can. There is a time and a place and a need to log, but not in that area.

When we shouldered our trapper Nelson's, with rifles in hand, and headed up the river, we didn't know what to expect. We both had a dog. Al had a big, rugged, long haired German Shepherd that he had strapped a pack on. I had a young, tan, half coyote, half dog I had picked up at the Stoney Creek Indian Reserve, near Vanderhoof. I got him as a pup from Mike Ketlo, a native guy I had worked with at one time. I had asked Mike how you said "Friend" in his Carrier language, and he told me, "Chetel", so Chetel he became. He wasn't a lap dog by any means. Like his ancestors, he was a survivor, and always stayed a little aloof, except when the dog food came out. But I liked that wild streak in him, and we got to be pretty good pals.

Bob, Al Fedor & their dogs

The Stein came in from the west, and the trail was pretty well beaten down for the first few miles. Then it started to change, and the canyon walls began to get steeper and squeeze in from the sides. As the mountains got higher and closer, it created a lot of shade which made for good growing conditions. There were a lot of big fir, birch and brush in the bottom and towering Ponderosa Pines scattered up on the steep, dry hillsides. The cool shaded areas were nice, but I was quickly discovering that my classy, flat crowned black felt cowboy hat was turning into a pressure cooker.

My dog, Chetel, was in his element, running ahead, snooping out all the nooks and crannies and mouse holes. Al's big German Shepherd was a real pack horse, struggling along like a real trooper, without a whimper of complaint. But when Al took his pack off, it was a different story, he was right on my dog's case. Al's dog was the dominant one. That had been plain from the start, but I think seeing my dog skipping around, having a good old time, while he had to slug along with that pack on his back, really ticked him off. I can't say as I blamed him, as I would have probably felt the same, but we had to watch him close.

I'm guessing we hiked up the river canyon about 20 miles. A lot of it was slow going where the river pushed you against the rock side walls, or where you had to pick your way across scree slopes where avalanches came down. As we got farther up, we started to run into trails where mountain goats had come to browse and water. You could see them high up on the sheer rock cliffs, small white dots jumping from ledge to ledge, and strolling around, thousands of feet above us. Skihist Mountain, the tallest mountain in the area, tops out at 9,759 feet, so these weren't rolling hills we were crawling around on.

On the afternoon of the third day we were seeing a lot of goat sign, so I decided I would test out my climbing ability and go after one. Looking back, I'm sure it was novelty more than necessity that brought on that decision, and, like a lot of ignorant things done in my younger years, something I wouldn't repeat. But at that time and place, and state of mind, it seemed like the thing to do. I took Al's rifle, as it had a shorter barrel than my long barrelled 38-55 Punkin slinger, and headed up the mountain. It was slow, tedious climbing, and as I worked my way up, it was a little dicey because of the loose shale. There were enough shrubs, rocks, and trees scattered around that you could probably find something to grab if you broke loose and started sliding, but that mountain was pretty steep.

I had worked my way up a thousand feet or so from the bottom when I looked across a little draw to my right, and there in the shade of a big Ponderosa pine, eyes half closed, chewing his cud, was Mr. Mountain Goat. I couldn't believe my eyes. He acted like I wasn't even there. I think at that time, in the early sixties, they were left pretty well undisturbed. Most of the time, they were in country that no predator would bother them.

I carefully lined him up and touched off the shot. He never knew what hit him. Now I was the one with a problem. A mature, male Mountain Goat is not a small animal. I was really surprised at how deep and narrow they are built, ideal for the terrain they inhabit. The goat was a tough looking old boy as he was starting to shed, and I was soon to find out he was a lot tougher on the inside than he was on the outside. Getting him down to camp was one wild ride. Once he started sliding there wasn't much you could do but hang on. I faintly remember arriving at the bottom in an avalanche of dust, rocks, a few shrubs, and bits of tree bark, with the goat on top. After the dust cleared and things settled down, I skinned him out, and whacked some nice tender steaks off one hind quarter for supper.

It was then we discovered that Al had forgotten the frying pan! Oh no! This was going from bad to worse. After a short discussion, (neither of us being too well versed on the finer points of cooking 50 year old Mountain Goat), we decided, since we had a big pot for cooking oatmeal, we would just boil it. It's important to remember here that all great explorers were not necessarily good cooks, and who knows, maybe Simon Fraser and Alexander MacKenzie forgot their frying pan too. Anyway, we boiled it and boiled it, and we boiled it some more. I wished for days after that that I had just left Old Billy sleeping under his tree. That meat was so tough it would have wore out 10 pair of boots if you had made boot soles out of it. That was all it was good for, the longer you chewed it, the bigger it got! Even the dogs turned up their noses. It was pretty stupid to shoot that goat. We had thought we would be in there for a week or so and could use the meat. It was getting pretty obvious the only livestock you could raise would be mountain goats. We were to find out later that the open area Al had seen on the aerial photo was actually alpine meadows that cover many square miles. On November 22, 1995 this area of the Stein River watershed was made into a B.C. provincial park, the Niaka'pamux Heritage Park, following a 25 year debate over development versus protection.

On the way out, the dog dominance thing got progressively worse. Al's dog was at Chetel every chance he got, and when we broke camp the last morning, my dog was gone. I guess he had enough and just reverted back to the wild. We stayed around for 4 or 5 extra days helping around the ranch at Earlscourt, and hoping Chetel would show up, but not a sign.

_____

We had met a husband and wife team working for Mundalls when we first arrived at Earlscourt. Their names were Jack and Viva Zachary, in their late fifties, real down to earth types. They had originally came from "Winterpeg", that city in Manitoba that makes the North Pole feel like Hawaii. Viva was a solid built lady with dark, pulled back hair, laughing eyes, and pleasant smile, who was fun to be around, and man could she cook perogies! and make good bread! She reminded me a lot of Maxine Jones, my cousin back in Vanderhoof. Her husband, Jack, was a Ukrainian. He had a full head of strikingly thick, wavy, snow white hair, and always kept it neatly combed.

I really liked Jack. He was a perfect example of the stubborn, determined people who overcame the immense hardships and challenges that came with farming the Canadian prairies. The story of his life, I was to learn later, is contained in a book "Into the Blizzard", by Olivine Bohner. It tells of his desire and dedication to share his Adventist faith with others, especially those of his own Ukrainian background. We liked working with Jack. He had that way of doing things that showed experience; planned out, and thought through. They were great people. Viva, with her outgoing personality, Jack more reserved. One thing that showed his prairie background was his bib overalls. They were a pinstripe grey and black that reminded me of those my Grandpa Batman wore. I enjoyed talking to him in the evening when we were setting around after Viva had made supper. They were very dedicated Christians and really into healthy living. His big kick was either alfalfa or carrot juice. We tried to convince him about the health benefits of boiled Mountain Goat, but he didn't seem to be interested. He was the perfect picture of dynamic, radiant health.

When we saw Earlscourt Farm, it was probably at its peak, starting to go downhill a little, but still in its glory. Later in 1963, the machine shed and all the machinery burned and the Mundalls returned to California. Then they moved to the country of Belize, where Dr. Mundall established, and operated, a hospital for several years. While in Belize, they added 5 more children to their family by adoption. This made a total of 12 children they raised and educated, so it was probably a good thing Mrs. Mundall ran the crew with a strong hand.

Earlscourt Farm was later leased out, and used for a self-supporting church school for several years. This school was later relocated closer to Lillooet, where it now operates as Fountainview Academy, a private parochial secondary boarding school that is affiliated with, but not owned or operated by the Seventh-day Adventist Church. It places a strong emphasis on its music program, with a youth orchestra and choir.

Unfortunately, fire seemed to be an ongoing problem at Earlscourt. On August 1, 1992, a forest fire burned a lot of the area on the west side of the Fraser River; burning along the west property line of Earlscourt, but sparing the farm and buildings. Then, on March 6, 1993, the Earlscourt mansion burned to the ground. Dr. Mundall had returned and retired on the place in 1991. After the fire, in true pioneer spirit, he managed to scrape together enough to rebuild, but not to the former glory of the original mansion. Sadly, Dr. Mundall passed away a few years later.

Merrit Mundall, one of the sons, and his wife Becky, and some of their children, continue to operate the ranch and run a herd of Black Angus/Gelbvieh cattle. The cattle, along with the orchards and a honey business, keep them busy. After Mrs. Louise Mundall remarried she continued to live at Earlscourt Farm with her second husband, Bryce Newell, until she passed away in her mid-nineties. I found Earlscourt to be a fascinating historical story and was thankful to be able to revisit Louise Mundall before she passed away.

Al Fedor & I finally ran out of time, and had to leave. My dog, Chetel, hadn't shown up, so I left a number to contact me if he came around, and we headed back north. Al had other things to do, and I needed to get back to Vanderhoof, get my rear in gear and make some money.

Catskinners, Chokersetters, and a Blue-headed Bear

The Interior of B.C. was just starting to open up to big scale logging in 1963. The province of B.C. was still one endless, untouched wilderness of merchantable timber, but the capacity to log and mill this goldmine was limited. As mentioned earlier, every stump farmer in the interior had a sawmill, but compared to what was to come, lumber production amounted to nothing. There were a few bigger sawmills around, at Fort Fraser, Vanderhoof, Prince George, and the Upper Fraser country, but nothing remotely close to the sawmills, pulp mills, and logging machinery of today. The time would come when there would literally be endless train loads of lumber pouring out of the Interior. Now, the gold came in the form of framing lumber, the best money could buy.

The majority of the timber around Vanderhoof, was Lodgepole, or what we called Jackpine. There was a lot of spruce as well, but from Prince George west to Smithers, and south through Quesnel and the Chilcotin, it was pine country. Logging the flat lands of the Interior is a lot easier than steep coastal logging. A large part of it is a big undulating plateau with a few low mountain ranges popping up here and there. Back then the trees were felled, limbed, and topped in the bush. A legal tree was 8 inches in diameter at chest height. A skid road was punched in about every hundred feet, and everything was felled, and topped in the road, so when the faller was finished, it looked like a "v", with the top of the tree towards the landing.

When I got back to Vanderhoof from Lytton, I found a summer job setting chokers for Gordie Peters, a logging contractor from Fraser Lake. My cousin Dick, had worked the previous winter in the Nulki Hills, setting chokers for him. Gordie supplied plywood shacks for the crew to live in, so that took care of the living quarters. Our favourite name for Gordie was "The General";

he was short and yappy, and his personality never improved much with age. But I give him credit where credit is due. He worked steady when it was possible to work. His money was good and if you did the job right, he left you alone, except to come around every day or two just to get on your nerves.

There was one other thing he did that was very important. Every spring during break-up, after a short vacation, he overhauled all his iron, so when it was time to roll again it was ready to go. He did the same thing in the fall before freeze up.

Some of the details from the summer of 1963 I worked for Gordie Peters get a little hazy, but as near as I can remember, there were 15 men in the crew. They were a real cross section of the ethnic mix that makes up Canada; Natives, Metis, Swedes, Norwegians, American D.P.'s (Dick and myself), and a German loader operator. Last, but not least, were the Scotchmen. We almost had enough of them to start a pipe band.

The Metis, the people of mixed European and native descent were tough, wiry men; the very backbone of the fur trade that opened up Canada. Though they were, as a rule, not big men, they took great pride in being tough, and when you read the history of their exploits, the feats of strength, in packing, paddling, and endurance, it's pretty impressive. Gordie Peters was Metis, and a successful logger.

Mark LaCerte, the cat skinner, was Metis, and I suspect was a throwback to those hardy canoe men who did the muscle work for the Hudson Bay and Northwest Company fur traders. I would have to say that when Mark crawled up on the seat of that little TD-9 International Cat, he didn't look too impressive. Greasy hat stuck on sideways, four day growth of beard, a jagged scar on one cheek, and dirty slouchy bush clothes that even the black flies wouldn't come close to. Then, to top it off, a lower lip that was crammed to the limit with Copenhagen snoose! Whew! What a sight. But in spite of his looks, when he went into action he was a good cat skinner. He could get more work out of that little TD-9 than you could believe. Not only was he fast, he was also careful and easy on the machine. When he came on to the landing with a big drag of logs, he would be hunched over in the seat with the black diesel smoke pouring out the stack, eyes dancing and a big, snoose stained grin from one ear to the other. My cousin Dick set chokers behind Mark, and they were always harassing each other, but they moved a lot of wood. You would never have believed it at the time, but after some difficult early years, Mark would go on to become a respected resident of Fraser Lake, working at Endako Mines, and serving for 25 years as a valued trustee for the School District.

George Teed was a tall, broad shouldered, sharp looking native guy that set chokers with us. He was educated at the LeJac Indian School on the south side of Fraser Lake. When we were working together he would challenge us with mathematical questions while we were waiting for the cat to come back for another drag. He would stump us every time.

One of the fallers was a Swede named Gus. He was an older experienced logger who along with doing a little falling helped Peters lay out the logging show. Being a Swede, he was a bit stubborn, but beyond this he had a more serious problem. Gus was an alcoholic, and followed a set routine. He would stay in the bush for three months at a stretch and never touch a drop. Then he would get into the after shave. One particular morning, he had fallen and hit his face on the chopping block which didn't improve his looks. This was the start of a 30 day binge. The boss would haul him to town and he would stay in the hotel for a month. Everyday he would put on his old fedora hat, sit in the pub and drink himself into oblivion. After a month he would be broke, come back to the bush for another three months, then do the whole thing over again. It was sad to see and a stark reminder of what booze can do.

The guy I set chokers behind for the first month or so that summer was a Scotchman, Butch McMaster. He looked every inch a Scotchman. Solid built, with a thick mop of straight sandy coloured hair, sharp, steady blue eyes staring out from under craggy eye brows, and a heavy jaw. He was plainly there to learn the logging business and make money, the "tight fisted" businessman! The only thing missing was a kilt and tam. Butch was just a young guy, probably around 18 years old. He was friendly enough, but clearly on a mission. It took us a little while to get it all sorted out, but he was a good safe machine operator. He eventually became a contractor for Fraser Lake Sawmills, logging in the Ootsa Lake country.

I didn't have much on the go when the weekend came, while working for Gordie Peters in the Nulki Hills, so I would stay Friday and Saturday night at the Jones'. I would then walk the couple of miles to George and Rene Tees to visit on Sunday. We would have long winded discussions on world affairs, religion, farming, etc. etc. I would pay George to run me back up to camp on Sunday afternoon so I could get a few things ready for work on Monday. Dick was busy courting Pam and never showed up for work until Monday morning. George and Rene were really nice people, and I enjoyed spending time with them.

One Sunday evening we had no more than arrived in Camp, when Gus, our old Swedish faller, came bursting out of his cabin chattering like a magpie! He was really wound up and I thought for a minute that he had got into the after shave again, but he was sober as a judge. He kept yelling something about a bear he had shot at that had a blue head. Wow! I thought he was having a late onset of the D.T.s but that wasn't the case. We had moved the Camp to a new spot a few days before and when Gus had gone back to pick up a few things, a big black bear with a blue head had attacked him. (This was his version of the episode). Fortunately, he had his rifle with him, and fired a couple of shots that scared the bear off, but poor old Gus was still shaking in his boots. A couple of days later, someone else saw this bear, and guess what! It did have a blue head! At that time, when the Forestry laid out the logging blocks, they used a spray can with light blue paint to mark the boundaries. Mr. Bear had found one of these, and, bears being bears, had picked it up in his mouth, given it a chomp, and got a dandy spray job. So, our old Swede wasn't seeing things after all!

Somewhere around the middle of the summer, Peters bought a new International TD-15. I guess it was new, at least it had a bright new yellow paint job. I ended up being the choker setter behind it. The guy operating it was Ted Johansson, Peters cousin from Fraser Lake, a top notch cat skinner. He was another one of those big, easy going, part Native guys, and reminded me of Jasper Thomas, the carpenter I had worked with building Al Simrose's dairy barn. Mark and Butch were good, but this guy was the best. I forget now how many chokers he flew behind that cat, but there was a pile of them. Ted would dump off one pile when he came in and I would hook up the ones I had set while he was gone. These chokers were shoe strings compared to the ones we used in Oregon. But though these were only 10 feet long and ½ inch in diameter, there was an awful pile of them to keep track of.

Dick and I worked hard that summer, and made good money. But one thing that just about drove us wacky were the black flies. It wasn't quite as bad when you were working, but when you had your chokers set and were waiting for the cat to come back, they crawled in your eyes, your ears, inside your shirt, even in your mouth. You never knew until a day later that they had bit you. That's when it would start itching and never quit. We used bug dope by the gallon, and they just licked it off and kept coming!

The last Scotchmen on the crew were the bucker men, Ken McInnis, and his partner, "Greasy" Graham. Ken was a nice enough guy, but he could go right off the deep end when he started drinking. Sadly, a few years later, both men were killed in a car wreck when Ken passed out at the wheel and ran off the highway near Vanderhoof.

Things were going pretty good, the dollars were rolling in, and I was starting to think of getting another set of wheels. Then we hit a roadblock. The cats were skidding into one big landing that was down in a kind of basin. From where we were working, on the side hills and flats above, we could look right down on the whole operation, like setting in the stands at a hockey game. It was a free-for-all down on that landing. Cats skidding in, bucker men ducking and dodging, trying to do their job with logs swinging overhead while trucks were being loaded.

Peters was a good logger, and things usually didn't hit a bottleneck like this, but sometimes it happens. Then the loader man went on strike. I'm not sure what the deal was, whether it was an issue over wages or he wanted to get some of his family's trucks in on the hauling, but the whole operation ground to a halt. Now we had a problem. The German loader man (a chronic bellyacher), versus the Metis General (a chronic bellyacher); both with the negotiating skills of a wounded wolverine! Ah, Great! I could see my dreams of prosperity fading fast. It must have taken a day or two for the "Nulki Hills Standoff" to end, but I'm quite sure that particular loader man never returned for another season. If there's one guy that's the kingpin, and better have his act together, it's the loaderman on a logging show.

I have to hand it to those old 966 operators, it was a high pressure, high stress job that took a special breed to keep everybody happy and not run over somebody. This deadlock that torpedoed us got me thinking. If I could get a falling job, I would be the one making the mess, not the choker setter cleaning it up. I would be completely independent, not relying on anything but me and my power saw. It would just be a case of making sure there was always wood on the ground. I stored that thought away for future consideration.

The Girl With The Auburn Hair

As the weeks wore on, I started to think of possible root picking partners again. Amazing how fast you recuperate.

My cousin Dick, and girlfriend Pam Brown, (who was now about to become his wife), would sometimes invite me along for a ride with them. On one of our "rose between two thorns" Sunday drives, Pam suggested we drop by the home of a school friend in Mapes, and see if she would like to go swimming. This was a brilliant idea on her part, as it would at least get me out of the front seat so you could tell who was with who. The two times I had ever seen this friend, Joan Snyder, was the time at the Sinkut Lake Hall, and then again, when she was riding her horse on her way to the Mapes picnic, when I had stopped to ask her about the missing skid horse. The girl with the nice smile and mop of auburn hair! Oh yes, there had been one other time shortly after the blonde breakup. I was riding around town with Clifford Evans one spring day when the high school kids were out for lunch, and we passed Joan, and Cliff's sister Linda, walking along the street, so he pulled over and picked them up. I had a standard clothes combination I always wore at that time. The once black Stetson had aged, and now had a 2" brim instead of a 4", (I had cut 2 inches off so I could get in a vehicle!) The vest was its own story. It was the most comfortable thing I'd ever worn, and something only a mother could love. I didn't even look at the girls when they got in, but there was a lot of giggling and muffled laughter in the back seat, and I was pretty sure it wasn't about Clifford. I was to learn later that in spite of my appearance, it was being pointed out to Joan Snyder that this was the guy who could sing like Elvis! (Not bad, not bad.)

When we pulled into the Snyder yard that day, with the little creek running behind the old log house, I was impressed. Nice day, nice spot, but I have to admit I wasn't dressed to wow a fussy 17 year old. She was 5 years younger, and becoming very popular among the guys her own age. I had on my regular seedy attire, complete with Stetson and sheep hide vest. I didn't think I really looked all that bad, as after all this was "cowboy country".

I got Dick to pull up to the house, then pulled down my Stetson, and headed for the door. Now they tell me it's quite an experience when the boys throw open the gate at a Rodeo and you're setting there on a 2000 pound bull. I would have gladly traded places right then with the cowboy on the meanest bull at the Calgary Stampede. I would find out later that the man who opened the door when I knocked could have a temperament very similar to one of those bulls!

But this day her Dad, Slim, was cordial, and invited me in. I took off my hat in true John Wayne fashion when I stepped through the door, and said "Howdy". Then I made my pitch, "mighty nice crick ya got runnin' through yer place". Well, needless to say, that threw Slim a little off balance, as I think he was wondering who I was, and what I was after. By this time, Joan's mother had also arrived on the scene with a puzzled look on her face. That's when I asked the question, "I just wondered if your daughter would like to go swimmin'?" Marj Snyder was a wonderful person. With remarkable poise, she calmly asked this bedraggled, knock kneed stranger, where we would be going, and who I was with. I told her the beach at the end of Sinkut Lake, and I was with Pam Brown and Dick Jones. This was where Lady Luck stepped in on my side, Marj had met Dick at a young people's house party they had held in the Snyder home a few months before. While Marj went to ask Joan if she wanted to go swimming with this derelict, her Dad and I exchanged small talk.

I think life must have been pretty boring that particular day, or she was fed up trying to boss her younger brothers around, or fighting with her younger sister about making sure her feet were washed before she came to bed, or maybe it was just plain curiosity about this tall, dark, handsome stranger. Whatever the reason, Joan decided to come, and in no time, we were loaded up and headed for Sinkut Lake. When we drove out of the yard, I happened to glance back, and it looked like something out of an old Ma and Pa Kettle movie. There, in a row, stood her younger siblings, from the tallest down to the shortest. There they stood, David, Brian, Paul, and Susan. As we drove off, not one smiled, but they all waved and they all seemed to have their fingers crossed. I thought that was kind of strange.

We had a good time at the lake, but she was pretty reserved and kept her distance (probably afraid something would jump on her from the sheep hide vest). But at least we got a little better acquainted. Her brothers and sister didn't seem all that happy when I brought her back so soon, but I just wrote that off to a case of power struggle. I did notice she looked pretty good in a swimsuit, so decided to make it a point to ask her out again sometime.

Later that summer I did arrange another swimming date with Joan, via Pam & Dick. We decided to take a run out west to Burns Lake to see the sights and then stop by Beaumont, the park at the east end of Fraser Lake, on the way home. It all went off with nary a problem. Her brothers and sister all stood in their Ma and Pa Kettle line up, when we left her home, and once again they all had their fingers crossed when they waved goodbye. This time they even smiled, hoping for the best. She looked even better than I remembered, and just to be nice after we got out of the lake, I put a dry towel over her shoulders and stood behind her and put my arms around her to keep her warm. (How thoughtful of me!) She didn't run away screaming for help, so I thought I was making progress.

But I did make a bad mistake that day. As we were riding along in Dick's car, I quietly told her that "It won't always be this way, I'm going to get a set of wheels before long". At least she didn't open the door and jump out while we were going full speed, but those words set off all the alarm bells. It turned out I was the third desperate old geezer that had told her something like this in the last few months! Well, needless to say, when we dropped her off that evening, she told me in a nice way that maybe I was a bit too old, and she was busy with other things for the next 10 years, so don't bother coming back.

———

It slowly dawned on me that I had probably overdone things a bit, so to make myself feel better, I headed into Prince George the next chance I got and bought myself a pick up. There are times when things go right, and this time they did. The guy had just traded it in when I walked through the door, and he was signing the papers on a new one. His name was Remo Ivor Lepitich, one of four brothers that owned a big ranch and timberland close to Quesnel. He was a middle aged man, and it was plain he came from a family that knew the meaning of hard work. When he realized I was looking at his pickup, he let me know in no uncertain terms what kind of care he had taken of that truck, and if I bought it, I had better do the same. It was a beauty, a solid black 1959 G.M.C. ½ ton, with a full length box, new tires, and four-on-the-floor.

Now I had a set of wheels again, and I was back in the race. Somewhere through the logging grapevine, I had heard that Eric Thomson, a sawmill operator up at Fort Fraser, was looking for a faller. I had been giving this timber falling some pretty serious consideration after the "Nulki Hills standoff", and decided I would give it a try. I still had my Pioneer 620 power saw, and a couple of wedges, so I jumped in my truck and headed west.

It's only a little over a 20 minute drive from Vanderhoof to Fort Fraser, but within a short radius of this small town a surprising number of important historical things have happened. In 1806, a North West Company fur trading post was established by Simon Fraser. This spot is now Beaumont Provincial Park, one of the nicest provincial campsites and swimming spots in the Interior. This was the place I had gone with Dick and Pam and my auburn haired girlfriend only a few short weeks before. Just down the road from Beaumont Park was the Nautley River, at just less than 1/2 mile long, the shortest river in the province of B.C., and one of the shortest rivers in the world. The Nautley River drains Fraser Lake into the Nechako River, and is the present location of an ancient village of the Dakelh, or Carrier, First Nations people. It is also a wintering area for a large flock of Trumpeter Swans. Thanks to local conservationist, Leo LaRocque, these majestic birds have been returning for years, in response to the feeding program he initiated.

No doubt, the most important event that took place in this area was on April 7, 1914, just east of the present town site of Fort Fraser, when Edson Chamberlain, President of the Grand Trunk Pacific, drove in the last spike on the Railway! The history of Fort Fraser is recorded in a book by local author, and long-time resident, Lenore Rudland. It has the rather unique title, Fort Fraser (Where the Hell's That?). It is an exceptional read, not just for the historical facts, but because she captures the very attitude and spirit of the community.

The thing I thought was pretty noticeable when I drove into the small town was Fraser Mountain. It basically marked the start of the Nechako valley when you came from the west. It was a steep, partially rock faced mountain that rose just west of the town site. Most of the mountains in the Interior are not too dramatic, but Fraser Mountain, especially on the east and north sides, looks like it was transplanted from the rock mesas of Utah or Arizona. Its sheer rock face rises almost straight out of the valley floor just a short distance from where the Nechako River runs past its base. Then it levels off at the top and tapers back to the south and west. This is where Eric Thomson's sawmill was located.

Hail Storms and Turnip Chompers

Well, if you're going to get rich, you can't be timid. I had never met Eric before and thought for a few minutes I had woke a sleeping grizzly, but it was a little early in the year for hibernating. I asked him about the possibilities of a falling job. With his personality, and the tough access to his mill site, I could see he probably wasn't swamped with job applications. Whatever the reason, he hired me.

Eric was a fairly tall, bull necked, barrel chested guy whose eyebrows pointed up to a peaked forehead. This gave him a slightly puzzled look. His ruddy, fat cheeked face and beady, close set eyes, reminded me of my good old Okie body guards from the dance hall days in California. He seldom smiled, and usually looked like he had just finished off a sour lollipop! A fast, explosive talker and hard worker, he was a surprisingly good boss if you did a decent job for him, and falling timber was now my job.

The south side of Fraser Mountain wasn't nearly as steep as the north side, so a lot of it was fairly easy ground to log. There were a lot of poplars mixed in with big heavy limbed Jackpine, but I had learned to keep my head up and eyes open so it went pretty good. One thing I had finally managed to find was a hard hat like Harold Bradley's. They sold them at Riches Saw Sales, and everybody wore them. I think they were called a "Chromalloy" brand, and were light as a feather and comfortable to wear. There was a plywood shack, with a cook stove, by the mill site where Eric told me I could stay during the week. So I brought my bedroll and supplies up, and moved in.

It was getting into late August 1963 when I started working for him and it was hot. You don't usually get much humid weather in the Interior, but if you do, that's when it comes, just before fall. We had cleaned up the easy ground, and he had punched in some skid trails straight up the mountain into a nice solid stand of tall clean pine. I had never really fell in any steep ground before and it was a little tricky. Falling the tree was no problem, but once you had some on the ground and dumped another one on top, it

223

could take off down the hill. But one thing you had as you worked your way toward the top of that mountain, was a view.

I could talk for hours on views. I have a thing about being up high where I can see out. These places have it all. The Nechako Valley is not a huge area like the Peace country or the prairies, but in this roughly 30 mile long by 10 to 20 mile wide area, there is everything. Mountains, lakes, rivers, timber, flat farmland, rolling farmland, hay meadows, ridges, valleys within valleys. If you want it, it's there. Wildlife? Oh, yes! Grizzlies, black bear, moose, elk, mule deer, white tails, cougar, lynx, on and on. There's even a few ground hogs left. It is a bountiful country, and I haven't even got into the fish and bird varieties.

Overall, the weather is fairly predictable, at least it used to be. Cold quiet winters, long slow springs, short hot summers, and nice falls. But what can make it awkward is the exception. I was getting right close to the top of one of my skid trails late one afternoon when I noticed it starting to get increasingly muggy. I was trying to get this trail finished so I could pack everything down and start another one at the bottom, in the morning. I was pushing things a little and not paying any real close attention to the weather until I heard a distant roll of thunder. When I looked off to the south, it was spooky. The sky was a strange dark green colour like I had never seen before, and moving toward me fast. I realized there was no chance of finishing before it hit, so I grabbed my pack sack and headed down the hill. You could feel the air turning colder by the minute, and just when I got to the shack, the storm hit.

If I had used my head I would have just jumped in the pickup and watched the show. That would have been the safest place. Everything had been logged off around the plywood shack so it was right out in the open. I dove into the shack, slammed the door, and sat down on the bed. That's when the big artillery opened up. I didn't stay setting on the bed long, I went under it! There's the old saying "there's no atheists in fox holes", and though I've never been a military man, I can assure you there were no atheists in that bush shack! That's the only thunder storm I've ever been through that I thought I'd had it. It was almost pitch black inside, and the thunder and lightning were deafening, both exploding at the same time. The shack was jumping up and down like a bucking horse, from the concussion, and the air reeked with a smell like gunpowder. What the thunder and lightning didn't do to keep you entertained, the wind did, and what the wind didn't do the rain and hail did. It was like a river coming down off that mountain.

———

A few weeks after the big storm, I got the word from Earlscourt Farms that someone thought they had seen my dog, Chetel. I had been hitting it pretty steady, trying to make my fortune in case I found some Crown land I could apply for. I had pretty well given up, for now, on root pickers, and a dog is fairly good company, and not near as fussy about how you smell!

It was a good trip down to Lytton. The weather had settled into early fall, with frosty nights, lazy, blue sky days that lull you into thinking you have 3 more months to get ready for winter. I had a good re-union with the Mundalls and Zacharys, and bragged a little about my new truck. I also seem to recall cleaning up most of the perogies and fresh baked bread Viva had laying around. But most of the 2 days were spent diligently looking for my dog, a long hike up the Stein Valley, all over the farm, morning to evening, looking, calling…not a trace of him. After the second day I had to leave, but while I was there, I did find out two more things.

The first was more Earlscourt history. Somehow, maybe it was information overload, I had missed the fact that along with owning the Earlscourt, Douglas Lake, Pavillion, and the Circle S Ranch at Dog Creek, the third Spencer in line, Colonel Victor Spencer ran Earlscourt as a registered Hereford ranch, bringing in imported Lionheart stock from England to improve the breed. But the critical thing I discovered was that the apples were ready! Wow! And what apples they were! Macs! That's what I was after. My brilliant business mind quickly realized this was the perfect way to pay for the trip down and back, so we loaded that shiny black G.M. down to where you couldn't cram another box on it. These apples were unreal. When you bit into one, the juice would squirt you right in the eye! It was like hauling a load of gold north to those fruit starved turnip chompers!

As the miles went by, I slowly realized there was a lot more potential to this load of apples than paying a gas bill. This was the perfect opportunity to casually drop by the Snyder farm in my new pickup and mention I had been down to Lytton and was selling these freshly picked MacIntosh apples from a famous orchard for a nominal fee. I didn't bother wearing my sheep hide vest this time. I scrubbed myself up until I sparkled, clean shirt, pants, low heeled shoes to avoid the "knock kneed" appearance, and headed for Snyders' to begin the apple selling tour. When I pulled into their yard, the boys had seen me coming around the top field but didn't know who it was, so they didn't have their fingers crossed… yet!. When I stopped, Slim came over to see who was there. As soon as I got out of the truck the boys all gathered around. When they recognized me, they quickly crossed their fingers, hoping. I explained my mission, dropped the tail gate, opened a box, and told them to try one.

I was quite surprised at how well behaved they were, they had obviously been taught some manners. It didn't take long until they were all oohing and aahing about the apples. I was still wearing my good black, trail worn, cowboy hat, so I know Joan was aware of who was there when she casually sidled out the door with her sister Susan. It has always been a mystery to me what a nice vehicle can do to improve your looks, and change your status among girls! When I was in church school in the 6th or 7th grade, we had a guy in Grade 9 that was about the homeliest human being I've ever known, and came complete with a minus zero personality. His Dad owned a very profitable business where the boy worked, and he always had money and the latest in a cool looking custom hot rod. The girls mobbed him, and he was the never ending rage as long as he went to school there.

Well, Slim bought a couple of boxes for the troops, and Joan, after helping herself to an apple, and carefully sizing up the pickup, volunteered to ride around and introduce me to the neighbours that might be interested. The "Get Lost" order seemed to have been lifted, and we had a great time riding around pedalling apples. She definitely had a sparkly personality and laughed a lot at my jokes, but asked a lot more questions about my truck than she did about me. When I took her home, I asked her if she would like to go to town for a hamburger. It wasn't too long before this became a fairly regular thing.

Sam Goodland and Family; Special Memories

My job for Eric Thomson ended for a few weeks, and an opportunity came to spend some time working for Sam Goodland out by Tatuk Lake. The first time I met Sam was the winter I worked for Harold Bradley. That was a bitter cold, deep snow winter, and I remember Sam coming up on the front porch covered with frost. He had just finished the last leg of breaking trail on a snow machine, through 35 or so miles of deep snow and north wind, and was about done in. Amy Bradley hustled him into the warm kitchen where she filled him up with hot food and tea, and got him thawed out so Harold could take him into Vanderhoof, where his parents and daughter now lived. It was a unique type of people that could be content, and endure living on a remote, isolated, ranch miles back in the boondocks, with no way out during the winter but snowshoes or a team and bobsled. In the later years, there were snow machines, but whatever they used, it was usually brutal, hard work to travel in winter.

Sam would have probably been in his mid-forties at that time, maybe a bit older. His face was thin and lined, and with his greying hair and black cowboy hat tipped back on his head, he looked every inch the backwoods homesteader. Like old Louis Kohse, he was tough as rawhide leather. His small ranch was roughly 35 miles south of Vanderhoof, and a couple of hundred yards east of the Tatuk Lake Road. It was a beautiful spot. The driveway wound down through big, scattered Bull pine to the log house and barn located on a low bench above the Chilako, (or Mud River). The river came out of the east end of Tatuk Lake, 9 miles to the south west, and was a big, clear bottomed creek at this point, with a fairly large willow fringed hay meadow across the creek from the house. Sam and his parents, Harry and Elizabeth Goodland had located here years before, and carved a homestead out of the surrounding wilderness. Harry Goodland, Sam's father, was an English cabinet maker by trade, and it showed in the tight dovetail corners of the house and barn. The overall appearance of the ranch was neat and tidy.

I had met Jean Goodland, Sam's former wife, when she was working at the McInnis General Store, a few miles west of Vanderhoof, where I bought my groceries on Sundays. Their specialty seemed to be freezer burned steaks and outdated bread, which I paid twice the going rate for, but I have always been a firm believer in supporting local enterprise, and besides, I liked the homey atmosphere and visiting with Jean.

I'm not sure when Sam and Jean met and married, but in his 2nd book, "Nothing too Good for a Cowboy", Rich Hobson tells of meeting Sam and Jean on one of his cattle drives from the Batnuni Ranch to Vanderhoof. He also tells of hiring Sam to do a lot of building and renovations for him when he bought the "Rimrock Ranch" a few years later. So, they had been together for a while, and had one daughter, Carol. It was a lonely life in the bush, and the story was that Jean had left the ranch in a huff after a disagreement, and walked out through the moose and grizzly infested backwoods in a pair of high heeled shoes! Now that may seem a little far fetched, but once you got acquainted with Jean, it wasn't that hard to imagine.

She was a tall, slender, finely built lady with high cheek bones and a soft, friendly voice. She always wore a long, full length skirt and blouse or shirt buttoned at the wrists, and her hair pulled back in a tight bun. Jean had a very slight overbite which only added charm and character to her smile, but behind the friendly smile, the smouldering flame of an independent spirit still burned in her dark eyes. I don't know what had happened in her life after she left Sam, but after being apart for many years, they were happily getting back together again. She asked if I would be interested in doing some falling for Sam's small sawmill operation and when the time came, I threw my power saw, guitar, the punkin slinger, and a few clothes in Sam's old lumber truck, and we headed for the ranch.

Their daughter, Carol, came along, as chief cook and bottle washer for the operation. I think she had spent most of her summers with Sam once she was old enough to help out, and the winters with her grandparents, who had moved into Vanderhoof. Carol was 3 years younger than I was, and we hit it off right from the start in a brother/sister kind of friendship. She was quite small with much the same friendly personality as her mother. One thing I noticed as we got better acquainted, was that she seemed to have a sense of maturity far beyond her years. I guess that came from spending a lot of time in the bush around older people. She was engaged to Corny Klassen, who lived near her Uncle Matt Goodland's farm in Mapes. Corny was a tall, husky Mennonite guy, with dark brown curly hair, wore glasses, and had a perpetual grin on his face. He fit somewhere in the middle of John and Mary Klassen's family of thirteen kids.

It was a quiet trip out to Sam's. We didn't talk much between the roar of the motor, and bouncing through the potholes. It was just a year or so before, that I had bounced down the same road with Louis Kohse and our talkative American hunters. When we arrived at Sam's ranch, they made a bed for me along one wall of the front entry porch, had supper, then hit the sack.

The two weeks I worked for Sam are treasured memories and I was able to catch a glimpse into the timeless way people lived before all the gadgetry that we now have. A Coleman lantern instead of a coal oil lamp was the only concession to modern ways. When we started logging, I went at it like a wild man. I was going to show Sam what a high production faller could do to these puny jackpine, and he wouldn't have to worry about having wood to skid for months to come. But that wasn't Sam's way. Like most people of that time, he was only interested in sawing enough lumber to make a living or subsidizing the income from his few cows. What I ended up doing was settling down and falling for a day or two, then packing slabs or stacking lumber, and once I got into the swing of things, I enjoyed it. He did the skidding with a little John Deere 40 Cat; I guess you could have called it "selective logging". He only took the bigger trees and left the smaller ones for another day.

Carol was a good cook, and after the chores were done and supper finished, we would sit around and visit for a while, or I would dig out my guitar and sing a few old cowboy tunes. Carol was an interesting person to visit with, and so was Sam, but he really wasn't much for small talk. He was a craftsman at log building and leather work; the harnesses and other things he made were the work of skilled hands. One of my most treasured possessions is a hand braided rawhide leather quirt he gave me when I finished working for him.

It was getting into late Fall when the job was done and I was keeping an eye out for a bull moose, as I still had the hunting fever pretty bad back then. I asked Sam if he would mind if I took a look around a piece of willow bottom behind his barn. He gave me the go ahead, so I dug out the punkin slinger. The morning before we headed into town, I slipped out the back door and down toward the meadow. It was still fairly dark when I got to the corral by the barn and I could see three big dark shapes through the rails of the corral. As it got lighter, I realized it was a big bull moose and 2 cows, and they were only about 50 yards away browsing on the willows. I waited until the light was good enough and lined up behind the bull's shoulder and squeezed the trigger. I'm sure Sam and Carol didn't need to wait for the alarm clock to go off that morning as I was only about a hundred feet from the house.

With the help of Sam's little John Deere Cat, we got him skidded out, and quartered up. Now I wouldn't need to buy any more freezer burned beef streaks for a while. When we left for town the next morning, there was a pile of moose meat lashed down on top of the load of lumber. This peaceful respite with Sam and Carol, and from my own cooking, was a real treat.

A Hard Headed Scotchman &
A Short Grass Goat Farmer

Eric Thomson, at Fort Fraser, was ready to have more timber fell for his sawmill, and I went back to work for him. Winter was approaching, and the old bunkhouse was too drafty so I rented a ramshackle house in Fort Fraser. Eric was looking for a second faller to get more timber down before winter, and a friend, Rod MacKenzie, was looking for a job, so he came up and we batched together. I was the one renting the house, so I laid down some strict rules on drinking, etc. for him to abide by. Rod agreed in his "Would I do anything wrong?" way, and moved in.

We hadn't shared the same house for a week, when he came up with the idea that he should bring his native girlfriend up to do the cooking. I wasn't at all interested, as I knew he still carried the scars of a gunshot wound in his side from an altercation at his brother's house in Vanderhoof earlier that spring. It had been brought on by brother Alex's involvement with a younger sister of Rod's girlfriend. Unfortunately for Alex, there was a young native ex-boyfriend who was not at all happy with this arrangement. He showed up at the house one Saturday night when the party was in full swing, walked through the door with a .22 rifle, and told Alex he was going to shoot him! Alex, who had been through the Korean War, calmly told him to "go ahead and shoot, I've been shot at before". The .22 bullet hit him slightly to the left side of the center of his forehead. Alex was setting in a chair, and slumped to one side. Rod sprang from the corner to grab the gun and was shot through the side. By this time, Bob Pool, one of the party goers, had dove into the large wood box by the side of the stove. From there, he would pop up and throw a piece of firewood at the intruder, and then duck back into the wood box. Everything was total chaos. The native man left, and they quickly called the ambulance for Alex and Rod. Alex was shipped to the hospital in Vancouver where he hovered between life and death for days. Fortunately, the bullet had hit just enough to one side that it travelled around the outside of his skull and had not gone into his brain. (There's something to be said for being a hard headed Scotchman!) It took him months to fully recover. He lost one eye, but eventually went back to work in the bush. True to his nature, Alex married his young native girlfriend. She passed away at a fairly early age, but they had one child, a girl they named Sheila. In later years, Alex took her on a tour of Scotland, England, and other nearby countries. He was very proud of his daughter, and rightly so – she is an attractive lady with a gentle air of refinement about her that matches the soft hint of her Gaelic heritage.

————

After talking things over with Rod, I decided it would be wise to move on to a less hazardous location, and left the house to him and his sweetheart. It was time to get a job closer to Vanderhoof, as by this time my auburn haired girlfriend and I were on pretty good terms, but not actually "going steady". We realized we actually liked each other, even though our personalities and habits were quite different. (Yes…quite different!) She was neat, clean, and organized all the time. I operated on the theory that it was easier to buy a new shirt than try to find the old one. There is a saying that "opposites attract" and that seemed to be the case.

Joan's Dad, Slim Snyder, and I, had initially hit it off pretty good because I was wearing my cowboy hat and boots when I came to take his daughter out. Slim was born in Youngstown, Alberta, and worked for farmers and ranchers in the Hand Hill area where he was raised. He had never lost the vision of himself as a "short grass" prairie cowboy.

One of the favourite family pictures is of Slim and his haying crew, taken on the Mapes farm in 1961. He is standing there with no shirt on, the points of his five tined, pitch fork stuck in the ground, and a "roll yer own" hanging out the corner of his mouth. He has his cowboy hat on, and all the kids gathered round. It's a classic. He had borrowed a team from Mat Goodland, a close neighbour. It must have been a very serious operation as Slim is the only one of the whole group with a faint smile. David is setting on the dump rake, Brian, (with a small cowboy hat on) is setting high on the shoulders of one of the team, while Joan is holding onto the bridle of the other horse. A very serious faced Susan is standing in front of her, while Paul is standing off to one side with his hands held together and looking like he would rather be somewhere else (probably the swimming hole). Janet and Dean weren't on the scene yet, but it is a great picture.

Slim Snyder and his haying crew

By the time I showed up, Slim had advanced to the point of having a two-cylinder Model "AR" 2 banger John Deere tractor, so there was a need for tractor fuel. This is where a problem came up. Joan and I were going to town for something, and Slim asked if I would pick up a barrel of fuel for him. Fuel? Well, certainly!! What better way to show him his daughter was going out with a responsible young man than to bring him a barrel of tractor fuel? We no sooner got out of the driveway than I completely forgot about the fuel barrel in the back. When we drifted in a couple of hours later after a leisurely hamburger and drive around town, Slim was nervously pacing up and down the driveway. I pulled up beside him and smiled. He quickly asked if we had his tractor fuel. Tractor fuel? Was I supposed to pick up some tractor fuel? That's when the cork came out of the bottle! There was one thing that was consistent about Slim ... his temper! That afternoon, I made one of the fastest recorded fuel deliveries in central B.C. history. I tried to make amends by unloading several hay racks of hay for him, but he never asked me to pick up a barrel of fuel for him again!

Bob Unloading Hay for Slim

A farm of course, is never really a farm without livestock. Slim took over the small herd of goats from his mother and step-father, Ellen & Ed Fisher, from their little farm at Bobtail Lake. There Ellen had all her garden and flower beds neatly fenced off to keep the goats out. Slim was thrilled to get this small herd of goats on the place. The goats, plus the milk cow, a dog, and a few stray cats, meant their place could now be classed as a Mapes "farm". The only thing lacking was some good reliable goat proof fencing.

I'm sure the goats couldn't believe their eyes when they were unloaded! This had to be goat heaven! All this stuff to get into and not a decent fence in sight. By the time I came along, the goats were long gone, but according to the kids, it had been quite the show! The family's favourite story was when someone shouted "The goats are out again!", and Slim sprang up from the table and took off after them in his sock feet. The goats had learned by this time that the best way to avoid capture was to whip across the bridge to the pasture on the far side of the creek, so while the whole family looked on, Slim made several trips back and forth through the creek in his sock feet trying to head them off and get them re-captured.

House Fire and Good Neighbours

Slim wasn't always the easiest guy to get along with, but he was a dedicated family man. When I came out of the bush one Friday afternoon in October 1963, I saw Joan crossing the main street in town with one of her legs covered in bandages. I stopped to find out what had happened, and she said their house had burned down. I couldn't believe it. They had lost everything. She put on a brave face, but it was a hard blow. There were 5 kids in the family and her mother was in the hospital right then due to complications with her sixth pregnancy. The one positive was that no one had been seriously injured in the fire. That was only because of Joan's quick thinking and actions.

All the Snyder kids were an independent bunch, and Joan being the oldest, took command of the troops when her parents were not home. When they got off the school bus that day, Marj was still in the hospital, and Slim wasn't home from work yet. Just before supper, Joan was busy in the kitchen, and her youngest brother Paul and a neighbour boy were in the breezeway porch in front of the kitchen window, where they were filling the Coleman lantern with white gas. This stuff was dynamite compared to the old coal oil lamp. Suddenly a sheet of flame exploded on the porch, and up the north wall of the house. Those old log houses with their dry shake roofs were a catastrophe waiting to happen. When the lamp exploded, it splashed white gas on Paul's shirt and pants which immediately burst into flame. He jumped up, let out a yell, and headed across the field in front of the house, screaming and swatting at the flames. Joan quickly tore out of the burning house after him. Paul was always very athletic, and normally could easily outrun her, but that day she chased him down, slammed him to the ground, and rolled him around until she got the flames out. She then ran up to the Mapes Road to get help. Although Joan suffered burns to her leg, and Paul had burns to his arms, it would have been a catastrophe if she hadn't been there.

In the meantime, Paul, and Sammy Dick, the neighbour boy, had managed to drag an old couch out of the door at the far end of the house before the roof caved in. By this time, some of the neighbours had shown up, and realizing her Dad would soon be coming home, Joan thought of sending someone up to tell him all the kids were safe, but it was already too late. Slim was a man of action, and when he came around the bend of the driveway and saw the smoke, he put the throttle to the floor and headed straight across the field toward the house. Unfortunately, there was a corral fence in the way, and when he hit the fence, corral rails flew in every direction! By this time all the neighbours who were gathered around, were running for cover.

It was a sad sight, but a lot of good can come out of a lot of bad. All his kids were safe, and that's what mattered. Everybody in the community rallied around. Brian, Paul, and Susan stayed with friends in Mapes, while Slim, Marj, Joan, and David stayed with Jack and Marg Roche and their family in Vanderhoof. Jack and Marg were long-time friends from Brandon, Manitoba, who had followed Slim and Marj out to Bobtail Lake, 30 miles south of Vanderhoof, in 1956. Jack had eventually found a job at Nechako Motors as a body and fender man, and they moved into town. It was difficult, but they all crowded into Roches small house, and immediately started the plan to rebuild.

Slim decided to build closer to the Mapes Road. It was a wise decision from a practical point of view, and would save a lot of snow plowing and road maintenance. It was also closer to the electrical power that came in a few years later. In some ways, though, it wasn't an easy decision. The old log house with the Virginia Creeper partly covering the walls, had been full of character. This beautiful spot, with the willow fringed creek slowly meandering its way through the summer shade of the poplar trees, radiated a sense of peacefulness and serenity, even though this spell had sometimes been broken when Slim came by chasing the goats.

The new house was built on a small knoll a hundred yards or so east of the Mapes Road. It was a perfect building site, with the land sloping gently away in every direction. The house wasn't fancy, but none of the houses in Mapes were fancy. It was a straight forward, rectangular building with 3 bedrooms across the back, a short wall separating the living room from the dining room, kitchen, and bathroom area. Slim was working full time at Nechako Motors, the Chev/G.M.C. dealer in town, as parts man, but spent every minute he could working on the house. A lot of people from the community pitched in to help. They not only gave their time, they also dug into their pockets and gave money. In the excitement of the whole thing, I even helped out for a couple of days. But the guys who really carried the load were two newly arrived Americans, Bryce Johnson and Ray Colley. Bryce and his family, along with Ray, a single man, had all recently immigrated to Canada from Montana. Neither Bryce nor Ray had a job at that point, so they worked on the house full time. They really put in the hours. It was late fall, winter was on the doorstep, and there was a ton of work to get done.

Bryce was a fairly short, solid built Finlander, with close cut blonde hair. He had a typical Scandinavian work ethic, and a lower lip crammed full of snoose. His partner, Ray Colley, was a thin faced, medium sized man, with iron grey crew cut hair and a real "old cowhand" look about him. Bryce and Ray worked like troopers, and kept everything on the move. If people came to help, Bryce put them to work, but if only the two of them were there, they just hammered on. They sheeted the outside frame of the house with heavy tongue and groove car decking, and once the wiring, insulation, and poly barrier were done, they finished off the inside with 1" x 6" shiplap. It was a good solid house with a big root cellar under the back side and you could keep the place warm with a candle.

The house warming party was a typical Mapes hoe-down celebration, and the whole family were finally back together again. But there was a mystery. Just after the house burned down, a tall, dark stranger had stopped by Nechako Motors and given Jack Roche a donation for the Snyder family Building Fund. This mysterious stranger wore a black cowboy hat, checkered wool bush shirt, and a pair of badly patched wool pants held up by heavy duty suspenders. There was also a peculiar odour about him that seemed to be a mixture of power saw gas, wood smoke, wet dog, moose meat stew, and poorly cooked beans. Jack was quite impressed with this generous stranger, as long as he kept down wind. He mentioned the encounter to Slim, and they racked their brains and finally decided it was Tony Evans, a somewhat reclusive horse wrangler and packer who lived a few miles down the Blackwater Road from Mapes. As the story of this mystery man circulated among the family, Joan immediately recognized the description, and kindly thanked me for the gift.

As things began to settle back in place after the house fire, it slowly dawned on me that this tall, willowy young lady with her dark auburn hair and attractive smile would make a perfect frontier wife! It was plain to see by the way she had calmly managed the situation during the fire that this girl was the kind who could hold off a band of hostile Indians or rustlers with a six gun in one hand, while casually flipping hot cakes for breakfast with the other! Well that might be overstating it a little, but there was definitely cool headed talent here. We began to get more serious, and started "going steady", which at that time was the step you took before becoming officially "engaged".

Bob & Joan with Trapper, goofing around.

But there were two major obstacles, the first being she was on the University Program in Grade 12, and planned on taking Nursing the next year. The second problem was that even though I was still in the very early stages of being a Christian, I wasn't too keen on marrying someone not of the same faith. In spite of the differences, I was more than happy to see her at the end of the week, when I came out of the bush. We continued at the "going steady" stage, as I needed more time to stabilize my financial condition (which meant I was always broke), and she wanted to finish high school and graduate.

My sister Judy had married Ellsworth Hilligoss, a bank employee, in 1962, and now they had written that they wanted to come up for a visit. They were very much into backpacking, and having never been to Canada, wanted to hike in the Jasper and Banff National Parks. We made plans for them to come up the next summer to see the country, and meet Joan and the Snyder family.

Ellsworth & Judy Hilligoss with their children Brent and Marissa, 1968

A Kind Heart &
The Dog Creek Hilton

When I quit my timber falling job for Eric Thomson and moved from Fort Fraser, I rented a cabin from my old Norwegian curling skip, Mel Lynum. I had stayed in this cabin while working for him back in February 1961.

I was now falling for Ed Bergen and Jake Teichroeb. I didn't know Ed that well, but was well acquainted with Jake. The Teichroebs' were a good bunch, and easy to work with. I really liked Jake, and his brothers Willy and Bernie. Jake and Ed were logging for Fred Adam's sawmill, which was several miles down the Dog Creek Road off the highway to Fort St. James. The Dog Creek road was in the same area as the original Hudson Bay Trail that cut cross country from Fort Fraser to Fort St. James.

––––––––

There was an older man, Ted Cook, and his wife, who lived on the east side of the highway to the Fort, (Fort St. James), near the Dog Creek turnoff. During the summer and fall he had a packing business where he used his string of pack horses to take supplies into the mining and hunting areas north of the Fort. The place where their log house was located had very little pasture. If he had a bred mare, or a few horses he wasn't using, he would pasture them out to local kids. A year or so before I came along, Joan heard of this and Slim took her up to meet Ted, and ended up with Belle, a pregnant mare to ride for the summer. This was the horse, as mentioned earlier, that she was riding the second time I saw her. Belle was the perfect, patient, horse for a new rider, and the whole family fell in love with her. Sadly, they lost her in mid-summer when she got into a patch of deadly water hemlock along the edge of the creek. Joan was heartbroken. Slim and Jack Roche took her up to tell Ted the bad news. His big concern was that no one else was hurt, and he wouldn't take a dime for his horse when they offered to pay him. Ted was a big man, even if he didn't stand very tall.

Dog Creek was a high divide that separated the Nechako water shed from the Stuart River watershed. The Stuart and Nechako Rivers join east of Vanderhoof at a historical Carrier site called Chinlac. Dog Creek was a snow belt. As you came from Vanderhoof or Fort St. James, you could see the snowbanks steadily building up along the sides of the highway. It was wet country, where summer rainfalls followed the high divide. All this moisture made for some nice spruce and pine timber.

Up to this point in my falling career, I had never worn snow shoes. Oh yes, I had seen a lot of pictures of trappers mushing along on these long, thin, neat looking things called cruisers, where they skimmed over the snow without breaking a sweat. But I had never worn a pair. While they looked like they might be fun to try out, they certainly didn't look like something you could work in. We were logging about two miles south of Fred Adam's mill. The road into it looked like a bobsled run because they were hauling the logs to the mill with an arch truck. A simple explanation of an arch truck is a big truck with an A-frame contraption on the back, and a winch that lifts the tops of a pile of logs off the ground, and then heads for the mill. The best arch truck drivers are those who have the mentality of a Kamikaze suicide pilot. One thing for sure, when you headed into camp, you wanted to be sure you didn't come face to face with the arch truck!

My humble abode in this world of white was a partitioned off section at one end of a large tool shed. I stayed in the bush during the week (to save money) and would come out to Mel Lynum's cabin for the weekend. My quarters measured roughly 16 X 20 feet. The rest of the shed was used for storing chokers, main lines, hydraulic hoses, different kinds of oil, a stove, and miscellaneous junk. There were also a couple of benches along the sides where the crew ate lunch. In my end of the Hilton Hotel was a large tin heater and a sturdy six foot bunk nailed to one wall. This consisted of four rough 1X8 boards and no mattress (saving money)! The window was a 3 foot wide by 4 foot high opening with a piece of 4 mil plastic over it. Not fancy, but at least the roof kept the snow out. It started off as a good winter, but then the snow came. Knee deep, crotch deep, then waist deep. Jake told me to get some snowshoes, but I was stubborn…"No thanks, I'm doing fine". It finally got to the point where I could barely wallow my way off to the side when I fell a tree. The clincher came when I fell a big pine and made the back cut too low. When the tree fell, it laid up against another tree, causing the butt to kick back over the stump and slide between my shaking knees. When it slid back, it took me along with it. Fortunately, when my steed came to a stop, it dropped down into the deep snow, and didn't move. I gave in then, and bought a pair of 32" bear paw snowshoes. Wearing those things was like walking around with two big garbage can lids tied to your feet. But I learned the tricks, and by spring I could get around through the bush like a 180 pound rabbit.

There was another thing I had heard about, but had never seen. It was called a rubber tire skidder. When I shut off my saw one afternoon, I could hear a steady high pitch humming noise coming from down by the tool shack. It was about quitting time, so I headed for the bunk house to see what was causing all the racket. When I came around a corner, there was a little C-3 Tree Farmer with its' motor howling at full pitch. It had two small logs on the back and the front tires were jumping up and down against a six inch windfall that was laying across the skid trail. It was pathetic. I smugly thought Ha!! So much for rubber tire skidders!

One of the cat operators that winter was Howlin' Hank Williams. He was from the hard scrabble jack pine country east of Vanderhoof, called Chilco. Like Mapes, it was a poor soil district that only through hard work and good farming practices, eventually became productive farm land. Red headed, Howlin' Hank, was operating a little TD-9 International and somehow in that deep snow country, always managed to get the job done. He was an optimist, and always seemed to have a crooked half smile on his long jawed face. He always had his hard hat cocked to one side on his head, and only when it was bitter cold would he snap the strap shut on his hard hat liner. Where Hank really hit his stride was telling stories. He always talked out of the side of his mouth in a confidential "This is just between you and me" manner that made everyone in the crew want to hear what he was saying. This is how he got everybody's attention and really made his day.

Just before starting work at Dog Creek, I had bought a purebred male German Shepherd pup from Emil Rauser out in Chilco. I named him Trapper, and we became good buddies. Things got pretty quiet in the bush at night after the crew left. I had worked my way through the moose I had shot at Sam's and was back to gnawing on freezer burned steaks from the McInnes store. When I came back from civilization after the weekend, I would throw these juicy morsels on the roof of "The Hilton". I kept my spuds and other stuff in a frost proof box I had made, and if a couple of potatoes froze, I would use them to teach Trapper to retrieve. This was our entertainment after supper. Doing this and spending some time studying my Bible by the light of the gas lamp filled out the evening.

Visitors were few and far between where we were at, so I was startled to hear a knock on the door of the tool shed one night. I ignored the first knock, thinking it was probably nothing more serious than a bull moose trying to knock his horns off against the side of the shed. But when there was a second knock, and the dog started growling, I picked up the punkin slinger and went to the door. There were two native guys standing there from Fred Adam's sawmill up the road. Fred hired quite a few native workers, and it seemed to work out well, but some of them lived pretty rough. They explained they had a friend at the camp who was seriously ill, and asked if I would take him to the hospital. They were obviously concerned, so I left the dog and we drove up to the mill site. There were a few shacks scattered around, and a young native man and woman climbed in after my two friends got out. The man was in pretty tough shape and could hardly breathe, so I took them to the hospital in Vanderhoof. He had pneumonia, and after he was admitted, I took his lady back to their camp. I heard later that he recovered, but he was in the hospital quite a while.

It was a deep snow winter that year, and Dog Creek lived up to its' reputation. Although there was a lot of snow we didn't have much cold weather. That's typical, and makes for poor snowshoeing. After wallowing around in the white stuff all day there was one thing I always looked forward to, and that was meeting the dog. He would spend all day lazing around The Hilton, bored stiff, chasing his frozen potato around the floor, or chewing up a pair of my new wool socks or anything else of value. His built-in alarm clock would go off when he knew it was time for me to come home. He would hide behind a high snowbank close to the shop, and wait to pounce on me. As I came down the road, I could see the tips of his ears, and his head would pop up, then jerk back down as he waited for me to come within range. I would come walking along, whistling, pretending I didn't have a clue there was a sixty pound dog waiting to jump on me. Suddenly he would give a sharp bark, tackle me, and down we would go in the middle of the road for a big wrestling match.

Stove Pipes & Wedding Bells

I had finally located a half section of land, a few miles east of Vanderhoof that I had filed on, and this, plus my "going steady" auburn haired girlfriend, who I was falling in love with, had caused me to consider every possible way to save money. In the fall of 1963, when I rented Mel Lynum's cabin, I suddenly realized there was a golden opportunity right in front of me. The stove pipes in Mel's cabin, and those in my shack at Dog Creek were exactly the same length and diameter ...perfect! All I had to do when I came down for the weekend or went back to the bush, was dismantle the stove pipes, move them to the other location, re-assemble them, get a fire going, and Bingo! Just like that I could save the price of three lengths of six inch stove pipe! Money in the bank! The first time I put this plan in operation, I realized I had made a serious mistake. If you have ever tried hooking up three pieces of stove pipe in the dark, by the feeble light of a flashlight lying on the table, and at 20 below F, you will know what I mean.

Pam & Dick did me a real favour that winter. They were married September 21, 1963, and rented a small house behind Audrey Smedley's Photo Studio on Stewart Street. Every Friday evening, they would kindly let me use their bathroom to take a shower and clean up. This may not seem like a big deal, but the bush smell mentioned earlier could be quite overwhelming in close quarters. They would go for a walk, or to the movie theatre, while I restored myself to something acceptable to society. Then I would take a drive up to the Royal Produce to pick up Joan. She was working on Friday evenings and Saturdays during her last year of high school for Peter Yip, owner of Royal Produce Foods. We would go back to Pam & Dicks' for a short visit, and then I would drive her home to Mapes.

There was a real stampede of engagements and marriages of local young people around this time. My petite cousin, Carma, had married Toby Millard, the rodeo cowboy, on July 6, 1963 and were living in Prince George. My oldest cousin Ed was engaged to be married to Carol Martin, but had been drafted to the U.S. army. His future mother-in-law, Gladys Martin, convinced him to go, so Carol would finish her nurse's training. They were married on June 4, 1966, after Ed served his 2 years in Germany, and Carol received her R.N. designation.

Joan and I were engaged, May 1964, just before she graduated from high school, with an October date for the wedding. Joan had decided to give up the idea of going away to take nursing and instead was planning on working at the Royal Bank in Vanderhoof as soon as school was out. This was mostly due to the fact that the nursing program would take 3 years, and by that time I would be an old man!!

Joan's High School graduation photo

When she walked down the aisle in June 1964 for her Graduation march, I thought she was beautiful. She was wearing a frilly pink dress, long white gloves, and her hair piled up in a fancy style. I was proud that this girl would soon be my wife. The tradition at the Nechako Valley Secondary School was to pass on a candle to a Grade 11 student before accepting your diploma. She gave her candle to Dick Goodland, Matt & Bernice's son, also from Mapes. Joan, and her closest friend, Carol Fasten, were in the center of their grad picture. They were both tall girls, taller than many of the boys in their class. But in the picture, they seemed to be noticeably shorter. Joan later confessed that they had their knees bent so they didn't tower over the boys!

Around the same time my youngest sister, Janice Kae, now attending Milo Academy sent me a picture of her and Mom at a Mother/Daughter tea at the school. Janice Kae was a horse person and spent most summers as a wrangler at summer camps. She was turning into a beautiful young woman and was very close to Mom & Dad, now that all of us older kids were gone.

Earlier that spring, I had made contact with the Irving Toombs family of Prince George, owners of a family construction business. I met Irving's sons, Kenneth and John, when I was working on the construction of the Vanderhoof Lumber dry kilns during spring break-up. They had the contract to spray the dry kilns, and I got to know them well. They invited me to church in Prince George and I decided I would go for the day, as Joan was working.

I wanted to show the church members I wasn't a total cave man, so I "put on the dog", so to speak, and dressed up in a clean white shirt, suit and tie (class!). I had arranged to drop Trapper off at my cousins' that morning, and as he hadn't eaten his dog food yet, I mixed warm water with it and carefully sat it down on the passenger side floor. He jumped up on the seat on the passenger side, and I got in on my side and away we went, off to church, dressed in style! I never quite made it to my cousins before I hit a patch of ice. The truck went in the ditch, and the dog and bowl of wet dog food lit on top of me. Oh yes, I really "put on the dog" that morning. Needless to say, by the time we got untangled, the dog food dug out of my ears, and the truck back on the road, we never made it to church.

Mapes & Sob Lake Communities

I was starting to get acquainted with some of the residents of the Mapes area, and found it had an interesting history and mixture of people. It was an old community dating back to the early 1900's. The name "Mapes" came from the George Mapes family that left Indian Head, Idaho, in a covered wagon in 1909, headed for the central interior of British Columbia. ("The Town that Couldn't Wait", page 31). They were actually headed for Ootsa Lake, but seeing a nice spot along the Blackwater Road, they decided to pull over and homestead. Eventually they opened a store, applied for a post office location, and Mapes was on the map! There were three families in the party, the George Mapes, the Elliots, and the Wilsons. It's a fascinating story; the community became a real mixture of English, American, Scandinavians, Mennonites, and a few other cultures and nationalities tossed in. But the Mennonite people were probably the majority. When they arrived on the scene in the early 1940's, it didn't take long to increase the population.

The Jake Teichroeb family that lived across the road from Slim Snyder was made up of 19 kids. Although a few of the Mennonite families kept to themselves, others, like the John Klassen and Jake Teichroeb families became very much part of the community. One of the winter highlights was when the Teichroeb boys stopped by the Snyder farm to see if any of the kids wanted to ride along on the stone boat when they hauled water from the Mapes School. For some reason, the water from the school well was exceptionally good, most likely because of a wide sandy ridge near where the well was located. (Years later the well was found to have a high arsenic content and a new well was drilled.) People from miles around hauled water from the school as a lot of local wells had a high mineral content. Henry Teichroeb was always the driver, and, though I'm quite sure he had never heard of Ben Hur and the chariot racers of Rome, boys will be boys. Everything was quite docile while Teichroeb's two forty-five gallon water barrels, and Snyder's three or four 10 gallon milk cans were being filled. This took some time as the water had to be hand pumped, but then the fun would begin. The horses, sensing the excitement, would be straining at the bit, ready to roll. Henry would get in position, snap the lines, let out a whoop, and let go. It's a miracle no one was injured or killed. The stone boat would careen around the school with the water sloshing, snow flying, kids screaming and falling off. After a couple of laps, Henry would pull the heaving horses in and anybody he had lost could get back on. Then they would calmly head out through the gate. This performance continued for several years until all the upcoming kids were initiated into the thrills, chills, and spills of water hauling. Somehow the parents never had a clue about what was going on!

Henry was not only a chariot racer; he was also a very talented fiddle player. At one point in their early years, he and his brothers, along with Oscar Walstrom, tried out, and were successful in securing a spot on the famous "Grand Old Opry" show in Nashville, Tennessee. Henry also told me the story of staying alone in a bush camp one fall, and taking his fiddle out in the evening. As he played, he suddenly realized he wasn't alone; birds and wildlife were gathering around the clearing to listen. He had a rare talent, but sadly, a few years later his life was cut short by a terminal illness.

Mapes was a much different community than the Lakes District where my cousins settled. It covered a larger area, was not as developed at that time, and was more ranch land than farm country. The people were from hard working pioneer stock, struggling to hack an existence from the land, and just a bit more hillbilly than the neighbouring Lakes District.

There were two major social events that everyone attended during the year. The first was the Mapes School Christmas Concert which was held in the main classroom. Families would be packed into the small stuffy room, noisy with the excited voices of the 25 or so students. This was usually a three ring circus, with the curtain falling down in the middle of a performance, the younger kids giggling, crying, falling off the stage, and a couple of the Grade 8 girls singing a badly off key, country western version of Silent Night. But everyone loved it! The highlight of the evening would be the candy bags and small gifts each child received, compliments of the Mapes PTA.

The second event was the annual Mapes Community Picnic, which was held in a field on Bert Welfare's place at the east end of Sinkut Lake. This was to end the school year, and was always a great event where all the families and young bucks from the community would come to demonstrate their physical prowess in front of all those standing by, especially the girls! It was also time for the old "has beens" to see who could limp over the finish line first in the "Over 40 Foot Race". But the main competition was to see who could gobble down the most pieces of Ivy Stampflee's fried chicken without making a complete fool of themselves!

The years I attended I lost more foot races than I won, but it was all good fun. The main event at the end of the Track and Field section was the High Jump. One year I do remember, everyone was weeded out to where only young Dave Klassen and I were left. Dave was about sixteen, one of the younger boys in the John and Mary Klassen family. Their farm was a few miles up the road from the Snyders', and the kids were all good friends. The Mennonite boys were a very competitive lot, and Dave could jump like a kangaroo.

His older brother, Henry, had beat me earlier in a foot race, and I was still smarting a bit from the defeat, so this was a chance to restore my self-esteem. Henry had good reason to appreciate speed. As a young boy he was riding his pony not far from home when he happened upon a moose calf. He thought the calf might be an orphan, and crawled off his horse to check it out. Momma Moose suddenly appeared, and was not happy with the situation. Henry leaped into the saddle, shifted into overdrive, and made a mad dash for home, with the moose striking at the rear end of his horse. She chased them right into the yard, almost to the front door of the house.

As the high jump competition continued the bar kept being raised until a sizable crowd had gathered. Dave had his style and I had mine for jumping over the bar. Eventually he complained that my style wasn't legal in Community Picnic Regulations, so the judges quickly gathered to discuss this serious problem, and finally agreed that my style was legal. On the next jump (or barrel roll), I managed to clear the bar. When his turn came, he knocked the bar off, and I had my revenge! We had a good laugh about it after, but I did learn one thing, Mennonite boys don't give up easy!

———

Mapes was a young, vibrant community. Jake Friesen and Albert Stampflee (who were extreme opposites in personality), started the Mapes 4H Club.

Head, Heart, Hands, Health, you might know the pledge. The kids from the hardpan, and hay meadow ranches and farms, knew their stuff. They were strong competitors in the big annual 4H Show at the Vanderhoof Fall Fair grounds. Cattle, sheep, goats (if you could catch them), chickens, rabbits, guinea pigs, whatever it was, their dedication to 4H gave them an opportunity to showcase their community.

Sarah Friesen, Jake's wife, was a motherly type, and also very dedicated to the community with her midweek Bible programs, and the summer Canadian Sunday School Mission Vacation Bible Schools. These programs had a long, lasting Christian influence on Joan, and other local girls who helped her with the younger children.

Along with these events, there were "box" socials at the school, and family parties in homes with lots of music. The latest in local footwear style in Mapes at that time was rolled down bobby socks and high heel shoes! Yes, Mapes district had their own style!

The Stampflees' were an industrious lot, and some of the earliest pioneers. Ivy Haddock came with her parents from Wisbech, England, and in 1920 settled in Mapes, where Pete Stampflee was living. Pete and Ivy were married in 1927. With only one boy, Albert, in the family, the girls, Muriel, Bertha, Gladys, Elsie and Sheila learned to do anything a man could do. This was still in the early days when everything was done with horses. With all the logging, saw milling, land clearing, hunting, gardening, canning, cooking and a hundred and one other things to do, the family established their farm. Visitors were always welcome and made to feel at home, with Ivy's fried chicken being a big attraction. In 1956 when Joan's parents, Marj and Slim Snyder, arrived from Brandon, Manitoba, Ivy was a real friend to Marj, who had lived a life of relative comfort in the city of Brandon. Now here she was, plopped down in the backwoods of B.C., with no running water, no power, and a passel of kids! Marj had suffered with asthma as a young girl, and was not always in the best of health. This, coupled with all the other stress, made life difficult, so it was Ivy to the rescue! She had been through the mill herself, and was a woman blessed with a natural gift of compassion and understanding; a great friend to have in time of need. Ivy would stop by for tea and a good talk on her occasional trip to town, and leave Marj feeling much encouraged. Sheila and Joan became good friends, cemented by their mutual love of horses.

Joan's grandparents, Ed & Ellen Fisher, lived a few miles from the Stampflees on their farm at Mapes, in later years. Before that they lived year round at Bobtail Lake, on the old Telegraph Trail, where Ed had a mink farm and ran a hunting and fishing business. Ed came into that area in the 1930's, running trap lines, and eventually settling on the ¼ section at the end of Bobtail Lake. Grandmother Ellen Snyder, widowed, and with her youngest son, George, met Ed at Sucker Creek, while traveling by team & wagon down to the Rasmussen Ranch at Butcher Flats on April 1,1941 to work as nanny and housekeeper. Ed & Ellen were married in the Anglican Church in Vanderhoof on October11, 1941 and spent the next 22 years happily living in their wilderness home at Bobtail.

––––––––

Other early pioneers settled in an area close to Mapes, the S.O.B. Lake community. The lake got its derogatory name from frustrated ranchers who lost livestock in the bottomless muskeg swamps around the lake edges. Fred and Rose Wright came in 1909 and lost their first home and two children in a fire. They rebuilt, with that indomitable spirit so necessary in those early days, and eventually had three sons, Dan, Alan, and Robin. I never met Robin or the old folks, but was well acquainted with Dan and Alan.

Dan was a tall, broad shouldered, dignified man, with a quiet sense of strength and good humour. After serving as a paratrooper during the Second World War, Dan came home to marry Leona Walstrom, and established a ranch that sat on a high bluff overlooking the infamous SOB Lake. Leona was a twin sister to Oscar Walstrom, who was always at the center of the country/western music world in Vanderhoof, and surrounding area. Leona was a short, solid built lady with a direct, straight forward gaze, and mischievous smile. Dan & Leona had two children, Clive and Kathy, and later sold their ranch to the Jiggs Blattner family from Ellensburg, Washington.

Dan's younger brother, Alan, served as a commando in the Second World War, and would tell the story of a "dud" shell that hit the truckload of artillery shells he was delivering to the front lines. Fortunately, the shell never went off. Fortunate for Bertha Stampflee, as well, who married him when he came home. Alan was the perfect stereotype of an old west cowboy; tall, lanky, easy going, with a ready laugh and smile. Bertha, or Bert as she was known, was a perfect match for Alan, and inherited her Mother Ivy's cooking abilities. Alan & Bert stayed on the old home ranch after the war, working with his parents, and building the ranch up.

Then, in 1958 George & Tiny Garrett bought the ranch, renaming it the 0-0. They came from Lakeview, Oregon, high desert cattle country. Like Fred and Rose Wright, they were not big people, only in vision. Tiny was a very attractive lady, and could rope and ride with the best. George, with his weathered face and short brimmed stockman's hat, looked like the sheriff of Deadwood City. Alan and Bert stayed on and worked for the Garretts' for a few years, eventually having three children, Ross, Roy, and Alene, while establishing their own place in the area.

George and Tiny worked hard on their ranch, and the 0-0 became a successful operation. George had a soft spot for kids and would sometimes hire them during haying season. Joan drove tractor for him for a few days one summer (so he had to have patience)! One thing he did that not too many were aware of was to loan five hundred dollars to a young local boy who was going to Ontario to attend College. Like most independent people, George loved enterprising thought and action. Another thing he loved was Hereford cattle. In later years, I bought a few bred cows from him that had a little Brockle around their eyes to prevent "Pinkeye". These cows, crossed with one of Clark Borth's good, easy calving Charolais bulls, produced some fine buckskin calves by sale time.

George and Tiny's son, Larry, began to take over the reins in 1980, and along with his wife Karen, operate the ranch today. Larry's sister, Elisa, and her husband, who is a lawyer, operate a business venture in Prince George.

———

Forest fires have had a big impact on much of the Interior plateau of B.C. With lightning strikes, and ranchers burning off grazing land, fires get away. Fire has always been the homesteader's best friend and worst enemy. If done right, it can do a lot of good, if done wrong, it can be a disaster, and leave a sterilized landscape that takes years to rebuild and become productive again. At one time, there were a lot of big Douglas Fir in the Mapes area. There are still a few of these along the ridges where the fires didn't get them. The Mapes Cemetery is such a place. There these great gnarled patriarchs stand guard over those sleeping under their protecting care. It's a peaceful spot, with only the occasional chatter of a red squirrel, or spring time drumming of a Ruffed Grouse to break the lingering quiet. It's also a practical spot, with its gentle south facing slope, and sandy soil that makes for easy digging. Many of the early pioneers are buried here, as well as friends and neighbours from later years, and Joan's grandparents, Ed & Ellen Fisher.

Slim and Marj Snyder had been baptized in the Mapes Baptist Church and now rest in this spot, awaiting the call of the Life Giver on the Resurrection Day. Slim passed away on April 28, 2005. We buried him the old way on May 3, 2005, (no backhoes allowed). The men of the family, took turns doing the digging in that soft, sandy soil. Jackets off, tears mixing with the sweat running down faces, laughing joking, crying a little; somehow, I think he would have liked the way it was done. After the service, we lowered his casket into the ground and covered him up. Now, the whole family took part. Sons, daughters, grandkids, great grandkids – some sprinkled handfuls and some shovelled. It was everyone's final tribute. After we tamped him in and mounded and rounded off the top of his grave, the 38 family members who were able to be there) hugged and crowded together in a long row for a family picture. It was the most meaningful service of this kind I've ever been involved in. In September, 2006, Marj's ashes were placed with him, just the way they would have wanted.

Pleasant Bay and Rough Water

After spring break-up in 1964 I heard of a Mormon logging contractor, Al Shaw, who was working up Stuart Lake, so I went up to check it out. Fort St. James was still quite a bit like the wild west at that time. The first time I saw Fort St. James was in the early spring of 1961. It was a cold, windy, dreary looking place at that time of year. I was job hunting, and rode up with Dr. Hugh Stephens from Vanderhoof. Dr. Stephens was on his weekly medical rounds to patch up assorted R.C.M.P. officers, Indians, loggers, mill workers, and stray dogs (not necessarily in that order) who had been injured, maimed, or wounded since his last visit.

We stopped at the local hotel for a cup of coffee after he was finished. As we walked in, I could feel the hackles on my neck start to rise. The pub in this establishment was locally known as "The Zoo"; apparently because someone had their finger bitten off during a fight in the bar. Drugs were also a problem, the restaurant was full of a mixture of white and native young people, who seemed to be at different stages in LaLa Land. After we left the restaurant we had one last call to make, to sew up a dog's badly ripped ear. I did the assistant part and held the dog down, while Dr. Stephens stitched it up. When we left that afternoon, I couldn't say I was all that impressed with the Fort.

When I drove up to check out this falling job in 1964, it was with reservations. This time it was early summer, and I have to admit I was impressed. It was beautiful, but the big negative was the wind. It has a direct shot at the village, down 60 miles of Stuart Lake, but it does keep most of the blood thirsty mosquitos, horse flies, bull dog flies, black flies, no-see-ums, and other varmints away. Established in 1806 by the Northwest Company, Fort St. James is the Gateway to a large section of wilderness, lakes, and rivers in northern B.C.

Al hired me on the spot. There seemed to be two main logging areas at that time on the north side of Stuart Lake; Peaceful Bay, and Pleasant Bay,

257

which were 36, and 40 miles by water from the Fort. There were no roads on the north side of the lake, and the logs were all moved to the mill at the east end by tug boat and log booms. There wasn't even a road into the Tachie Indian Village, which was 28 miles by water west of the Fort. These bays were protected spots that were big enough to assemble log booms and have enough room along the shore line for landings and camps. Log booms are made up of logs that are chained end to end to form a large circle. The inside of the circle is filled with logs that are bucked to length.

Al was a nice guy, medium height, round ruddy face, wire rim glasses, and a congenial personality. Behind the mild mannered exterior were the keen dark eyes of a get it done, businessman. He ran a topnotch camp, best of food, good bunkhouses, and no horse play. He hired you on contract and expected you to produce. He was the Bishop of the Mormon Church in Fort St. James, and had an attractive young wife and several children. When the crew went up the lake, they stayed in for 2 weeks at a time. I explained to him that I was getting married that fall and there was planning to do, so he made a concession. He would let me use a leaky, decrepit river boat to come out every Friday afternoon, provided I pay for the gas and was back on the job Monday morning. That was more than fair.

I was on the dock, ready to go the next Sunday evening when he went up the lake (I picked up my river boat the next time we came down). Al was spread pretty thin. He was responsible for his church, his wife and young family, and a logging camp and crew. He was a busy man. I don't remember how many of us were waiting on the dock that Sunday evening to head up the lake, but there were too many. He had a good size cabin cruiser with two fifty horse motors on it, but when everybody and everything was loaded, he couldn't get it out of the water to plane. He finally got two or three guys out on the end of the bow to hold the nose down while he opened everything up, and very slowly the boat finally lifted out of the water.

One other faller that got on board that evening was a small sandy haired man named Art Johnson. Art was a harmless looking fellow who looked more like a shoe salesman or first grade teacher, than a red neck logger. He had a puny little twenty inch bar on his saw that was obviously too short to do the job. As I looked at Art and myself, it was clear that Al Shaw must be desperate for fallers.

The next morning after we got everything lined out, Al ran Art and I around the corner to the boom landing. He pulled up sideways to let us out on a boom log fairly close to shore, as the bay was full of logs and he couldn't let us out on shore. The landing crew were lined up against the bank waiting for the cats to come down with a drag, but more than that, they were waiting for Art and I to make our ballerina trip along the boom sticks to shore. Art went first, axe in one hand, power saw in the other, pack sack on his back. He never made two steps before he started to wobble and lost his balance. Suddenly, with a cry of despair, he jumped from the relatively stable boom log out onto the loose logs that were bumping and bobbing around inside the boom. By this time, the landing crew were on their feet cheering him on. Art took off like a tap dancer, not toward the shore, but in a total panic, straight toward the center of the boom. Finally, in desperation, he threw himself out in a spread-eagle position across the logs, axe in one hand, power saw in the other and began to cry for help. By this time the landing crew were rolling on the ground howling with laughter! Well, I couldn't in all good conscience leave my friend in this predicament, so I jumped out on the logs, ran to him, grabbed his saw and somehow made it to the landing. By some miracle, he managed to get up on the logs and finally made it to shore.

Now it was my turn. I was pretty quick on my feet at that time, and managed to get back to the boat, but when I picked up my stuff and stepped out on the boom log, my foot slipped, and in I went, power saw, axe and packsack, right up to my armpits. This whole performance was clearly out of control until the landing crew finally came to my rescue. A few minutes later, a skid cat came in and two soaking wet fallers climbed on board for the ride to the top. Welcome Wetbacks! Your first day of logging at Pleasant Bay!

The first week was a learning curve. The big firs were almost twice as long as our Vanderhoof Jack Pine. Everything was top skidded, and I was dumping my trees at too sharp an angle, and the tops were crossing the skid trail, but after a few days, I got used to the extra length. They were skidding with those big, long nosed 2 U Model D-8 cats. Most of the choker setters were native guys from the Fort or Tachie village. The cats were pulling a big wheel arch and when they broke over the edge at the top, and started down the steep grade to the lake with a drag of big fir logs fanned out behind, it was quite a sight. The fallers caught a ride up with the cats in the morning, as it was a lot easier than packing your stuff up on foot, but with supper waiting, it didn't take us long to get down at night. Our top faller was Gordon Bissel, a sandy haired, solid built logger out of Prince George.

Gordon's wife was the cook and knew what and how to feed loggers. She was a small gracious, attractive lady who always wore a fresh clean cotton dress, full white apron, and friendly smile. When mealtime came, everything was steaming hot, and ready to go, with the help of a "bull" cook. While the men were eating, she would stand along the wall and the minute anything was close to empty, it was immediately refilled. She was a topline professional cook, and there wasn't a man that didn't treat her with respect. As usual, I was always the first to the table, and the last to leave.

———

The bunk houses were comfortable, but some of the occupants left a little to be desired. Loggers enjoy a good story; it can even be embellished a little to bring out the good parts, but they don't have much patience or tolerance for braggers and outright liars. One of the guys in our bunkhouse was an Italian. He was a professional ski bum who worked as a faller in the off season to support himself. The most entertaining thing to him, was bragging about his skiing, and other daring exploits. He looked like an athlete, and in spite of his stories, he was also a hard worker. One evening he decided to mix up a 5 gallon can of power saw gas and pack it on his shoulder up the mountain, as there were times he would go up after supper and work for an hour or so during the long summer days. All seemed to go well, and as we lazed around on our bunks, we could hear his power saw in the distance, but when he came in that night he had a strained look on his face, and after taking a shower went straight to bed. During the night, he woke us up with his moans and groans of suffering. When morning came, he grudgingly told us what his problem was. Apparently the 5 gallon can of gas he packed up the hill had a leak in it, and the gas had soaked through his shirt and dribbled down the crack of his rear end. Not realizing what had happened, he put in his hour or two of falling and by the time he got back to camp, he had a king size case of bleeding hemorrhoids. Loggers by the very nature of their jobs, are victims of numerous cuts, scrapes and scratches; so they immediately began to sympathize and suggest various home cures.

The first thing of course, was to cleanse the wound. Everyone agreed the high pressure spray washer would be an ideal solution. Then of course there would have to be a salve of some kind applied. Some suggested "Old Spice" after shave lotion, some thought pine tar, or balsam pitch, (the idea being that this would burn so bad he would forget all about the hemorrhoids). There was finally a consultation, and all agreed the best ointment would probably be a generous application of top quality, all-purpose, ball bearing lubricant; so someone headed off to get the grease gun! By this time, the Italian's face had turned a pasty white, and he was begging Al to just take him to town. So that's what was done and strangely enough we never saw him again.

––––––––

Most of the guys in camp were a good bunch. There was one cat operator in the crew that gave me the cold chills. He was a big, slope shouldered, hulking older man who was bald headed except for a heavy fringe of black hair around the sides. He was a reclusive type with a bad attitude. But most of all, he wasn't careful. Charlie Joseph, a young native guy from Tachie village was his choker setter. Charlie was in his early twenties, with the quick, smooth reflexes and tall athletic build of a basketball player. With his high forehead, wavy black hair, long handsome face, and aloof bearing, he looked more Hawaiian than native. He always wore a full brim aluminum hard hat and blue denim jean jacket on the job. Every day at work was a cat and mouse game, with Charlie as the mouse, but he always managed to stay one jump ahead. The native boys all stayed in one bunk house; there were five or six of them. They were cordial, but kept to themselves and most worked as choker setters. On other jobs I worked, they also made good fallers.

There was a big, flabby younger guy in our bunkhouse who had a Martin guitar he wanted to sell. He said it was a Jumbo Martin, and when you hit the top string it sounded like a bass drum. I don't know where he got it from, and didn't ask, but he wanted a hundred dollars for it. I wanted that guitar in the worst way, but didn't have the cash or a check on me. He had decided to quit and was catching a ride out with Al the next morning and seemed to need the money, so he just tore a piece off the lid of a cardboard box and said "Write me a check on this." I had never heard of such a thing, but when he left the next morning he had his piece of card board (which the bank did cash) and I had the guitar. I never saw or heard from him again.

————

Friday afternoons I would head down the lake in my leaky scow for the Fort, as arranged earlier with Al. Going down the lake, or coming back, could be a joy ride or a nightmare, all depending on the weather. If you hit it just right in the old river boat, it was like riding a surf board; you could catch the crest of a wave and throttle the motor up or down to ride it. Stuart Lake has drowned a lot of people over the years, through carelessness and over confidence, and some through just plain stupidity. Not surprisingly, my experience fit in the stupidity class.

We got a lot of wet weather that summer, and when the wind and rain came over the Babine divide at the west end of Stuart Lake, it created very rough water at the east end. I came back on a Sunday afternoon to head up the lake in my river boat, and found it was too rough. I waited a while and decided I would try to stay as close to the north shore as I could, and if I tipped over, I could make it to shore, with my life jacket on. It was an awkward position as I wasn't headed straight into the west wind, but quartering into it. It was a delicate balance because I had to go north west before I could head straight west up the lake to Pleasant Bay. Another disadvantage was when I opened the throttle up, the old 50 horse kicker throttle handle wanted to pull sideways. This problem was quickly solved by tying a small cord to the handle and running it through a slat on the side of the boat. I could steer it by hanging onto the throttle arm with one hand, and pulling or slacking off on the cord with the other (kind of a gee/haw effect). This wasn't the standard means to steer a boat of course, but I was getting pretty good at it! I figured that by placing my full, ten gallon, fuel barrel on the opposite side of the boat from where I was sitting, it would balance things out perfectly. There were two glaring errors in my calculations; the first was that I didn't tie the fuel barrel down, the second was what I would do if I got broadsided by a rogue wave! When I started up the lake, it was rougher than I expected, and the waves were hitting the south side more than planned. It was a fine line. I had my old 38 – 55 punkin slinger laying on the same side as the fuel barrel. Then, it happened! A rogue wave slammed into the side, and knocked the fuel barrel over to the same side I was sitting on! For a couple of seconds, the boat stood up on its side, and I thought I might have to go for a swim. I released the throttle, let go of the steering arm, dropped my unique steering cord, then leaped up on the top edge of the boat. It fell back down to where the bottom was at least level with the lake, and I quickly began to assess the damage. I hadn't taken any additional water on board, so there was still hope. I quickly wrestled the fuel barrel back where it belonged, tied it in place with my steering cord, and headed at a sharper angle into the waves.

Looking back, I think the only thing that kept the boat from tipping over, was the water on the bottom that helped stabilize it. The water had collected because most of the caulking had fell out between the first two rows of planking in the bow. This allowed a considerable amount of water to shoot between the cracks, which acted as a bit of a sea anchor. Farther up the lake the wind tends to drop, so the rest of the trip was fairly uneventful. Although what had happened was pretty scary, I soon discovered all the hazards didn't come from rough water. Most of my comings and goings on the lake were pure enjoyment. Sometimes I would go down the south side just for a little variety. It was a beautiful trip, with several islands jutting up here and there. Back in the summer of 1961, I had helped my Mapes friend, Henry Klassen, build a small cabin for Norm Pauley, on one of these islands. Norm was helping Henry with his education at that time, and was a close friend of Bill Wineberg, who I was working for at Nulki Lake.

One particular sunny Friday afternoon on my way down the lake, I was surfing the clear green roller coaster waves toward the east end, and enjoying the freedom from a week of hard work. The big wedding day was drawing closer and that would bring my days of free range living to an end, but I was looking forward to seeing my future bride. Lost in thought, I was passing an island when I heard a faint call for help. It's strange how a voice carries over water, but as I looked toward a narrow beach on an island to my left, I could see a figure jumping up and down, arms waving. You can never tell what kind of an emergency you'll run across out in the boondocks, so I opened up the old kicker and headed for the beach. As I got closer, I could see it was a native woman who seemed to be in distress.

263

When I ran the bow up on the beach and got out, she came running at me yelling, "You take me Fort St. James, you take me Fort St. James!" I quickly realized she was so plastered, she could hardly stand up. Oh yeah! I thought, this is just what I need in my leaky river boat that's already about to sink on its' own! She finally managed to get the story out that her sweetheart had left her on her own while he buzzed off to the Fort to replenish their fast dwindling alcohol supply, and now she was afraid he might forget where he had left her. This was clearly an emergency situation! I checked things out and made sure she had plenty of food and water, jumped in my trusty boat, and before she could crawl in with me, opened the old 50 horse up and the last I saw of her, she was still waving me to come back. When I got to the Fort, I reported the incident to the R.C.M.P., and then headed for the bright lights of Vanderhoof.

––––––––

I ran into one major head butting contest with Al, toward the end of the season, that was partly my fault. I had got the hang of laying those nice big firs down in the skid trail where they belonged, and the cat skinners and choker men seemed happy enough. Then I ran into a situation I didn't know how to handle. There were some short ridges that ran out toward the lake from the high plateau we were logging. These ridges were like your fingers sticking out from your hand when it's laid flat on the table. The trees on top of the ridges were straight enough to fall and be skidded by the top. The trees on the steep sides were a nightmare. They were all heavy limbed on the downhill side, and leaned backwards away from where they needed to go. I tried. I beat my plastic wedges to a pulp. It was a steep side hill, and hard to get a good swing, but I wedged them from the side, from the back, and every other direction, trying to get them to go up the hill and into the road, but it was hopeless. I had wedges sticking out of those trees until they looked like pin cushions.

Al wasn't around, and wouldn't be for a couple of days. I told the foreman what I was up against and he seemed to be occupied with other things. So, after spending more money than I was making, buying wedges at the commissary, I just sawed 'em off and let 'em go. I had those big fir trees going over like dominoes, all in the wrong direction, but I had tried my best and

264

saw no other way. The next time I dropped in at the office, Al was there and I could see the smoke coming out from under his hard hat and his face was quite flushed. I had the uneasy feeling he was perturbed about something. I told him I had come to pick up my check, and when I looked at it, there was hardly anything there. I asked him what the problem was, and he told me he had docked my pay for all the extra hassle it had been to winch those big trees out by the butt. Well, that's when the dog fight began. When it was over, the hair was knee deep around the office, but I got all my money, and never felt any guilt over it.

Al was a dedicated man, but he was spread pretty thin. Late one evening, just as it was getting dark, he suddenly remembered he had to pick up a part or do something at the Fort, so he jumped in his boat and took off, throttle wide open. I think he had a spot light on the boat. But with all the booms going down the lake and drift floating around, it was taking a big chance. About half way down, he nailed a log that knocked a big hole in his boat and left him floating around in the middle of the lake until daybreak, when he was finally rescued.

September 1964, and a lot of the native boys had shut it down as it was time to forget the white man's work schedule and time to go fishing. That's something that I always found fascinating, before the white man showed up the natives didn't have watches, didn't go by the hour, but by the sun and season. They had a tribal, hunter-gatherer culture, and probably not too many of them had ulcers. My last week in September, I really poured it on. The last day I worked that fall was miserable – cold, wet, and windy. But I had stuck it out, and when I gathered all my stuff together for the last trip down the lake, I felt like I had finally finished my apprenticeship as a faller.

Fort St. James was then, is now, and always will be a frontier town. Its characters are as big as the country. The magnitude of what was attempted and done in this area is truly astonishing. The fur trade, the gold rush, the logging and sawmill ventures, the bush pilots, the freighters, the paddle wheelers that weaseled their way impossible distances up the lakes and rivers, you name it, it has been done or tried. When I worked for Al Shaw the summer of 1964, not a lot had changed. The only thing now that's still the same, is the sheer rock face and bald head of Mt. Pope that looms above the town. In 1964, it was still river boat or airplane access to the lakes and rivers, Tachie, Trembleur, Takla, Tezzron, Tachie River, Middle River, and Driftwood. In 1964, the north road goat trail ran 135 miles to the gold claims at Germansen Landing and Manson Creek. Now it is a road that carries up to 250 loads of logs a day to sawmills as far south as Dunkley Lumber, between Prince George and Quesnel. There is now a feeding frenzy of logging that will result in nothing left in a few short years. Yes, I'm glad I was able to see it when I did.

This was my last job as a foot loose single man. In less than a month, I would be getting married, with all the responsibilities that come with it. But at least I wouldn't have to face my own cooking!

Bob falling for Al Shaw

La-a-a-nd Fever

By this time, the homesteading quest had reached a fever pitch. I had heard back from the B.C. government on the half section I had applied for east of town. I was disappointed as they excluded the west quarter section because it had too much timber and wanted forty one hundred dollars for the front quarter. Outrageous! Never heard of such a thing! No one ever paid over fifteen hundred dollars for a quarter section, even if it was wall to wall timber. I was really upset, so went on a land hunting expedition with my old friend J.V. Bangs.

J.V., his wife Lois, and three of their children, Beverly, Larry, and Jack moved to the Lakes District from the Oregon coast not long after my cousins came in late 1960. They lived in the old Hargreaves place just west of Red & Maxine. Originally from Pennsylvania, they had an older daughter, Polly, living in southern California. J.V. was quite tall, with close-cut, reddish hair, thin lips, and hooded eyes. His wife, Lois, was a short, conservative lady, who played the organ at the United Church for many years. J.V. was one of those people who could fall face down in a pig pen and come up without a spot on him, and smelling like a rose. He and his wife were always neatly dressed and everything they did from gardening to building was done to perfection. But J.V. had one weakness, he was land hungry. Not in the way greedy speculators are land hungry; it was deeper than that. Just to see such great quantities of land available was a thrill of its own. I think in a way it was like prospectors, the thrill of the search is worth more than the gold, chasing the dream worth more than realizing it. When he said the word "laaand" it was with respect, almost reverence.

We didn't find anything right off, but we were brothers in the quest! Joan had started work as a teller in the new Royal Bank in Vanderhoof right after graduation from high school. She looked very sharp and trim in her royal blue coat, and grey skirt. Looking to the future, I could see some real advantages in having a wife that worked for a bank. The Royal Bank manager in Vanderhoof at that time was Gary Valance. His son Jim, as a teenager, was involved in local bands, and later wrote songs for entertainer Bryan Adams, and others.

My parents and younger sister Janice Kae came up a couple of days before the wedding to get acquainted with the "soon to be" new relatives and see what the country was like. They were impressed. Slim and Marj were the perfect hosts.

Joan and I, with my Dad, made a quick run to Prince George on Friday, the day before the wedding, to get a few things. I had made what I thought was a wise decision a week or so earlier, and traded my good black '59 G.M.C. pickup, with its four on the floor transmission, for a light blue, short box 1963 Ford F-100, with a 3 speed standard column shift. What a mistake! I made this decision for three reasons. I wanted my new wife to be able to sit close to me, with no gear shift in the way, at least on the honeymoon. I thought everyone would be impressed with the "rags to riches" story of me now owning an almost new pickup, and having a pretty young wife! The third reason was that the gas tank on the G.M.C. had a leak, and rather than get it fixed, it gave me a good reason to trade it in.

After finishing our shopping trip, we had just started out of Prince George when I saw a guy hitchhiking toward Vanderhoof. I never thought of giving anyone a ride because the cab was crammed full, but as we passed him, I suddenly realized the hitch hiker was Charlie Joseph, the young native choker setter from Al Shaw's logging camp at Pleasant Bay. I pulled over and he came staggering up to the truck. He was a sad sight. The young, handsome, athletic guy with the air of a confident and capable logger was now a staggering drunk. I could hardly believe it was him. I explained we would be glad to give him a lift as far as Mapes Road if he didn't mind riding in the back. He seemed happy enough for the offer and crawled in. When we pulled off at the Mapes corner, he climbed over the tail gate, took a couple of wobbly one legged jumps, and piled up in the ditch. After we helped him get untangled and stabilized enough to hitchhike again, he shook my hand, thanked me profusely for the ride, and we took off. I hated having to leave him like that, but there wasn't much more we could do.

The Wedding Celebration

The morning of the wedding, October 3, 1964, I got up early, jammed all my clothes (suit, shirt, tie, etc.) in a suitcase, put on my black cowboy hat, and headed over to my cousins. The tradition was that the future bride and groom were not supposed to see each other on their wedding day. I actually had other things planned anyway. J.V. Bangs and I were going land hunting!

The wedding was to take place promptly at 8:00 p.m. Saturday night. At 6:00 p.m., J.V. and I were still badly stuck in a bog hole somewhere out in the middle of the Nechako Valley. Somehow, by using Archimedes "Law of the Lever", and a couple of windfall poplar trees we managed to get unstuck, back to the Jones', and cleaned up before the wedding. But it was close!

The wedding itself went off without a hitch. Pastor Calvin Buehler from the Gospel Chapel was the officiating minister. Joan had asked her best friends, Carol Fasten, Anna Schultz, and Linda Evans, to be her bridesmaids. They were lovely, all wearing light blue dresses with matching veils, white high heel shoes, and nylons (no bobby sox!). They each carried bouquets of white flowers, held together with flowing blue satin ribbons. Joan was beautiful. Full length white wedding dress, white shoulder length veil, and a beautiful bouquet of cascade, long stem red roses. Sally Williams sang "Because" and "I Love You Truly" accompanied by her sister Gale Broen. Both young ladies, recently married, were daughters of Nels & Midge Cruthers.

I had conscripted my three cousins to serve as best men. Good old cousin Dick and his two younger brothers Dwayne, and Donnie. We were all dressed up in black suits, white shirts, and black ties, (those were the orders). We also wore boutonnieres of white flowers (which my backwoods cousins had to sniff to make sure they were real).

After the wedding ceremony, Audrey Smedley took the wedding pictures, then we came back to the recreation building, right next to the Gospel Chapel, for the reception. The long table for the wedding party was located at the far end of the hall, with the guests seated at tables along both sides. As the wedding party made its entry, the bride and groom came first, followed by the bridesmaids, who were escorted by the best men. Joan's youngest sister, Janet, had been born 5 months before, so when Slim and Marj came in behind the wedding party pushing a baby buggy, a muffled ripple of laughter went through the crowd, some said later that all the scene needed was for Slim to be carrying a shotgun!

Wedding Picture: Donnie, Dwayne, Dick Jones; Bob & Joan Mumford;
Carol Fasten, Anna Schultz, Linda Evans

It was a great wedding supper, a hot turkey buffet for over one hundred guests, all prepared by family and friends. Joan's grandmother, Ellen Fisher, made the three tier wedding cake, which was then decorated by Rene Tee. Both our mothers looked especially nice; It was hard to imagine these ladies being old enough to be mothers of the bride and groom. Pastor Buehler and his wife were wonderful down-to-earth Christian people. He wished us well in this new venture in life, and asked Gods' blessing on the food. Then, since the food was free, and this whole thing was taking so long, all the starving locals dug in and ate as much as they could hold. The Vanderhoof Kinnettes served the food and kept the kitchen organized, doing a great job. That's one good thing about a small community, everybody pitches in, and you can laugh, cry, and celebrate together, just like a big family. There were a few speeches, and telegrams read, but no one got carried away. By this time, most people were full of turkey and beginning to snore, as it was now past eleven o'clock at night.

Joan's parents: Slim & Marj Snyder

After the well wishes were finished, we got in the almost new Ford F-100 and headed for the room we had reserved at Bednesti Lake. After we left, we hadn't gone a mile when a strange smell began to waft through the cab of the truck. We stopped and looked everywhere, glove box, behind the seat, under the seat, everywhere but in the ashtray. It finally got so bad we had to drive with the windows rolled down. The next morning, we discovered the ashtray was crammed to the top with mothballs! Compliments of Jack Roche!

Bob's parents: Lois & Wayne Mumford

Meanwhile, back at the Snyder farm, the locals had woken up, and the wedding celebration was going full swing. The Mapes crew didn't go to bed at midnight if there was a wedding to be celebrated (even if they had filled up on a turkey dinner). Probably the high point of the celebration was when big John Klassen fell down the well. Actually, he didn't fall down the well, he fell in the well! Slim was attempting another one of those 'dig your own well' projects, to save money, and was down about six feet through the hard pan. Typically, in the rush of the wedding preparation, someone forgot to pull the plywood cover over the well, and for whatever reason, big John fell in. After they fished him out, he didn't appear to be in any worse shape than when he fell in so the celebration continued. Dad played his fiddle, Oscar Walstrom his guitar, and Jack Roche his accordion, while everyone sat around visiting and having a few drinks. It seems they had quite the celebration!

Honeymoon and Life After

Our honeymoon trip to Dawson Creek and points north (which meant Taylor and Fort St. John) was somewhat disappointing, but then who is looking for scenery on their honeymoon!!! Joan & I had disagreed which way we should go for our honeymoon; she wanted to go south and I wanted to go north. For me, the main attraction was no doubt the Peace River Dam site at Hudson Hope, which was all the talk in 1964. Fortunately, Joan's sense of humour, which she inherited from her Irish grandmother, saved the day and we had a wonderful time exploring the area. Impressive as the Peace River area was, it just wasn't my kind of country, too flat and no mountains! Even the Peace River farmland, nice as it was, just didn't click. In the end, we had a good time, and after almost ruining our honeymoon because of my babbling about land, I came to the decision to go ahead with the quarter section east of Vanderhoof. Somehow the Nechako Valley was where I felt at home, and Joan was in full agreement.

My family had spent a few days staying with my cousins at Sinkut Lake while we were gone, no doubt re-living the McDowell Creek days of Oregon. When we got back, Dwayne and I took Dad on a quick hunt out to the east end of Tatuk Lake. Within thirty minutes, he had a nice two year old bull moose on the ground. I used my tag and we had our winter's meat.

The next weekend, Dad, Slim, and I went on a trip to Lavoie Lake that lays southwest of Tatuk. We got there in the late afternoon, found a leaky rowboat stashed in the willows, and within an hour had more big, fat, shiny three and four pound rainbows than we knew what to do with. That night we built a roaring fire in front of the root wad of a big spruce windfall, cut chunks off those big fat solid rainbows, stuck them on a willow stick, and roasted them over the hot coals. The best rainbow trout I've ever eaten.

The whole visit turned out really well; wedding, reception, Mapes celebration, and John Klassen still going strong after his trip down the well.

There was a little glitch over the land worries on the honeymoon, but now that was settled. We took a couple of pictures with the folks in front of the Government office before they left. Joan had her hair in curlers and covered with a blue hairnet (quite a change from the white wedding veil), but this was real life. Yes, real life! Now we were on our own.

Mom, the Newlyweds, Janice Kae

The first major disagreement had taken place before the wedding, and was about where we would live immediately after the wedding. Joan had sensibly suggested we rent an apartment in town as she was working a lot of overtime at the Royal Bank. Living in town I could get out of my cold, wet bush clothes, have a nice hot shower, and we could live like civilized human beings. I wouldn't hear of it. If we were going to be pioneers, then we needed to live like pioneers!

We rented a little eighteen by twenty- four foot cabin from Marg & Jack Roche, ten miles east of Vanderhoof. The heat was a small wood cook stove, no power, no telephone, and no plumbing (just the famous "outside biffy"). I had made a slight miscalculation earlier and spent the money we were going to buy furniture with on the "almost new" Ford F-100 pickup. This created a minor dilemma, but we managed to find a small table, 2 chairs, and easy chair of sorts, and a World War II single army cot for a bed. The house was divided into two rooms but we eventually ended up living in the main room, which was much easier to heat.

Once we were moved in, our day went something like this; up at 5 a.m. to start a fire in the small firebox of the wood cook stove (only heat in the house). Try and eat lukewarm porridge with your mitts on, and wade out through the 200 yards of three foot deep snow in the driveway to the pickup parked by the highway. This early morning walk was made while packing at least one large empty cream can, for water. Then we shoveled out the pickup the snowplows had buried during the night and hoped the truck would start.

At night when we got home, the schedule was reversed, but with a couple of slight variations. The first was when I got off work and came to pick up Joan, and she would still be working. They would let me inside the Bank so I could at least keep warm. As I sat in a chair, my frozen clothes would thaw out, and the water would run into my boots and insoles (oh, great!) When we got home, the snow plows would have filled up the parking spot, the cream can I had to pack to the house was now full, and I had to warm up a house that had sat all day at -20 to -30 degrees (F) with no heat in it. Oh yes, I was starting to weaken, and thinking about that heated apartment in town!

The last big hurdle to face was cooking supper. It took forever for the wood cook stove to get hot enough to thaw out a package of moose burger and fry some spuds. Just about the last straw was when we opened up a package of what we thought was moose steaks and found it was sawed up moose bones! My cousins, especially Maxine, had thought doing this, as well as putting a large pencil through a package of moose burger, was a hilarious joke to play on the newlyweds. They had made up these packages while helping cut up the moose Dad had shot.

But the final straw came the night we came home and I let Joan off so she could crawl over the snowbank, down through the grader ditch, and up the other side to the unplowed driveway (a shorter route to the cabin). Being considerate, I waited to make sure she got across to the driveway before going up the highway to park the truck. She had on all her Royal Bank finery as she headed down over the bank, but when she got half way across the ditch, she broke through the crust, and in she went right up to her waist. She was a tough one that winter, that's for sure, but this was too much. As she stood there buried in snow up to her waist with her nice Royal Bank skirt spread out around her, and her drawers full of snow, she began to cry. Well, there is nothing in the world that touches the soft spot in an old logger's heart than seeing a lady cry. I managed to haul her out and get her to the cabin, but I had enough of this, so then decided to find an apartment in town. There weren't any, not a single one. So, we just toughed it out.

That winter was the coldest winter I've ever seen. In January, it went down to -60 degrees F for 2 weeks. I must be a wimp, but I don't know how those old timers handled it. They were tougher than I am. We didn't work in that kind of cold because nothing would start, and Workmen's Compensation wouldn't cover you anyway. But the bank teller insisted she had to go to work, as they were short staffed. She caught a ride on the school bus in the morning, which had to run its route in all weather in those days, and then travelled back home with a neighbour, but I was happy just feeding the fire and making supper.

Homesteaders

When spring finally came in 1965, and the grass turned green, I couldn't wait to get to our homestead. It was in May when the paperwork from the B.C. Government Lands Branch was finally completed. I had decided to go ahead with the pre-emption for $4100.00, as I knew there was more than enough timber on the quarter section to cover the price. The Land Act had been changed a few years back and you could no longer get an actual "homestead". I have used the word "homestead" because it sounds better than "pre-emption", which it was now called. Our homestead was located 3 miles east of Vanderhoof, and ¼ mile off Highway 16, which was still gravel at that time.

Now, as I walked the ¼ mile in, to have a good look at the quarter section, (160 acres), that would be our homestead, I was pretty cranked up and full of plans. The hogback ridge I walked in on was a perfect place to build an access road. When I walked down the crest of that ridge, through the big poplars, and out on the point, I could see this would make a perfect building site. I clearly remember the thrill when I looked through the big poplars and saw the meadow below. I knew I was far enough from our east line that when the poplars were cleared off we would be able to see the whole ¼ section spread out around us, and Sinkut Mountain to the south. I would soon be the proud owner of 160 acres of crown land that no man had ever held title to.

As I stood on the spot that would soon be a home for my wife, myself, and eventually our three kids, I thanked the Lord for what He had done. He had brought me a long way from where I had been a few years before when I stepped off that Greyhound bus in Prince George that cold January morning in 1961.

The End

Acknowledgments

I would like to thank and acknowledge the following:

Paul Andrews and his wife Rosalind Scovill for their support and encouragement. Thanks is not a big enough word for the time Rosalind spent deciphering and typing my unreadable manuscript.

Carol Gardarson of the North Thompson Star Journal for taking on the challenge of typing out my first few chapters.

Lynne Frizzle for bringing the manuscript together at a crucial time.

My immediate family (siblings & cousins), friends and McDowell Creek neighbours, for sharing photos, stories, and family history.

My wife, Joan, for her support throughout the writing of this book, and help with the final edit and interaction with the publishers.

Printed in Canada